INSIDE THE MIND OF THE SEX KILLER

John Sanders

truecrimelibrary

Published by True Crime Library,
the paperback division of Magazine Design
and Publishing Ltd.
PO Box 735, London SE26 5NQ, UK

An imprint of True Crime Library
© 2008 True Crime Library
© 2008 John Sanders
All rights reserved

This book is sold subject to the condition that it shall
not, by way of trade or otherwise, be lent, re-sold,
hired out or otherwise circulated without the
publisher's prior consent in any form of binding or
cover other than that in which it is published and
without a similar condition including this condition
being imposed on the subsequent purchaser

Cover design by Ben James
Designed and typeset by Declan Meehan
Printed and bound in Great Britain by
CPI Cox & Wyman, Reading, Berkshire

ISBN 978-1-874358-40-4

For Barbara, Ben, David, Declan, Jacqueline, Jayne, Jeanette, Louise, Martin, Mike and Phil

Other titles in the
TRUE CRIME LIBRARY

WOMEN ON DEATH ROW

A DATE WITH THE HANGMAN

MURDER MYTH AND MAKE-BELIEVE

MURDER WITH VENOM

BRITAIN'S GODFATHER

FROM WALL STREET TO NEWGATE

CAMINADA THE CRIME BUSTER

FROM THE X FILES OF MURDER

FAR FROM THE LAND

THE BOOTLEGGERS

STRANGE TALES FROM STRANGEWAYS

FORENSIC CASEBOOK OF CRIME

TONY MARTIN AND THE BLEAK HOUSE TRAGEDY

CELEBRITY SLAYINGS THAT SHOCKED THE WORLD

BRITAIN'S LAST HANGMAN

WOMEN ON DEATH ROW 2

CONTENTS

1. Sado-masochism; history and sexual implications of flogging; "spanking;" bondage 1
   Neville Heath, Graham Young, Ben Fawley

2. Homosexual sadism; mythomania; torture 19
   Dennis Nilsen, Steven Bailey, Randy Kraft

3. Fetishism 39
   Ted Bundy, Jerry Brudos, Frederick Ducharme

4. Necrophilia; sadism without aggression; insanity; vampirism 65
   Peter Kurten, Robert Black, David Rulo, Gerald Gallego, Jacques Algarron

5. Sexual myths: pornography, castration, rehabilitation, lunar killing 81
   The murder of Jane Longhurst, Paul Beart, Bobby Long

6. Mutilation for sexual satisfaction; symbolic sadism; prostitution; erotomania 105
   Jack the Ripper, "Jack the Stripper," Robert Hoskins, Arthur Jackson

7. Paedophilia; child abuse 123
   Morss and Tyler, Mark Valera

8. Domination; physical inadequacy; fear of women 143
   Leonard Lake, John Duffy, Christian Jungers, Manfred Wittmann, Bernardo/Homolka

9. Voyeurism; Peeping Toms; flashing; mother hatred; Oedipus complex 161
   Patrick Byrne, Gary Hopkins, George Reilley, Niels Falster, Kevin Fitch, Werner Boost, Richard Evonitz, Elmo Lee Smith, John Balaban

10. Animals; post-mortem voyeurism 193
    Ed Kemper, Alan Victor Wills, Richard Chase, David Rulo, John Norman Collins

11. Are sexual killers born or made? VMPC – damage to the prefrontal lobe 207
    Phineas Gage, Donta Page, Jeremy Skocz, Steven Parkus

Appendix. Two sexual killers discuss themselves 227
   Carl Panzram, Ian Brady

INSIDE THE MIND
OF THE
SEX KILLER

Every week we read reports about horrific sexual murders. We know that men rape and kill, but how much do we know about the inner workings of their minds – the factors that drive them to commit crimes which for normal people would be unthinkable?

Juxtaposing psychiatric findings with case studies of high profile sexual killers, this book analyses sexual deviancies such as flashing, necrophilia, sado-masochism, fetishism, erotomania, bondage and voyeurism, among others, in their relationship to sexual crimes, in order to bring a better understanding to the age-old puzzle: what makes them kill?

Its findings are sometimes shocking, and often deeply revealing about the dark jungle of the criminal mind.

CHAPTER ONE

SADO-MASOCHISM; HISTORY AND SEXUAL IMPLICATIONS OF FLOGGING; "SPANKING;" BONDAGE
Neville Heath, Graham Young, Ben Fawley

By the time she was 33 and separated from her husband, Margery Gardner had established a reputation for herself as a fun girl, always ready for a party, always good for a laugh. She had been an art student and was a talented artist, a film extra, something of a socialite, and her career, when all the pieces were put together, revealed a woman who was like a natural butterfly on the green leaves of life.

All this was to come to a sudden, abrupt and appalling end in a tragedy discovered by the manageress of the Pembridge Court Hotel, Bayswater, when, at around two o'clock in the afternoon of June 21st, 1946, she decided to find out why the occupant of Room No. 4 had not appeared that day.

She found the room in darkness with the curtains still drawn. The form in the bed did not move. The manageress walked past the bed to the curtains, opened them, and then returned to the bed, pulling back the sheet that covered the recumbent form.

What she saw nearly made her faint. In the bed was a woman. She was naked and dead and her death had been one of unspeakable violence.

Although the manageress had never seen the woman before, the police had no difficulty in establishing her as Margery Gardner. She had been beaten with a lead-tipped thong – 17 lashes from it were found on the front and back of her body.

A seven-inch-long wound in her vagina had been caused by a metal poker, inserted, then pulled sharply upwards, ripping open the soft flesh and causing her to bleed to death. Her ankles were firmly tied together and both arms crossed underneath her body. Marks on her wrists indicated that they had been bound together and subsequently released. Other marks on her body revealed that she had been severely bitten.

All these injuries, it was noted, were inflicted before she died.

She had then been held by a pinning grip under her chin and suffocated, either by having her face pressed down against a pillow, or through being gagged, or possibly both.

Margery Gardner was the victim of the sexual-sadist killer Neville Heath, who was hanged at Pentonville Prison on October 26th, 1946. What was unusual about her murder was that she already knew when Heath took her to that hotel room that he was a vicious sadist. She had, in the classic contemporary cliché, been down that road before with him. She had found a tormentor she enjoyed, for just as he was a true sadist, she was a true masochist.

Shortly after Heath was hanged a detective employed by a different hotel from the one in which she died revealed her dark secret. The detective told how, just a month before her death, Mrs. Gardner had to be rescued from Heath's savagery. She had gone with him to a West End hotel, where they registered as husband and wife.

They dined there, and after visiting clubs in the neighbourhood, returned to their room about midnight. An hour later a guest heard Mrs. Gardner scream. Finding the bedroom door locked, he called for help, and the hotel detective entered with a passkey.

Margery Gardner lay naked and spread-eagled on the bed. Her feet and hands were tied to the bed and she had been severely thrashed. There were bruises on her face and body. Heath was standing over her in maniacal frenzy, and had to be held back while she was set free.

The hotel detective suggested she could lay a charge against Heath, but she stalled. She was married to someone else, she said, and the scandal of being found with another man would kill him.

"I could not bear my husband to know about this," she said.

Both were told to get out of the hotel on the spot

– and they both went.

"She must have known she would be thrashed when she went to the Pembridge Court Hotel," said the detective. "She must have been aware of the woven thong and its purpose. Almost certainly she went to the hotel with Heath prepared for his abnormalities."

If all this behaviour seems at least bizarre, it is well understood by sexual psychiatrists. The pursuit of happiness, the desire to experience pleasurable sensations, is a yearning inherent in everyone. Together with the pleasure principle there is also a pain principle, and because everyone is different the mixture of the two is never quite the same in each individual. There is a little bit of a desire to cause pain in every one of us and it is most apparent in the sex act. But in most individuals it is kept under strict control. When that control is lost, as it was in this case with Neville Heath, and inflicting pain becomes the object of sexual gratification, we are in the realms of the abnormal. We call this sadism, after the infamous exploits of the Marquis de Sade who was finally condemned to death in the 18th century for his sexual perversions. Psychiatrists prefer to call it *active algolagneia*, from the Greek *algos*, pain, and *lagneia*, lust.

The interesting thing about Heath and Mrs. Gardner was that they found each other and were able to become a perfect team in which their two perversions fitted together like a key in a lock. She was a true masochist because she was excited by his abnormal behaviour and found pleasure in becoming the instrument of his gratification – she was his slave, getting her sexual excitement by refusing to defend herself.

The case of Margery Gardner is an extreme one; there are many degrees of masochism just as there are of sadism. In its mildest form a woman enjoying a playful nip on the ear by her partner during a love embrace, or simply enjoying being undressed by her partner, may manifest it. This willing defencelessness makes the masochist the passive counterpart of the sadist – hence psychiatrists call masochism *passive algolagneia* as distinct from *active algolagneia*.

In a 1919 essay, Sigmund Freud described masochism as a universal human fantasy. Nonetheless, he appeared to be surprised by male masochism. He thought submission was for women only and never understood why the male should suffer it.

Since both males and females pass through a subordinate phase when young, the capacity for masochism must be universal. We all indulge in a form of social masochism when we read newspaper and magazine accounts of people who manifest today's twin icons of wealth and celebrity. Everyone has to obey someone – there is always the boss, and then the boss of bosses, and then his (or her) boss, and so on ever upwards.

Masochism is complete submission and it comes to males as well as females early in their lives when they obey their teachers, their parents, and the strongest of their own peers. They know they have to obey because the consequences of not doing so would be to strike back, which would create anarchy. They therefore recognise their subordinate position and in many cases actually enjoy the helplessness of it.

For young men especially, a capacity for submission, and therefore masochism, is vital for social and often for career survival. It is, however, a capacity that does not have to be realised. Freud's judgment on the acting-out of fantasies, including masochistic fantasies, was that although they may be universal, their acting-out in real life is a perversion.

We don't know much about the character of Margery Gardner beyond her being something of a good-time girl, but as a typical sexual masochist she would have suffered from low self-esteem, and intense feelings of inferiority, against which would have been striving a desire not just to be dominated but actually to dominate herself, just as conversely there is in many sadists a desire to protect their partner and to devote themselves to her. Thus there is a bit of masochism in every sadist and a bit of sadism in every masochist.

Sado-masochism; history and sexual implications of flogging; "spanking;" bondage

Neville Heath was more than a masochist – he was a fantasiser who carried his fantasies into real life. At various times he called himself Lieutenant-Colonel George Heath, Lord Dudley, the writer Bruce Lockhart, Captain Selway, MC, Group Captain Rupert Brooke and Major James Armstrong. Like many another fantasist, he had no need for these masquerades – he was handsome enough and more than attractive to women. It was also a reflection of the erratic personality revealed in his sexual life that he had gained what surely must have been the unique distinction of being commissioned in the RAF, the British Army and the South African Air Force, and being thrown out of all three of them.

After the savage murder of Margery Gardner, Heath went on the run via Brighton to Bournemouth, where he picked up another girl, Doreen Marshall, whose body was later found horribly mutilated under bushes in Branksome Chine.

At his trial at the Old Bailey he did not deny murder – he pleaded that he was insane. His counsel took the almost unprecedented course of deliberately putting the prisoner's earlier criminal history before the jury: Heath had been a Borstal boy and had been convicted of fraud and bouncing cheques. This was to lay the foundations for the courtroom battle over Heath's mind.

The defence called the psychotherapist at Wormwood Scrubs Prison, who said that while he found nothing to indicate ordinary insanity in the accused man's character, he was suffering from moral insanity. At times he was unaware of what he was doing and he showed no remorse or appreciation of what other people would think of his behaviour.

The senior medical officer at Brixton Prison thought Heath wasn't insane, but a psychopathic personality and a most abnormal individual. Being a psychopath, according to this doctor, was not a disease of the mind; it was "temperamental."

Another prison doctor who gave evidence also thought Heath wasn't insane. He described him as "a psychopathic personality and a sadist." He knew what he was doing when he was killing, and he knew it was wrong.

Some of the composure and studied understatement that were part of Heath's superficially endearing personality surfaced just before he was executed, when he asked the prison governor for a glass of whisky. Then he added, and these were his last words, "In the circumstances, you might make that a double."

•

The woman who likes to be tied up by the man who likes tying up women is not as unusual as might be thought. Tying up, or bondage, is pure sado-masochism, enjoyed by both consenting partners, the one dominating, the other wanting to be dominated, and as such a manifestation of primitive humankind's deepest urges. This is why the story told by Ben Fawley, an unemployed father of two who suffered from bipolar disorder, seemed to be plausible enough when he was asked to explain the disappearance of his 17-year-old girl friend, Taylor Behl. Her decayed body was found in a ditch and a post-mortem established that Fawley's semen was inside her.

They had had consensual rough sex, he explained. After that, he told police: "All I remember was her saying she would tell her mother and the police that I raped her. She wanted me to help her commit a crime before her eighteenth birthday and we drove round Richmond [Virginia] having sex and all the time her begging me to break into buildings and I kept refusing."

They ended up on a beach where Fawley tied Taylor's hands together and bound her legs to the car with sticky tape, before he stuck a plastic bag over her mouth – all this allegedly at her request. He claimed he took the bag off when she started choking.

"That's when she started cussing me out and calling me a wimp and saying I just didn't have what it takes to, you know...She said she wanted to choke and gasp for air. That she wanted to think she was gonna die. All I remember then was trying to get her on to the car seat."

Fawley dumped her body in the ditch. "I panicked," he said. "I couldn't believe she was dead."

His account of Taylor's last moments cannot of course ever be corroborated, and according to the district attorney it was "all garbage." But if Taylor really did ask him to tie her up and stick a plastic bag over her mouth until she started choking, she wouldn't have been the first person to come up with such a request. She could already have known, as many others know, that such behaviour can result in an enhanced sexual thrill – though be warned, if it interests you, it is extremely dangerous and should be avoided. Certainly Taylor wasn't entirely innocent. In her internet blog diary, which was how Fawley met her, she said: "I am just coming aware of my body and the power I can have over men. I hope I use it wisely. Still, the temptation is there. Maybe bad girls have more fun than good ones."

In another entry she revealed that, "bad boys call me jailbait." Ben Fawley became one of 92 "friends" she listed on MySpace, a popular social networking website. Signing herself Tiabliaj – jailbait spelt backwards – she began a digital conversation with Fawley that eventually led to meetings and sex between them. None of her family was aware that she posed for photos he then posted on his website. *Deviantart.com* specialised in seductive pictures of girls in school uniform wearing short skirts and eating sweets.

Police seized items including a box of animal bones, sex toys, women's clothing, guns, burglary tools, chains, a machete and hatchet from Fawley's home. Several of his seven computers contained child pornography. Website images revealed his freakish obsession with death, fire and decay, often in the form of animal bones and rotting human flesh. He had also signed up for a fetish convention in Florida for "specialists" in bondage and S and M. He was convicted of first-degree murder in August, 2006, and sentenced to 40 years in prison, 10 of them suspended.

•

How do you recognise a sado-masochist? He may be emotionally repressed and sexually undeveloped. His sexual deviations almost always result from an inhibition in his development.

Freud considered that many of the experiences of childhood are so painful that we cannot tolerate their memory. As examples: you discover your father has a mistress, your parents ignore you, your mother favours your younger sister. We use defence mechanisms, such as repression, to drive these experiences into the unconscious. But these ghosts of childhood continue to cloud our minds, and we must analyse them if we want to be free as adults to make realistic choices in our lives.

The desires and fears established early in childhood drive our lives. You may think you can make decisions of your own free will, but Freud didn't think you could. He said our erotic lives were governed by our secret, unconscious, pre-formed allegiances to our parents.

He believed that our lives centred on our genitals; they are in our minds and they guide our lives. He said: "Anatomy is destiny." He observed that many of his male patients expressed anxiety about their penis, and feared having it cut off. Such fears were partly based on actual threats in 19th century pedagogy, where boys caught masturbating were threatened with having their penis amputated, and partly, according to Freud, on a son's fear that his penis might be bigger than his father's and consequently his father would cut it off.

Freud created a tripartite model of the mind, the id, the superego and the ego. The id is the primitive, animalistic, instinctual element, demanding instant gratification, thus: "I have seen an attractive blonde walking across the road and I want to ravage her." The id struggles with the superego, the part of the psyche concerned with ethical and moral conduct, thus: "That would be wrong, my conscience tells me so." The ego, representing the cognitive and perceptual processes that inform behaviour, settles the matter between the two warring elements, thus: "It's not such a good idea after all." In the sexual criminal the superego and the ego are overwhelmed by the id.

Can psychoanalysis do anything in such cases? Freud himself maintained that even the most severe psychotic illness could be transformed through psychoanalysis. But he also found that people are creatures of habit. A man with a collection of mistresses is unlikely to settle for one; similarly, a man who rapes a woman is likely to rape another one. He coined the phrase "repetition compulsion" to describe the phenomenon of patients who repeated their behaviour and did so compulsively, even when it was not in their best interests.

•

Sado-masochists may not actually be sexual sadists, for sado-masochism exists outside the range of sexual attitudes, just as it exists outside the range of crime. Many people we can categorise as sadists practise what is called ideal sadism, where the outlet is in writing pornographic literature or drawing dirty pictures in which torture and sexual scenes predominate. It has been said that the best criminologists (and this must include Sherlock Holmes) are often sadists. They love intrigue and are emotionally glacial. The building blocks they compose in their imaginations are founded on suspicion and cemented with sexual symbolism. Occasionally they even spill over into crime.

Such a one was Graham Young, an eager young man who poisoned his pets, his family and then his friends at work. He was a classic psychopathic ideal sadist, and revealed himself as such in his confession when he was finally arrested.

All his workmates at Hadlands, makers of photographic equipment, knew about Young's obsession with "morbid" subjects. His main topics of conversation were poisons, the Second World War, witchcraft and Adolf Hitler. He was a devotee of Hitler and Nazism and collected books on the Hitler period in Germany.

When police searched his flat in Maynard Road, Hemel Hempstead, they found "macabre drawings" which Young said he made while under the influence of inhaling ether. One of the drawings depicted a graveyard and a man with a bottle of poison and a genie coming out of the neck of the bottle. The drawing also showed two bald-headed men. Young readily admitted his obsession with the macabre and said: "I seem to have been a misfit when I was young." He was then only 23.

People referred to in his diary by their initials, he told police, were "figments of my imagination. I was preparing to write a novel and they are my notes."

But psychologists recognised the clinical, criminologist-type mind when he added: "I know you found poison in my flat but that does not mean I poisoned anyone. You first have to identify the poison and show the opportunity. You say I did it. How did I do it? Lastly comes the motive. I suggest you have to prove all three: means, opportunity, motive."

When one of his victims, his workmate Fred Biggs, was dying horrifically, Young wrote in his secret diary: "I have administered a fatal dose of the special compound and anticipate reports of his illness on Monday. He should die within a week. I gave him three separate doses: the total absorbed should be about 15 to 16 grams." A couple of days later he wrote: "He is surviving too long for my piece [sic] of mind." And another entry read: "It is better that he should die. It will be a merciful release for him, as if he should survive he will be permanently damaged." Biggs did in fact die a week later.

What, a sane person will ask, could a man like Young possibly get out of this? Although it doesn't seem at once apparent, one answer is a sexual thrill. For ideal sadists usually accompany their fantasies (in this case Young was of course realising his fantasies) with masturbation, although ejaculation is not uncommon without masturbation. For them, ideal sadism is equivalent to sexual intercourse.

Young was asked if he felt any remorse for his two victims, who had died from poisoning by thallium, which he had served them in their morning coffee, and for the several others whose health he had permanently damaged by poisoning them with heavy metal. He replied: "That would be hypocritical. What I feel is the emptiness of my soul. I suppose I had ceased to see them as people, or at least a part of me had. They had become guinea pigs."

When Young was found guilty at his trial the court heard that he had arrived at his first job as the tea-boy at Hadlands, fresh from nine years in Broadmoor, where he was sent at the age of 14. He was only 13 when he killed his stepmother by poisoning her. Then he administered belladonna to his sister and antimony to his father and a school friend. Unfortunately, no one at Hadlands was told about these offences or about his Broadmoor background when he arrived at the photographic equipment firm at the age of 23. So they had no reason to suspect, until the work force began to fall ill, that the new recruit was stark raving mad.

Young, who had the dubious distinction of being Britain's worst poisoner, was jailed for life for the murder of the two men at Hadlands. He served 18 years and died in prison in 1990.

•

The practice of sado-masochism is not in itself a crime, nor could it ever be, although several years ago it was categorised by the Italian Parliament as a sufficient reason for a woman to get a divorce if she were the victim of it and didn't like it. Sado-masochistic practices are often quite a healthy escape for some couples. The much-revered Victorian author and clergyman Charles Kingsley, who wrote the classic *The Water Babies*, interwove kinky sexuality and religious symbolism in his private life; he used to rope his wife Fanny naked to a large cross before having intercourse, and Fanny apparently loved every minute of it. Kingsley, who was also a good artist, drew erotic pictures of naked nuns and monks copulating, demonstrating that even among clergymen religious emotions are not necessarily a substitute for sexual feeling. The billionaire American store owner Alfred Bloomingdale could get no satisfaction from his favourite sexual partner, model girl Vicki Morgan, until he had first stripped and thrashed several prostitutes hired for the occasion, and then beaten the long-suffering Vicki as well.

Beating one's partner, sometimes euphemistically described as "spanking," is much more popular than might be imagined, and while it is clearly sexual deviancy there is no great harm in it. The celebrated 20th century writer and critic Kenneth Tynan happily confessed to his enjoyment of spanking. "There is no sport to touch it," he wrote. "It is not just a nocturnal relaxation, it is a way of life." Although married, he had met an actress named Nicole who shared his passion for beating sessions and joined in the spanking even when a third party was present. Tynan recalls an incident when he spanked a woman named Sophie while Nicole looked on: "I put her over my knee, opened the slit of her knicks and gave her chubby bum twenty-five smacks. Nicole sat two yards away, starring at the reddening globes. She then replaced me and gave Sophie twelve stingers with the hairbrush."

Tynan, with his descriptive gifts, should have been able to explain more than most why anyone should enjoy spanking, and he did try. The pain, he explained, is the price one pays for the anticipation and the recollection afterwards. This may not be too helpful; to many of us it may seem rather like the man who was beating his head against a wall because he felt so relieved when he stopped.

For those who may have some difficulty in understanding the pleasure–pain principle, one of the best explanations was given by E. Wulffen, a psychologist, just before the outbreak of the First World War:

"Although the heavy blows may not at first induce erotic pleasure, the initial pain soon gives way to a sensation of warmth which envelops the whole of the seat like a soft, warm blanket, producing a pleasurable sensation, and this may easily connect up with the sexual area. Boys...for this reason sometimes endeavour to obtain a repetition of the chastisement which may ultimately affect them sexually."

Wulffen was writing with the public schools in mind. of course, for public thrashings reached their zenith in these bastions of private learning. Before the public schools institutionalised flogging, it was already being widely practised in the armed forces. In the 18th century Royal Navy men were stripped to the waist, roped to the mast and flogged unconscious before the whole crew. It is difficult to believe that this was simply about punishment and that sadistic pleasure was not involved. It was, of course, supposed to be a deterrent, and as such it possibly worked. When Private Robert Hackett, serving at Millbay Barracks, Plymouth, objected to a remark made by Sergeant Henry Jones about a friend of his, he told the sergeant: "It's only the thought that I would get 40 lashes for it that stops me beating you up right here." The disaffected private then strode away, but came back with his rifle 15 minutes later and shot the sergeant dead. He was hanged for it outside Exeter Prison in March, 1861.

During the 1860s large-scale military flogging started to be phased out. Of all the soldiers court martialled in the 1850s, 10% were flogged. Ten years later this had dropped to 3%.

By then flogging, allegedly as a deterrent for breaking the rules but, from the available evidence, as much for sadistic pleasure as for any other reason, was being heartily embraced by the public schools. Anyone who was anyone in 19th century England had been flogged at public school, and many of them were proud of it. When a boy at Eton refused to be flogged by the headmaster, he was immediately expelled, and when his father protested, readers of *The Times* and other newspapers sent their opinions to the letters page over a period of several weeks. Almost all of them were for flogging the boy. One wrote to the *Morning Post*: "Flogging, used with sound judgment, is the only fundamental principle upon which our large schools can be properly conducted. I am the better for it and am, therefore, one who has been well swished."

When schooldays were over the young victims who had found masochist pleasure in flogging and being flogged had plenty of outlets in which to indulge themselves as adults in the big cities of Britain. Some brothels specialised in flogging. Mrs. Theresa Berkeley, the owner of one of them in Charlotte Street, London, saved on labour costs by inventing a flogging machine. Customers who preferred not to use the "Horse," as the machine was called, could either flog the in-house prostitutes – they had such names as Sally Taylor, One-Eyed Peg, Miss Ring, and Hannah Jones – or be flogged by one or several of them. Needless to say, Mrs. Berkeley made a huge fortune from her brothel and retired to the easy life of a refined Victorian gentlewoman.

The English public school was created originally for the young sons of officers serving in the far-flung corners of the Empire. When they resorted to flogging – called in France the English vice – the young scions of the military were simply enacting what their fathers were about. The many references to it in literature suggest that it was enjoyed by the floggers, the flogged, and the audience who crowded into the school hall to watch the fun. It might be concluded that one reason why so many British males are emotionally repressed today is because they bear the hereditary burden of this alternative sexual experience. Neville Heath's partner Margery Gardner was not the only victim to have been killed in a sexually inspired flogging session and indeed flogging remains merely an esoteric pastime until someone is killed. Then it becomes a sexual murder.

Sado-masochism; history and sexual implications of flogging; "spanking;" bondage

Flogging's long history certainly includes other murders, masquerading as judicial murders, in its embrace, triggered, as we have already seen, by sexual impulses. Sentencing a woman to a whipping, the notorious 17th century Judge George Jeffreys ordered the whipper: "I charge you to pay particular attention to this lady. Scourge her soundly, man. Scourge her till her blood runs down! It is Christmas, a cold time for madam to strip. See that you warm her shoulders thoroughly!"

On another occasion Jeffreys sentenced a man named Tutchin to seven years' imprisonment, during which he was to be whipped each year through every town in Dorset. This meant that for seven years he was to be flogged once a fortnight.

The severity of whipping often amounted to a death sentence. A prisoner named Dangerfield was whipped so ferociously all the way from London's Aldgate to Newgate that he died a few days later.

Whipping became an officially encouraged form of punishment in England in 1530 in a move to control vagrancy. Under the Whipping Act, any vagrant was to be taken to the nearest market place and "there tied to the end of a cart naked, and beaten with whips throughout each market town or other place till the body shall be bloody by reason of such whipping." Half a century later the punishment generally took place at whipping-posts set up in towns and villages throughout the country.

The whip was usually the infamous cat-o-nine-tails, also employed for many years on adult offenders as a means of maintaining discipline in prisons. Birch-rods were used on young offenders. Magistrates in England and Wales (but not Scotland) could order any juvenile delinquent aged eight to 16 to be given six strokes on the bare buttocks – the child's parents had the right to be present. A police constable usually wielded the rod, and some courts allowed the father to inflict the punishment in the presence of a police officer.

Where the miscreant lived had a distinct bearing on

whether he might receive this form of chastisement. In 1935 no birchings were ordered by the juvenile courts in London, Birmingham, Bradford, Bristol, Cardiff, Leeds, Leicester, Liverpool, Newcastle, Nottingham, Plymouth, Portsmouth, Salford and Sheffield. But in that same year Wallasey birched 14 young offenders, Windsor birched seven, Warrington six, and Ramsgate, Accrington and Blackburn each birched two.

Although whipping was frequently administered by our forefathers for sexual satisfaction disguised as punishment, in moderation it was considered therapeutic. In Ancient Greece it was common knowledge that flagellation on the buttocks stimulated sexual appetite, and it became a popular treatment for impotence in men and sterility in women. It was also considered efficacious in cases of constipation – in the baths of ancient Bosnia girls beat naked men to open their pores and prompt the evacuation of their bowels, and a 16th-century Italian philosopher recorded the case of a gentleman unable to pass a motion unless he was whipped.

A 17th-century Danish doctor, Caspar Bartholin, noted: "I have observed that boys, and men too, have been cured of pissing in bed by whipping." In 19th-century Germany a case was recorded of a 15-year-old boy who was fastened to a whipping-bench and thrashed on his naked buttocks until blood flowed, in an attempt to cure him of nocturnal bed-wetting. Whether the treatment worked or not was not recorded.

In Great Staughton, Huntingdonshire, whipping was apparently considered a panacea for just about everything. In 1690 the town council paid eight shillings and sixpence for the guarding and whipping of a woman lunatic, and 20 years later the same council paid a man eight pence for whipping two people suffering from smallpox.

Curiously, although specialist brothels proliferated in Britain for whipping customers, whipping was a routine punishment for prostitution both in Britain and on the Continent. Procuresses arrested in France were placed

Sado-masochism; history and sexual implications of flogging; "spanking;" bondage

on donkeys, their offence was written on their backs, and they were whipped through the streets all the way from the court to the prison. In Spain, prostitutes were stripped naked and thrashed with the birch; in Italy they were branded and whipped, and in Germany any man found with a whore was made to carry her on his shoulders to the whipping-bench.

Women in Britain could be whipped in public until 1817, after which an Act of Parliament prohibited the punishment. Earlier that year a young woman in Scotland became the last of her sex in Britain to receive a public whipping. Convicted of being drunk and disorderly, she was whipped through the streets of Inverness on three separate occasions. Three years later, in 1820, the thrashing of women was prohibited altogether by the Whipping of Female Offenders Abolition Act.

At the beginning of the 20th century American jailers used razor-edged "paddles" to thrash recalcitrant prisoners. A convict at Ohio State Penitentiary recorded that such punishments were known as "seventy-fives," from the number of lashes inflicted. One inmate died after one of these beatings. Bound hand and foot, he had been placed across a trough and flogged until his flesh hung in ribbons and he lost consciousness.

An official investigation into conditions at convict camps in Georgia found they each had a "whipping boss." It was customary for the whipping boss to sand his leather thong to make it sting.

A whipping boss named Goode was resolved to whip Abe Winn, a 16-year-old white boy serving time for stealing two tins of potted ham. Described by witnesses as "a frail little fellow," he had angered Goode by spilling hot coffee on the backs of his pigs. Goode got four Negroes to hold the boy while he gave him 57 licks with his sanded strap.

"I saw young Abe stagger to the hospital steps," said a witness. "He could not lie on his back and died on his stomach. They said he died of consumption."

Corporal punishment was last used in a United Kingdom prison in 1962, and five years later the

Criminal Justice Act, 1967, abolished it. But the English vice continues to flourish all over the world to this day. In February 2007 a Chinese businessman advertised on the internet for a stand-in mistress to be beaten up by his wife to vent her anger and to thus protect his real mistress. The "successful" candidate would be paid 3,000 yuan (£200) per 10 minutes. According to the *Beijing Youth Daily*, more than 10 women applied.

CHAPTER TWO

HOMOSEXUAL SADISM; MYTHOMANIA; TORTURE
Dennis Nilsen, Steven Bailey, Randy Kraft

Since psychological profiling was pioneered by the FBI in the 1970s, and later followed up by Scotland Yard, we have learned a good deal about identifying serial killers. Psychiatrists know that many murderers have a pattern of offending which begins with relatively minor crimes and grows increasingly violent until the offender rapes or murders.

It is frequently noted that these offenders have often had a disturbed childhood. Many children who have grown up to be serial killers have begun by torturing animals. Edmund Emi Kemper, a Californian cannibal convicted in 1973 of killing eight women including his mother, killed cats in his neighbourhood when he was 13, sometimes burying them alive, and putting their heads on poles as trophies. He sliced off the top of one cat's head with a machete, and decapitated another. He also killed his own cat, cutting it into small pieces. Years later he did precisely the same thing to his mother.

Kemper would have felt at home with Carroll Edward Cole, executed in Texas in 1985 for five of the 35 murders of which he was accused. Cole's first act of violence, he recalled, was committed when he was a child and strangled a puppy.

It was also as a child that the cannibalistic sexual serial killer Jeffrey Dahmer impaled frogs, decapitated dogs and staked cats in trees in his back garden. He moved on to killing young men and boys, and confessed to murdering 17 of them at his Milwaukee home. He committed his first murder in 1978, was finally arrested in 1991, given a number of life sentences and murdered in prison two years later by another inmate.

The serial killer Ted Bundy, whose career is dealt with in the next chapter, is another example. In his childhood he witnessed his grandfather's brutality to animals, before he took to torturing them himself.

People who abuse their partners at home are much more likely to commit violent crimes outside the home, as did the Soham murderer Ian Huntley and the M25 rapist Antoni Imiela. One in 12 domestic abusers have convictions for sex attacks on strangers. In common with many domestic abusers, some murderers can be charming and cunning, and extremely adept at manipulating people, including the police.

Psychiatrists try to fit serial killers into categories and then examine the profile of the category: these can include mental health problems, involvement with prostitutes, alcoholism, child murders and of course sexual killing. Some killers may fit into several profiling categories, such as Anthony Hardy, the so-called Camden Ripper, jailed for life in 2003 for murdering three prostitutes whose dismembered remains were found in bin bags. He had a history of domestic violence, mental illness, alcoholism, and obsession with prostitutes and convictions for motor offences.

Although we should try to avoid all strict categorisation where criminals are concerned, the typical sadistic sexual killer is generally young – usually under 35. He tends to be a quiet, withdrawn sort of person, even sometimes a social misfit. This is a problem for him because he yearns to be something that he isn't – he longs to exercise power over others. And he also fantasises about killing long before he actually turns to murder.

This is a profile that fitted like a glove the homosexual serial killer Dennis Nilsen. He was the sort of man who couldn't get on well with anyone. He went into the army and came out again because he didn't like it, then he became a policeman and didn't fit in. Interestingly, both these jobs put him in uniform, which bolstered his very low self-esteem and gave him the sense of power he needed.

Finally he became a clerk in a government department. No one at work liked him much, finding him truculent and inaccessible. Yet Nilsen craved the company of his fellows, whom he so much desired to dominate. To fulfil that desire, he was prepared to kill.

He picked up his first victim, a teenage Irishman, in a pub a few days after Christmas and took the lad back to his apartment, where they continued drinking until they were both in a state of collapse on the bed. Nilsen awoke two or three hours later, pulled back the blankets and gazed at his companion, asleep in an alcoholic stupor. Within a few more hours, he told himself, his new friend would wake up, shake himself down, and disappear out of his life.

"I remember thinking that I wanted him to stay with me over the New Year, whether he wanted to or not," Nilsen was to say later. Overcome by the desire to possess, he strangled the youth with a tie, but failed to kill him. He finally forced the young man's head into a bucket of water and drowned him.

Nilsen gave the corpse a bath, shampooed its hair, laid it on the bed and had sex with it. He had entered into a state of total possession that would last until he would tire of his dead companion. After that he would bury him under the floorboards, and go off in search of a new victim.

At one point he had six bodies under the floorboards of his north London flat. Some of them he cut into pieces and flushed down the lavatory. Others he took out occasionally in order to masturbate over them. He sat them in an armchair to watch TV with him and he would talk to them. One corpse stayed in his armchair for a week, because, said Nilsen, "it was so nice to have someone to come home to."

While under arrest Nilsen decided to psychoanalyse himself. He wrote:

"I may be a creative psychopath who, when in a loss of rationality situation, lapses temporarily into a destructive psychopath. At the subconscious root lies a sense of total social isolation and a desperate search for sexual identity. God only knows what thoughts go through my mind when it's captive within a destructive binge. Maybe the cunning, stalking killer instinct is the only single concentration released from a mind which in that state knows no morality."

At his trial a defence psychiatrist thought that Nilsen suffered "a severe personality disorder," and that when he was killing he was in a state known as dissociation, which meant that it seemed to him he was watching someone else committing murder.

Dissociation, however, is no more than a state of allowing repressed sexual feelings to become so overwhelming that they rule out rational behaviour; the killer is more than happy to pass on the act to "someone else" in his imagination, arguing that it can't be him who is doing these things. It may be a reason, but it isn't an excuse for murder.

It was held that because Nilsen had spared 14 of the young men he picked up he could desist from killing when he wanted to, so he was able to choose between right and wrong. Another medical witness said Nilsen suffered from a "false self syndrome" which was merely a Jekyll and Hyde situation, not dissimilar from dissociation. This type of personality can cope with the world when things are going well, but falls apart under stress.

•

Homosexual sadism is as old as homosexuality, which is as old as time. In the mid-20th century some scientists doubted that homosexuals were born that way, arguing that all the factors that made up a homosexual were environmental. Since the "outing" of so many homosexuals a good deal more has been learned about homosexuality, and the sin that dares not speak its name is finally something that can be spoken about. We know for instance that in the decade from 1990 to 2000 it became much more prevalent. The National Survey of Social Attitudes and Lifestyles, which questioned 11,161 people aged 16 to 44, disclosed that the number of men who reported ever having a homosexual encounter rose from one in 28 in 1990 to one in 19 in the year 2000. For women, the incidence almost tripled, from one in 56 in 1990 to one in 20 in the year 2000.

This represents a quantum leap forward in sexual social history. Sodomy was a serious criminal offence until the mid-20th century, in public and even in private. Males who indulged in mere improper intimacies were not prosecuted, but determined policemen looking for evidence of criminal intercourse sometimes followed them.

Viewed in its historical context, public acceptance of homosexuality depends entirely on the age in which the homosexual happens to be born. If he were born in Sparta, rather than Athens of the Golden Age, he would have been welcomed literally with open arms, for the Spartans expected a man to have sex with another man in preference to a woman. Heterosexual relationships were regarded as second-rate compared to homosexual friendships; heterosexual relations were a tiresome business, which existed only for procreation, certainly not for recreation. If he had served at the court of any of the great Roman emperors of the first century, with the exception of Claudius, he would have been welcomed in the emperor's bedchamber.

If he were born in Victorian England and went to a public school he would have been in his element – homosexuality was endemic throughout all the public schools. Discussing Dean Farrar, the 19th-century author, in his book *The Victorians*, A.N. Wilson wrote: "The school in which he [Farrar] was actually teaching was a hotbed of homosexual bullying, where every pretty boy was given a girl's name and faced the possibility of either being labelled public property – in which case he was frequently compelled into (often public) acts of incredible obscenity – or of being taken over and becoming the exclusive 'bitch' of an older boy."

Contrast this with the situation just a hundred years after that at East Sussex Quarter Sessions, when I was a young journalist reporting on the trial of Rupert Croft-Cooke, a distinguished novelist. Croft-Cooke had picked up two sailors, both adults, and taken them to his private home for homosexual purposes, to which they consented. The village bobby later waylaid the two sailors on their way back to their ship. Having had a good evening's fun, spliced with a drink or two, they told the bobby all about their night of sex up at the author's big house.

None of this was of the slightest interest to the public, no one was harmed, but the morally schismatic British now considered what would have been accepted as a very private affair in a different age as an outrage. Croft-Cooke was sentenced to nine months' imprisonment and his distinguished career was in tatters. A few years later the Wolfenden Report put an end to such nonsense, and what was a custodial offence now became a free-for-all. If there is an element of emotional confusion in the psyche of homosexuals it hasn't been much helped over the centuries by the attitude of legislators and law-enforcement officers.

•

Homosexual love is as obsessive as heterosexual love, lesbian love perhaps even more so. Lesbian love, which has "come out" as a discussion subject in the last few years, is much more often created than congenital – it derives less from an innate impulse than through environmental and cultivation factors. For that reason it frequently does not last for life, as it does with male homosexuality. A girl may develop a "crush" on an older person, for instance, and the environmental support for the development of such a relationship exists in places where women are thrown together, such as schools, universities and prisons. Or a woman may be desperately unhappy with a heterosexual relationship that has gone all wrong, particularly on the physical side, and in desperation seek solace in the arms of another woman, where she knows she can receive respect, gentleness, and love. At most times these partnerships are short-lived, but sometimes they are unbreakable.

Indeed, anyone who tries to break up a lesbian love affair is taking a considerable risk and should beware. Annie Williams, who lived in the Miami suburb of Carol

City, discovered in 1990 that her daughter Cassandra, 19, was having an affair with Valerie Rhodes, also 19, and expressed a mother's natural disaffection. The two teenagers discussed their predicament and then decided to act. On the night of March 19th, 1991, Valerie, who had been hiding in Cassandra's wardrobe, walked up to the sleeping Annie Williams and shot her several times.

"I couldn't watch it," Cassandra Williams said. Nor could she help Valerie drag the body out to Annie's car. They drove to a local park and left the car there with the corpse of its owner inside it. A note predating the murder was found later in the Williamses' home. It was signed by Cassandra, and in it she took full responsibility for drawing Valerie Rhodes into the conspiracy and murder plot. Despite that, both were given life sentences for first-degree murder.

The case was an echo of the infamous New Zealand killing by Pauline Parker, 16, and Juliet Hulme, 15, who in 1954 bludgeoned Pauline's mother to death in a Christchurch park after she had taken steps to have them separated. Pauline and Juliet may not have been de facto lesbian lovers, but they meant the whole world to each other, and their bond, when threatened, was strong enough for them to kill to preserve it. They were sentenced to be detained during Her Majesty's pleasure in separate detention centres. They have since been released.

One of the more intriguing aspects of homosexuality is the gender attitude to it. Men as a rule accept lesbian relationships – they even sometimes find lesbian love erotic. Heterosexual women tend to be affronted by it. Men find it much harder to accept male homosexuality, which women can accept more easily, often feeling "safer" when talking to a male homosexual. The reason is that male homosexuality challenges the essence of heterosexual male virility. When a woman is in the company of a homosexual she knows that the subliminal "battle of the sexes" does not exist, so she can relax.

The sexes close ranks, however, when confronted by a transsexual. In a case some years ago where a male office employee wanted to change sex, his male boss asked some of his staff, men and women, if they would accept the transsexual in their department. They willingly agreed, even upbraiding the boss for his language of circumspection, telling him that he did not understand that these things happened in modern life, and he should learn to accept them.

Three weeks later they sent a deputation, three men and three women, back to the boss, complaining that it was impossible to live in an office with someone of a "third sex;" that the "freak" had been forced upon them, that no one could concentrate on their work, and asking that the transsexual should be removed at once. In such cases the transsexual emerges as a subliminal threat to the sexuality of both the male and female employees; in this particularly case the staff did not recognise this at once.

•

In his film *Psycho* director Alfred Hitchcock portrayed a young man so obsessed with his dead mother that he wears her clothes and a female wig to murder a woman while she is showering, effectively adopting the role of a transvestite in order to kill. The "mother figure" he becomes is avenging herself on the unfortunate victim, for the young man is aware that his mother (even though she is dead) doesn't want him to love or lust after another woman.

The psychiatry is very real, for transvestites exist, as actor Anthony Perkins existed in *Psycho*, in a wholly fictitious universe. When he succumbs to an overwhelming sexual urge to dress in women's clothes the transvestite is completely unaware of the end result, of the gross parody he represents. In his own mind he has become a woman; he has locked out reality and his mind is encompassed in his fiction. In some cases, where he is cross-dressing in private, sudden exposure may bring him sharply and agonisingly to his senses; in other cases, where he goes out into the street and has congress with other transvestites, the lie is so fixed in his mind that he is ready to believe that others believe it too: he is in fact a woman.

Well, some others, perhaps, but not all. In her book *Quai des Ombres* (Fuyard, Paris), Dr. Dominique Leconte, who is in charge of the Paris morgue, tells a sad story of a man brought into the morgue after dying of a heart attack in a nightclub. Before his wife could be summoned to view the body the morgue assistants had to remove the female attire he was dressed in, "including the tennis balls fixed inside his bra." They had rightly decided that the dead man's wife probably knew nothing about her husband's nocturnal activities, and that his sudden death was not the best time to inform her of them.

Transvestites are no more sexual killers than any other deviant group; the similarity is that many sexual killers also experience the living lie that prevents them from confronting all the realities of the world. Psychiatrists recognise that between the ages of three and four some children begin to "arrange" the truth – for example, to avoid being punished. From these arrangements the lie is born – the lie which all of us make use of more or less at some time during our lives. Through an unconscious decision and to avoid frustrations, the ability to construct myths about oneself is also created. This is called mythomania, and has been defined as "a form of psychiatric disequilibrium characterised by a tendency to fabricate, to lie, to simulate."

The mythomane is not, however, a true liar. The true liar knows that he is lying – he has every intention of deceiving someone and acts with the full knowledge of what he is doing. A mythomane, on the other hand, believes what he is saying – he doesn't lie to deceive but to convince himself. The reason for this is that he cannot live with himself as he is. He wants to be recognised for what he isn't, he has to adopt all the traits of someone else to give him his own right to exist.

In 2004 a pretty blonde Frenchwoman, Florence Le Vot, stunned television viewers when she went on a chat show, sub-titled "Living for 20 years with a Severe Illness," to describe her experiences. For 10 years, she told the audience, she had suffered from successive cancers caused by a birth control product that had been prescribed to her mother in pregnancy.

The product, Florence explained, had caused malformations in other children whose mothers had taken it, but in her case nothing happened until she reached adolescence. "Then, at that time, I was stricken with illness. First my uterus, then my ovaries, next my intestines..."

The 12 operations she had undergone were a nightmare of pain. As the audience listened to her story, it was clear that her courage was shining through. Determined not to go under, Florence took up one of the most demanding and spectacular of modern sports – jet-skiing. You can see jet-skiers hard at work off most of the fashionable Mediterranean beaches, drawing figures in the sea on their high-powered scooters. Florence not only joined their ranks, she twice won the world jet-ski championship.

Such was her fame that she was chosen as stand-in to Lara Croft in the movie *Tomb Raider*, and posed nude for a magazine – all this while crippled with pain. The TV studio audience, all cancer sufferers themselves, listened enthralled at this triumph of the human mind over matter. What they didn't know was that the whole story was a tissue of lies.

Florence in fact was born a boy, named Geoffroy Le Vot. She (or he) had already told her story 10 years earlier in another TV programme in which she began with the words: "I was born a boy, but I very quickly realised that this was an error of nature..."

As a child the boy wanted to wear a dress, to play with dolls, and as an adolescent his masculine genitals bemused him. To this equally fascinated TV audience he described the mental torture caused by his dilemma. "I'm going to England for an operation," he told them. "When I come back I shall be a woman."

In truth, and this was the truth, he did go to England

and was surgically transformed into a woman. Back in France he needed more operations, with painful side effects. He was now inevitably feeling the acute isolation of the transvestite who becomes a transsexual, who must suffer alone, who cannot confide in family or old friends, because none of them can really understand this abnormality. So he began to lie, re-inventing his life just as his body had been re-invented. Henceforth he was Florence. He (or she) worked for a cosmetics company in Bayonne, in the French Basque country. To explain his frequent absences for his corrective operations, he invented cancer. But he also had to invent a past, one that corresponded with the lie that he had been a girl all his life.

Probably unlike most people in her situation, Florence couldn't stop talking, and as she talked she embellished.

•

Recently an experiment was carried out in America where a boy twin was dressed as a girl from birth and raised and educated as such; the theory being that boys could be "turned into" girls if you started early enough. But the unhappy subject of his experiment finally threw off this false shroud after 18 years of misery, cut his hair short, bought a suit of clothes and has lived happily ever after as a male person.

Subsequently a medical researcher claimed to have discovered that a minuscule part of the human brain is different in women than in men – in other words, girls are born girls and boys are born boys, and all the evidence for that is written in the structure of their brains. The research showed that in some cases some homosexual men have the distinctive brain mark of women; hence, it was argued, homosexuals may be born as such.

Few have much doubt about that these days, the consensus being that both nature and nurture can create homosexuality. The causes of homosexual sadistic murder are, however, scarcely different from the causes of heterosexual sadistic murder – primarily they are jealousy, theft, blackmail and, as was the case with Nilsen, loneliness coupled with pure erotic stimulation. As with all sexual murder, a perversion of the sexual impulse within the killer has to find an outlet through aggression, through inflicting torture and severe pain on the victim. Frequently the seat of the sadistic homosexual killer's aggression is his victim's penis, suggesting that this is a substitute for sexual intercourse, the sadistic killer being released from sexual tension through sadistic acts of torture.

When the sense of being "different" dawns upon a homosexual it can give rise to a cocktail of emotions including fear, despair, shame, and particularly loneliness, the desire for company that was so evident in the case of Dennis Nilsen. It is because of these linked emotions that the homosexual finds release in alcohol as a lever to his sadism; again, this was apparent in the Nilsen case.

In a recent American case of homosexual murder the prisoner's statement to police after his arrest was very typical of this type of sadistic killing. "I knew the fellow about two days," the statement read. "He gave me a lift in his car. We stopped and bought three or four bottles of wine. We then went to a hotel in a nearby town and arrived there about dusk. We got a room and got undressed and went to bed. We indulged in the act of mutual masturbation and an attempt of sodomy was made after fooling around for some time and drinking and quarrelling.

"Then everything seemed to go blank on me. I can remember standing over him – he was bleeding. I remember we had drunk all the wine and the knife was lying on the table. I remember hitting him on the chest. Then I stabbed him and he hollered, 'My God, you've stabbed me!' Then he began yelling for help, and I kept beating him over the head with a wine bottle. Then someone came to the door and I went out of the window by the fire escape. I didn't intend to kill him, but when I got started, I couldn't stop."

What was happening here was characteristic of the sadist: the build-up to a sexual frenzy which, as it moved towards its apogee, was unstoppable; the uncontrolled frenzy was a substitute for the final sex act. The killer was described by psychiatrists who examined him as "temperamentally cold, perverted and hyper-sexual."

•

Male-to-male sexual crime often depends on the instigator employing deceptive charm. This was the chief weapon in the armoury employed by Steven Bailey, who was known around the internet world as the great master of dangerous sexual fantasy. After his arrest following a torture session that went disastrously wrong, he boasted: "I was flown several times to people's homes for my various talents – and because I'm a nice guy."

After he was diagnosed with the HIV virus in 1991, the physically ravaged Bailey began to find his salvation on the internet. He posted a profile on his website telling interested readers he was looking for adult men to play, among other things, fantasy strangulation. There were exchanges of phone calls, photos and meetings that took place in the applicants' homes, or in his own one-bedroom flat in St. Paul, Minnesota.

At home Bailey created a torture chamber in his bedroom, equipping it with a harness and accessories such as handcuffs, ropes and similar bondage gear to restrain a person during sex. He used ligatures and nooses in order to restrict his willing victim's flow of blood, and oxygen to heighten the death-defying thrill of the sex act. And he would soak a gag in chloroform and place it over the victim's nose and mouth.

It was a kinky interest in erotic asphyxiation that drew Maceo Brodnax, aged 53, to visit Bailey. Brodnax travelled across the United States from his home in West Hollywood, California, to spend some time with the "great master."

The two had already made contact in an internet chat room aimed at those interested in sexual domination and asphyxia. They talked a few times on the phone, and Brodnax e-mailed a photo of himself to Bailey before his arrival at the start of what was supposed to be a three-day visit. In fact, it was a visit that was to end in lies, videotape and death.

In the early hours of November 6th, 2002, a neighbour spotted Bailey dragging a naked body, partially covered with a blanket, and later identified as Maceo Brodnax, through the car park of his block of flats. The neighbour called the police and officers arrived just as Bailey was attempting to pull the body into a passenger seat of his car with the help of a rope he had tied around the corpse. Caught red-handed, he was arrested and admitted to having killed Brodnax.

Police took away four boxes of evidence from Bailey's flat. They included paraphernalia more associated with a medieval torture chamber than a small apartment in a quiet, middle-class suburb. They also found a videotape which Bailey had recorded of a sex act with Brodnax.

Forensic tests on the decomposing body established that Brodnax died within hours of his arrival at Bailey's home, and that the body had been kept there for four days before Bailey attempted to dispose of it. Although it was clear that the body had been moved around the apartment several times in those four days, police declined to elaborate on Bailey's motives for keeping it for so long.

Bailey at first insisted that Brodnax attacked him with an ashtray and while defending himself he killed his visitor. This is the classic defence in such cases, and it was soon changed. The new story was that Brodnax died because Bailey had gone to answer the phone while he was asphyxiating his visitor with a gasmask, plastic bag and chloroform-soaked rag. He said he then forgot to revive him until it was too late.

Incredibly, phone records revealed that he was on the phone for nearly an hour.

Bailey told police his only mistake was that he did not

contact them immediately. The prosecutor said: "He was a big talker. I think he's used to being in control and I think he perceived himself as being in control of the interview when we talked to him. He may not be a predator as such, but you can't help wondering what kind of harm other visitors to his chamber of horrors have endured."

The case raised legal questions about how to prosecute an accused man when two consenting adults engage in a sex act that ends in tragedy. Describing Bailey's modus operandi, Peter Erlinder, professor of law at St. Paul, Minnesota, University, explained: "It's part of the sex act – part of it is causing bodily harm and there must therefore be a certain amount of risk, and that being so, there has also to be a certain amount of co-operation.

"The question then becomes whether this was beyond consent, and whether the individual who survived was doing more than what was consented to."

While Bailey had no criminal record, police found an e-mail he wrote shortly before meeting Brodnax. It detailed his fascination with sexual violence, "especially if it ends in the slow, brutal death of one or more of the men involved." The e-mail invited men to contact him for "brutal games."

Bailey said the e-mail was taken out of context and was part of the sheer fantasy that practitioners like him use on the internet. He added: "Because I have AIDS, I always use a condom. I'm very responsible. I'm into this rough stuff, but I don't kill people. That is not my world."

He was charged with third-degree murder. When his trial began in April , 2003, he elected to be heard before a judge rather than a jury.

There was no evidence that Bailey ever received money for performing his sex acts, and Judge George Stephenson ruled that the state couldn't prove that the accused was in a depraved state of mind when Brodnax met his death. The state hadn't shown beyond reasonable doubt that Bailey acted without regard for human life.

But he had caused the death of Brodnax by creating an unreasonable risk and consciously taking a chance of causing death or great bodily harm, and as a result he was acquitted of the murder charge but found guilty of manslaughter. He was sentenced to serve between four and seven years in prison.

The judge noted that Bailey tried to revive the unconscious Brodnax and that he then went on to issue e-mail alerts about the use of chloroform. This indicated that the death caught him by surprise. He would not by any means have been the first of the many performers in acts of erotic asphyxiation who have been caught by surprise when someone dies. Their satisfaction comes when the oxygen supply to the brain is cut off at the moment of orgasm, providing an extra sexual thrill. Perhaps it goes without saying that this is a highly dangerous practice.

Steven Bailey was a particularly unsafe man for internet respondents because he embodied the primary assets of a dangerous homosexual criminal – his notable charm, which he boasted about, and his desire to control, which was remarked upon by the prosecutor at his trial. He told police he had been with 5,000 men during his lifetime. It seems that 4,999 can count themselves very fortunate that they didn't meet the same fate as the luckless Maceo Brodnax.

•

Randy Stephen Kraft, a 38-year-old computer analyst in California, was another homosexual charmer. In his case his gloss of urbanity and good looks hid a maniacal sexual killer, and when he was finally arrested LA Police breathed a sigh of relief. For years they had been trying to catch a predator who picked up lone men on the freeways, tortured and defiled them, and then threw them out of his car window. The bodies of no fewer than 30 young men had been found dumped by the side of freeways, the seemingly endless ribbons of multi-lane motorways that spread like a spider's web over southern

California, and other corpses were found in wasteland and desert scrub. Now at last they had the man they had been hunting.

Kraft was caught by a routine police patrol as he was cruising the San Diego freeway. When he was pulled over on to the hard shoulder he got out of his car and walked towards the police car – a sure sign to the officers that there was something in his vehicle that he hoped they wouldn't find. There was, and they did find it. It was the body of Terry Lee Gambrel, a 25-year-old marine. His trousers were open and wet and there were ligature marks on his neck. "He thumbed a lift and I just picked him up," Kraft explained unconvincingly.

There were plenty more incriminating things in Kraft's car, including beers, a knife, a can of spray that could be used as an aphrodisiac on a prospective gay lover, nine different prescription drugs, 47 photographs of young men, some of them naked, some clothed, some apparently dead, and the belt that had been used to strangle the young marine. There was also a notebook in code which, deciphered, suggested that Kraft had killed 67 men.

So what kind of man was Randy Kraft, who from all outward appearances was an all-American boy, but who, if his coded claim were true, would rate among the worst homosexual killers of all time? Curiously, his very ordinariness was remarkable. His father was an aircraft factory worker, and Randy was an only son, who got on well with his three sisters. He was a good sportsman and an academic achiever. At university he studied economics and there, after a few parties involving sadomasochistic bondage, declared his homosexuality. He was 22. Seven years later he rented a flat with a gay friend, Jeff Seelig, who he had already known for several years, and set up home with him. After that his rise to a highly paid job in the computer industry was meteoric.

A few hours after Kraft's arrest on the freeway Jeff Seelig arrived home to find his shared house overrun by policemen in overalls. There was plenty more evidence on hand, including the possessions of several young men whose bodies had been picked up alongside the freeway system. Suspicion naturally also fell on Seelig, who at 29 was 10 years younger than Kraft, but after hours of questioning detectives were satisfied that he had no idea of his flat-mate's nocturnal encounters with strangers. Yes, they were both into sado-masochism; they occasionally had threesomes, and sometimes Kraft brought home strangers for his own sexual gratification. But their "domestic" sex life had hit a bad patch over the past 10 weeks, and Kraft had gone off most nights on his own.

An examination of Kraft's victims revealed a streak of delight in torture within him that was never apparent to many of his friends, for whom he was always the life and soul of the party, the very popular one.

One victim, Cruz Mestas, an art student, had a toothpick jammed into his penis before he died. When his body was found both hands had been cut off and the stumps wrapped in plastic bags. Another victim, Malcolm Little, a truck driver, was found with his legs spread apart revealing all too obviously that his genitals had been cut off. A tree branch had been forced into his rectum. The naked body of another, Anthony Silveira, aged 29, had a toothbrush inserted into his anus. The body of Mike Inderbieten, another truck driver, had been emasculated, his nipples burned by a cigarette lighter, and a large blunt object forced into his rectum. The body of Mark Hall was found with its penis chopped off and a cocktail stick had been jammed into the penis with such ferocity that it was lodged in the bladder. His face and one of his nipples were badly burned with a cigarette lighter and the evidence suggested that the torture had taken place while he was still alive.

Some of the victims died from an overdose of pills, others were strangled. In most cases Kraft incapacitated his victims with alcohol and pills, tied them up, sodomised them and then tortured them before strangling them.

He was bought to trial in September, 1988. His defence was that someone else, and not him, was the freeway killer, and as the seemingly limitless catalogue of horror was recited he sat calmly taking notes. After an 11-day retirement the jury found him guilty of 16 murders between 1972 and 1983, and on August 3rd, 1989, he was sentenced to death.

How Randy Kraft, who had so much going for him, became a psychopath, torturing and killing, is hard to fathom. He was the product of a good home with loving parents, he did not torture animals as a boy, he had no previous criminal record, he was articulate, highly intelligent, good-looking, and popular in his circle of homosexual friends. While many serial sexual killers can be profiled and categorised, Kraft remains one who doesn't fit in anywhere.

CHAPTER THREE

FETISHISM
Ted Bundy, Jerry Brudos, Frederick Ducharme

We have seen how Dennis Nilsen was a chronic misfit who desperately wanted to fit in. He was hopelessly weak yet he craved power. He was desperately lonely but wanted companionship. So he turned to corpses for sexual comfort.

Paradoxically, turning to an inanimate object for comfort can also be a rejection of human company. This is the motivation of the fetishist, who actually wants to retreat from the reality of a sexual partner. He takes his inanimate object – usually a piece of clothing like lingerie or shoes – and uses it as the focus of his sexual desire.

It is generally held that only men can be fetishists because the subconscious purpose of a fetish is that it is a rejection of women, a refuge in some object connected with a female but out of her physical presence. This object of the fetish becomes a symbol behind which the sexual partner entirely disappears, and the symbol becomes itself an adequate stimulus for masturbation and orgasm. However, some psychiatrists argue that a woman can be a fetishist because cases are documented where shy, self-effacing women who hold themselves in low self-esteem have achieved erotic thrills from unlikely inanimate objects like rings and necklaces, particularly if they have stolen them.

The reason why a male fetishist rejects women can be complex. It may arise out of some repression in childhood. It may be fear. It may be a conditioning influence. For instance, a sensitive boy may become anxious in adolescence about the size of his genitalia; for him, one scoffing remark in a communal changing room can have a devastating effect on the psyche and produce in him an everlasting dread of revealing himself in front of a woman. Locked in his world of angst, he turns to a vicarious object, a fetish.

For other fetishists it may be a sense of inadequacy about sexual performance, or it may be deep-rooted guilt. For others still it may be a substitute for normal sex because they see the sex act as an affront to their sense of morality.

Whatever the cause, the driving force is imagination and fantasy and the fetish object is the outlet for it. The fetish object becomes magical in his mind and if it is a body fetish it may transmute to the fetishist as a revelation of all that is pure and good about the female in his mind, to whom the fetish belonged. The fetish object prevents him having to face the humiliation of rejection. Note here that the fetishist is probably a sensitive person. Human beings differ hugely in their ability to use their imaginations, which is why some are great artists and writers, while others cannot draw a line or write a note. If we apply the same breadth of imagination to sexual stimulus we should not wonder that even a lock of hair, cut from the head of an admired girl, might drive some fetishists to sexual frenzy.

Jerry Brudos's fetish was for women's high-heeled shoes. When he was five years old he found a pair of them on a rubbish dump, took them home, and clumped around the house in them, much to the annoyance of his mother. When he was 16 he planned to capture a young woman, hide her in a secret place and do whatever he wanted with her – the theme of John Fowles's novel *The Collector*.

Still in his teens, he became a clothes thief. Then he was charged with assault after trying to force a young girl to take off her clothes.

Brudos was married and the father of two children when, one night in January, 1968, a girl called at his home in Portland, Oregon, selling encyclopaedias. He invited her in, took her to his workshop, and strangled her. He undressed her and tried lingerie and high-heeled shoes from his collection on her still warm corpse. Then he cut off her left foot, slipped it into a high-heeled shoe, and put it in a basement freezer. He got rid of the rest of her body by throwing it into a nearby river.

For Brudos the supreme sexual thrill was to remove the severed foot in its high-heeled shoe from his refrigerator and masturbate in front of it, He thus had all the accoutrements he needed for female desire without the complexities of the female herself.

Ten months later he killed again. He cut off one breast from his victim's body. Before throwing the rest of the corpse into the same river he photographed it hanging on a hook in his workshop – a photograph that was later to trap him because it revealed his own image reflected in a mirror. Psychiatrists easily recognised the voyeuristic conduct in this second murder. Fetishists frequently enjoy watching themselves, and mirrors and photography figure largely in their scheme of things. A few months later Brudos picked up another girl, raped her, strangled her, cut off both her breasts, and then raped her dead body.

In April, 1969, his last murder was a carbon copy of the third one. A tip-off from a young woman alerted police, who raided Brudos's home and found plenty of evidence to condemn him. He received three life sentences.

The rapes which accompanied the murders in the later cases were not characteristic of the fetishist, who generally does not seek the gratification of his normal sexual impulse by such obvious violence. But just as the severed foot was a fetish for him, so were the severed breasts. These were not just the anatomical parts of a woman, they were symbolic.

Why should the fetishist be at such pains to escape from the reality of women? One answer is fear, arising from emotional under-development. The fetishist adopts his perversion through a profound fear of being rejected by the real object of his attraction, his sensitive nature being unable to face the humiliation of rejection. Another answer is hatred – a desire to kill and destroy the object that was once the focus of love, and retain just a part of it for sexual satisfaction.

Brudos's conduct was extreme for a fetishist but the motivation was essentially fetishism. The fetishist cannot always get satisfaction from normal intercourse – his "supreme thrill" is entirely in his imagination, using a prop, in this case the severed foot in the high-heeled shoe, or the severed breast, to create his dream pictures.

Shoe fetishism is common among fetishists, the shoe probably symbolising the need for the fetishist to be dominated by a female, since he is unable to dominate her himself. In one case examined in America a man with a shoe fetish discovered that when he masturbated he could only achieve orgasm while holding one of his girl friend's high-heeled shoes – the girl friend did not have to be present. When she went off and married another man she understandably took all her shoes with her. The fetishist then began stealing high-heeled shoes from a shop. He took only one each time rather than a pair, but soon came to need a new shoe each time he masturbated. Asked why this was so, after he was arrested for shoplifting, he said that in his mind's eye each new shoe represented a virgin.

Fetishism in fact comes in a variety of ways. A fetish can be a flower, or it may be a picture, or it may even be simply a particular smell. Any unusual fixation on any object, such as stockings (object fetishism), or part of the female body (body fetishism) like the buttocks, is a form of fetishism where the attraction makes the fetishist more passionate. Hair is a particularly common form of fetish. In a recent case in America a serial killer murdered only dark-haired girls (this was a hate fetish); his divorced wife and his current girl friend were both redheads, and there was no history of him having molested them.

A. Binet, a Victorian psychologist, described fetishism as what a man saw during an early sexual encounter. Because most early sexual encounters are associated with lingerie, this may explain why some sexual killers retain "trophies", generally knickers, belonging to their victims. The fact that most men have a perfectly healthy interest in lingerie demonstrates that fetishism is nothing to worry about unduly in its early stages – like flogging, it only becomes dangerous when it is used as a vehicle for killing.

Fetishism in its milder form is self-contained and does no harm, except that it keeps the fetishist in a state of tension, which may lead to overt personality problems. Male X, for example, may be erotically excited when Female Y wears a black suspender belt. Stimulated by the suspender belt, the fetish, he makes love to her, and throughout she remains the object of his desire; she is the loved one. However, when Male X begins to regard Female Y as merely an adjunct to the suspender belt, which then becomes all-prevailing as his erotic stimulus, he may become psychopathic.

The fetishist's obsession also becomes a nuisance when, intent on a body object, he steals from clotheslines. In a recent case police arrested a man of 56 who was caught stealing women's underwear that had been hung out to dry. When they raided his home they found over a hundred articles of women's underclothes neatly folded away in drawers. All had been stolen from the washing hung out in local gardens and were used regularly as objects of sexual stimulation. Psychiatrists have noted that once a fetishism is formed it will often last into old age and will be kept by the fetishist even when he is impotent – he will continue to get erotic delight simply by stroking it.

Fetishism in its more severe form can be extremely dangerous. Detectives investigating the violent sexual murder of Blanche Fisher, a single 45-year-old who lived in the prosperous Grandview district of Vancouver in 1950, were surprised when on a routine patrol they saw a man walking along the pavement without his trousers on.

The man wore a light raincoat, a scarf and a pair of short rubber boots. But his legs were bare.

The detectives pulled alongside, whereupon the raincoat man suddenly sprinted across a car park. The officers took off after him in a breakneck race that ended only when the man stumbled into a rabbit-hole, giving them an extra moment to overtake him. They found that the only clothing he had on under his raincoat was a silk shirt.

At police headquarters the stocky, redheaded prisoner claimed that he had blacked out that night and had regained his senses just moments before the chase, only to discover that most of his clothes were gone, along with all his money. "I was on my way home when you saw me," he said. "I ran away from you because I was bewildered."

The prisoner called himself Frederick Farnsworth, 34, although it later transpired that his real name was Frederick Ducharme. When he said he lived on a houseboat beneath Burrard Bridge, the detectives were instantly on the alert – Burrard Bridge was the place where Blanche Fisher's battered body was found.

Her body was pulled from the water two hours after her killer had thrown it in. She was covered with lacerations and bruises, and she had been drowned after being strangled. The lacerations, particularly on her throat, and irregular scratches on her forehead caused by a knife-like instrument, indicated she had been tortured during a violent and prolonged sexual attack.

It took time for the officers to ascertain that Ducharme's story was phoney, and that in fact he had been out prowling for a woman to attack. He stuck to a line that he often had black-out spells which lasted several hours; it was because of these attacks, he claimed, he had been discharged from the Royal Canadian Air Force three years earlier.

"I ate dinner at home last evening," he insisted. "I can't remember anything after that until I came out of the spell and was on the street. I don't know what happened to my clothes or my money."

Ducharme's houseboat turned out to be a crude, one-room affair built on a barge-like hull. Inside it was littered with newspaper, clothing, pots and pans and a crazy assortment of junk, none of which looked very interesting. But behind a chest of drawers investigators found a pair of women's black shoes which were later found to have belonged to Blanche Fisher. On top of the chest were news clippings about the murder. And in a drawer they found a collection of trinkets, among them a woman's Bulova watch mounted on a silver ring. It matched perfectly the description of Blanche Fisher's ring.

That Ducharme was involved in the murder of Blanche was put beyond all doubt when the investigators found a button under some debris in a corner of the houseboat. It was one of the buttons torn from her coat – two were ripped off as she struggled for her life.

He was arrested and charged with Blanche's murder. But the evidence of what had led him to the ultimate crime, his obsessive object fetishism, was clear for all to see. On a clothesline on the houseboat half a dozen pairs of women's knickers were waving in the breeze. Ducharme was a single man and he had no girl friends.

Shoes, knickers – the fetishist lamely tried to explain them all away. He had obtained the knickers in various ways. He stole some from clotheslines, others he kept as "souvenirs" from various girls he had known. He found the shoes in the street a couple of weeks earlier.

The picture that emerged was of a man who was probably once placid, gradually feeding his imagination with object fetishes until his mind was overwhelmed, until he was prepared to kill to satisfy his overheated lust. This extreme condition is thankfully rare, but the case shows that fetishism, like all sexual deviancies, has no limits unless it is kept sensibly in check.

Ducharme paid for his crime with his life. After a 14-day trial he was hanged at the provincial prison of Oakalla on June 30th, 1950.

•

One new variant of fetishism that has arisen in recent years is the "chat line," where customers call women for a sexually explicit conversation. In these instances the fetish is the caressing, disembodied voice and the fetishist, distant from the reality of the female object, gives full rein to his imagination under the stimulus of the fetishist words as he brings himself to a state of high excitement, if not to orgasm. The other winner, of course, is the owner of the chat line, who charges a premium rate for it.

The profile of the fetishist is not a difficult one to draw. He generally keeps a low profile and is shy and introverted, particularly in the presence of women. He may have been brought up in a strict and repressed family at odds perhaps with his sensitive nature. He tends to be obsessed with his perversion and uses his fetish more frequently than a normal heterosexual person engages in sexual intercourse; he will sometimes repeatedly masturbate over his fetish until he is exhausted.

He is narcissistic. Being afraid of straight sexual encounters, he sees himself, rather than any girl friend, as an object of true love. He is generally timid, easily slighted and humiliated, suspecting affronts that cause him to retreat into himself. This creates in him a block to understanding other people's meanings, which may be completely harmless; hence, too, he is unable to understand a woman partner. He is often afraid of impotency in a realistic heterosexual situation.

The fetish condition is much more widespread than one might believe and for that reason it should not be supposed that just because a man is a fetishist he is therefore an embryonic sexual criminal. A glance down the list of "chat line" operators reveals that they are in abundance – they could not be in abundance unless there were an abundant number of clients, a number far greater than the number of sexual criminals. The truth is we live in a society where sexual outlets and sexual repression are strictly controlled; we do not always know our way through the minefield of rules. As a result many men grow up emotionally repressed, a condition not helped by the rapid emancipation of women, now demanding their "fair share" of anything on offer.

A noted German psychiatrist has suggested that in some cases fetishism may be an outlet from a previous perversion which has since been repressed. Prevented by a parent from satisfying his visual curiosity by looking at his half-dressed sister, for example, a sensitive boy may find an outlet for this repression in his sister's clothing, objects which would not normally have any erotic significance. The danger here is that the boy has substituted one repressed perversion with another.

•

The sexual criminal who develops by way of fetishism becomes a fantasiser who develops physical urges that are not satisfied by his fantasies alone and which therefore need to be fulfilled in the world of reality. Such a sexual criminal was Ted Bundy. Besides being one of the most fiendish killers in US history, Bundy was a fetishist, a sadist, a necrophiliac and probably a paedophile. He raped and killed at least 15 college students – the FBI estimate that the number of his victims was as high as 36. They were of a kind – dark-haired with a parting in the middle of the head – indicating his fetish for this particular type. After killing some of them he applied make-up to their faces, washed their hair and committed acts of necrophilia on them, even when their bodies were decomposing.

Often he strangled them during the sexual act, stuffing their vaginas with mud and dirt and sodomising them with bottles and aerosol cans.

Bundy was 15 and doing an early-morning paper round when nine-year-old Anne Marie Burr, a neighbour's daughter, disappeared without trace. He never came under suspicion, but she was probably his first victim.

Characteristics of a fetishist were incised in his personality. He had a high IQ and there was an unusual factor in his early life that intrigued psychiatrists. Bundy was illegitimate, a fact that so worried his highly religious mother that she left town for his birth.

For the first three months of his life Bundy was left without his mother in the nursing home where he was born, while she talked to her parents about adoption possibilities. It is believed that if an animal is deprived of mother love even for the first few days of its life it loses the ability to form bonds of affection. Was this the time, it has been suggested, that his career as a serial killer was determined? It is not unusual for a fetishist to be fearful of the intimate company of women, although this is not always outwardly visible. In Bundy's case his mother's rejection would act as a conditioning influence, causing him to close himself in with his sex impulse.

Ted Bundy grew up as a presentable, handsome, athletic man. He gained a degree and went to law school. He seemed to have many qualities to attract women, and women were certainly attracted to him. But, like a true fetishist, he was shy, over-sensitive and immature in his relationships, and he had an overwhelming fear of dealing with women in conventional courtship. As a result he saw them only as objects over which he had to have complete and violent sexual control.

None of this was visible. His friends at law school were awed by his confidence and his knowledge. One professor put him in the top one per cent of students. Some, though, saw his confidence differently. For District Attorney Frank Tucker, "He was the most cocky person I have ever faced."

His regular girl friend Meg Anders said that he insisted on practising sodomy and bondage on her, but she stopped it when on one occasion he half strangled her while she was tied up. A previous girl friend described how he used to tie her up with her stockings before sex.

Experts agree that such acts are for the most part within the normal range of sexuality, that everyone has a degree of sado-masochism in their make-up. But when such deviancy is totally relied upon, its practitioner is wandering into the psychopathic. A striving for power and sexual mastery develops, coupled with a striving for appreciation.

The Florida neighbourhood where Bundy was to claim his last victims certainly appeared peaceful enough, if somewhat shabby. It was at least a comfortable shabbiness, familiar to most old Southern college towns. The former gentry who once called it home have departed, but its broad streets, shaded by ancient oaks, are still much in evidence.

Many of the old mansions still stand, too, their white columns or wide verandas set back on generous lawns. Their elegance, however, has departed along with the cotton aristocrats who built them. Most have been divided up into boarding-houses, small apartments, or taken over by the fraternities and sororities of Florida State University.

In any era this was an unlikely setting for the kind of violence that was visited on it in the 1970s. It began here on September 29th, 1969, when a female medical student was found dead in her bed in her flat in West LaFayette Street. Her nightdress was hiked up around her head and she had been raped before being beaten to death with a blunt instrument.

While, five years later, police were still searching for the brutal killer, an art student living in St. Augustine Street took her Irish setter for a walk and disappeared. Both she and the dog were found dead on May 17th, 1975, the dog on the back seat of a car, the raped and partly dressed body of its mistress in the boot. She had been shot four times with a .22 pistol.

Not far from where the art student's car was discovered in Apalachicola National Forest, another student was found on May 1st, 1977. She had been beaten senseless and dragged to a campus car park. She survived, recovered and returned to her parents' home in the Midwest. But "she couldn't remember a thing; it was a case of total amnesia," the police announced.

While this young girl was struggling for her life in a Tallahassee hospital, one of her closest college friends, Margaret Bowman, from St. Petersburg, Florida, visited her frequently. A university professor who taught both girls said, "Margaret Bowman was emotionally distraught that her student friend couldn't attend classes for several weeks. I know it upset her terribly. They were very close."

The battered student did not return to Florida for

the autumn and winter terms in 1977-78, but Margaret Bowman did. She moved to a new sorority house named the Chi Omega (a sorority house in the US is essentially a female dormitory; the male equivalent is a fraternity house) that was a short distance from where her friend was attacked, and just a few blocks from the West LaFayette and St. Augustine Street addresses where the two earlier victims lived.

Built in the early 70s, the Chi Omega, a brick and white painted building, was a comparative newcomer among the stately but decaying homes of an earlier era. In the winter of 1978 it housed about 40 girl students.

Margaret Bowman, 21, was studying fashion merchandising, and had been elected to the student senate. She was born in Honolulu, the daughter of a career Air Force officer. She also worked part-time at The Colony, a clothes shop, to help pay for her studies.

The room next door to hers was occupied by 20-year-old Lisa Levy, who was also studying fashion merchandising and also worked part-time at The Colony to help pay for her education. The room across the hall from the two girls was shared by Karen Chandler, a fashion design student, and petite Kathy Kleiner. Karen had taken the previous year's sex assault on her sorority house sister almost as hard as Margaret Bowman, and worried endlessly about the safety of the girls living in the house.

On Saturday night, January 14th, 1978, most of the girls were out on dates. They straggled back in ones and twos, some of them not getting home until early Sunday morning, January 15th. Generally, they entered by the back door, which had a push-button combination lock that was supposed to be kept fastened after midnight.

Karen Chandler was one of the early ones in. She'd had dinner with her parents and got back to her room about 10.30 p.m. After watching TV for a while she went to sleep about midnight. Kathy Kleiner was already in bed. She went to a wedding earlier in the day and retired by 11.30 p.m. Lisa Levy made it an early evening too. After a nightcap with another student at a bar next door, the two girls returned to the house at about 10.30 p.m.

Lisa went to bed. The other girl sat up talking to Margaret Bowman until about 2.45 p.m. She remembered noting the time on her digital clock as she got into bed.

Student Nita Neary got back from a party at 3 a.m. and found the rear door ajar, which was contrary to regulations. Even more strange, the hall lights upstairs were turned off.

Nita changed into her nightclothes and went to the bathroom, which, as in most dormitories, was shared, and opened into the common hallway. While she was brushing her teeth she heard the closed bathroom door squeak.

"It only does that when someone walks by," she later explained. "But when I came out, there was no one there." Nita then went into the shared living-room to turn off the lights. As she did so, she heard a thump and footsteps from the floor above. The footsteps hurried down the stairs.

Nita turned towards the foyer, and then paused. A man was standing by the door. His left hand was under the doorknob; in his right hand he grasped a club, holding it in the centre so that both ends protruded from his fist. "It looked like a log because of the texture. It was rough, like tree bark. I thought he was either a burglar or one of the girls had got up enough courage to sneak a guy up."

The man appeared "frozen." As she was standing in the now darkened living room, "three or four yards away," she could see that he was motionless. For a matter of seconds the silent tableau held, then the man disappeared through the door.

"I don't think he saw me," Nita later told the police. His face was turned away the whole time, his profile to her. But as an art student she was trained to observe. She remembered he was a white man wearing white trousers and a dark coat. A knitted ski cap covered most of his face. He had a sharp triangular nose, thin but prominent.

Concerned, Nita ran upstairs to wake her roommate and alert her to the possible burglary. The roommate grabbed her umbrella from a cupboard and thus armed the two girls ventured downstairs to check the front door. It was locked. They peered out of the window. The front garden and street were deserted. Still concerned, however, they went back upstairs to wake the sorority president.

Down the hallway, they saw Karen Chandler stagger out of her room, bent over, her head in her hands as if she were ill. They ran to help her and saw that blood covered her face and hands. Through the open dormitory door they saw Kathy Kleiner sitting up in bed, "moaning and groaning."

The police arrived at 3.23 a.m. and were admitted by Nita, who told the officers that the intruder was a white male, young, five-foot-eight, 12 stone, slender build, clean shaven, prominent nose, knitted cap, and carrying a large stick with a dark cloth or stocking around it.

Investigating, the officers discovered that upstairs they had a body. Margaret Bowman was lying face down on her bed, her yellow nightie hiked up, her arms twisted around and her body on her back. Around her neck was a tightly wound stocking. Her body, head, bed, walls and floor were splattered with blood. Her knickers lay on the floor by the bed.

Trailed by the housemother, the officers began a room-by-room search. When they entered room number 8 they discovered a figure lying covered up on the bed.

"That's Lisa Levy," murmured the housemother from the doorway. One of the officers reached down and pulled away the bed covers to reveal Lisa's battered and bloody head.

On the beds of both victims, on their pillows and in their hair were fragments of tree bark. Police found similar fragments by the front door. By this time an emergency rescue team had arrived. They took over from the girl who was holding a plastic cup under Kathy's chin to catch her blood. She was still sitting up in bed, moaning and incoherent, when the rescue men eased her into an ambulance. Karen Chandler was now unconscious.

The emergency team leader pointed out a puncture wound near Lisa's right nipple. To the police it looked like a bite mark. Her nipple had been almost severed. There was a similar mark on Lisa's left buttock, and on Margaret's thigh there was an abrasion similar to a rope burn.

Margaret Bowman was pronounced dead at the scene. Lisa Levy died in the ambulance on the way to hospital. Mercifully Kathy and Karen recovered, although they never fully remembered what happened that night.

Meanwhile, at an apartment block just a short distance away, two girls who occupied one of the flats came home at about 2.00 a.m. As they went through the door they made loud catty remarks about the volume of their neighbour's TV, hoping to be overheard. It was a bone of contention between the two roommates and the TV owner, a girl ballet student from Virginia named Cheryl Thomas who lived on her own. The volume was lowered and the roommates went to sleep.

At about 4.30 a.m. one of the girls was awakened by loud thumping noises coming from Cheryl's room. "We then heard Cheryl. She wasn't crying, she was whimpering. I phoned a guy I was going out with and asked him what I should do. He told me to phone Cheryl's room to see if she was all right."

The two roommates called Cheryl on the phone. "We let it ring five times. As soon as the phone started ringing I heard real wild noises, like running, and I could hear Cheryl both crying and laughing. She didn't answer the phone so I thought something was wrong."

The two girls called the police, and 12 police cars arrived within minutes, while the dispatcher kept the girls talking on the phone, urging them to stay calm and sit tight. It was now about 4.40 a.m., just a little more than an hour after the first call from the Chi Omega house only a short distance away.

The police found Cheryl Thomas crossways on her bed, a pair of tights entangled in the bedding. "She was in a semi-conscious state; she did not respond to any of our commands and there was blood all over her body and bed."

Cheryl did not recover consciousness for nearly a week, and as with Karen and Kathy she could not remember much about the attack. She had been severely battered, perhaps with a length of board she used during the summer to keep her window propped open. She had lost the hearing in one ear, and what was tragically worse, damage to her inner ear threatened to impair her sense of balance and end her ambition to become a dancer. She underwent brain surgery.

Reconstructing the crime, the police believed the intruder, whom they assumed to be the same man who had invaded Chi Omega, had removed the screen on the door, bent back a curtain rod, and thrust himself into Cheryl's apartment. They also believed that the ringing telephone saved her life.

By 5 a.m. all the girls living in Chi Omega had been fingerprinted, so that their prints could be eliminated by technicians processing the house. All available police personnel were set to comb the neighbourhood. In the next few years 40 different police districts were to become involved in the manhunt.

"We have a deranged murderer on our hands, a crazy man," horrified officials warned the 22,000-student campus. "We don't know where he is or what he will do next, but you must not go out by yourselves."

Fraternity students armed with bats volunteered as extra security guards for the residences. Many parents withdrew their daughters from the university, and students walked in groups to classrooms. A police command post was set up near the university campus. Officers checked every acquaintance of the five women who had been attacked and ran a house-to-house check trying to find a trace, any trace, of the killer. Was he a student? Did he live in that neighbourhood?

There were no suspects, although the police began the tedious process of checking more than 100 possibilities. Inevitably, they explored the possibility of a link between these crimes and the attack on the student the previous year. All the girls were bludgeoned and at least two, possibly three of them, were sexually assaulted.

A few bits of information were gathered. Three of the girls, the two who were killed and the ballet dancer Cheryl Thomas, had all been at Big Daddy's bar earlier in the evening of the attack. Other students who were also at the bistro spoke of a young man with a thin, sharp face staring at them offensively.

An intensive search did not recover the murder weapon, but police thought it must have been the branch of an oak tree. There were many old trees in that neighbourhood, and a pile of oak timber was stacked by the back door of the Chi Omega building.

All the girls had been severely battered. The two who were killed were, according to Dr. Thomas Wood, a police doctor, first clubbed unconscious. His theory was borne out by the lack of any signs of a struggle in their rooms. Lisa Levy had strangulation marks on her neck and suffered trauma to her anal and genital areas. Police recovered a hair spray bottle from the floor of her room on which lab technicians found blood and faecal matter, leading to the surmise that her assailant had used this to assault her sexually. She had also been bitten on the breast and buttocks.

"But in all likelihood," said Dr. Wood, "she was first rendered unconscious by the blows to the head, then bitten, then penetrated by an object and finally strangled to death." He theorised that the abrasion on Margaret Bowman's left thigh was caused by the forcible removal of her knickers, and she was hit so hard on the head that her skull was depressed. She was then strangled with the tights found tightly knotted around her neck.

The bite marks on Lisa's body were photographed and measured. The bite on her buttocks was surgically removed for preservation.

The tights found on the bed in Margaret Bowman's room had one leg cut off, the other tied, and holes cut out for eyes. Lab technicians found brown curly hairs inside.

According to the police reconstruction, the Chi Omega killer walked through a recreation room after entering by the back door, which he found unlatched. He then went up the stairs. At the top was a corridor with doors along both sides.

"He did in fact pass over several rooms before entering one of them. It is quite possible he looked in on the others, but he was probably looking for a room with just one person in it," said a detective.

Working from Nita's description of the man whose profile she had glimpsed, a university professor of art drew a sketch that the police released widely. When she was able to talk, Cheryl Thomas told the police that she returned home that night shortly before 2 a.m. She heard the girls in the next room come in and complain loudly about her TV. After making herself a snack, she went to bed. Some time later she was awakened by a noise.

"During the night I heard a plant being knocked over, but I had a cat myself and I thought it might have knocked something over. So I went back to sleep." She remembered nothing more until she woke up in hospital several days later.

Despite many hours of police overtime and accompanying frustration, the search for the maniac killer yielded no clues worth following up for the best part of a month. Then one of those chance things happened that underline the value of police vigilance. At about 1.30 a.m. on Wednesday, February 15th, 1978, Police Officer Robert Lee, on routine road patrol near Pensacola, 220 miles west of Tallahassee, spotted an orange Volkswagen Beetle.

Something about the vehicle made Officer Lee suspicious. He radioed in to see if it were stolen, then stopped the driver near a restaurant and asked for identification. As the driver, a young man, produced a student card issued by Florida State University, the patrol car radio crackled back the information that the Beetle had been stolen from Tallahassee the previous Sunday.

Officer Lee ordered the young man to lie down on the ground and started to handcuff him. But the policeman thought someone else was hiding in the car, and his attention was diverted. In a swift moment, the captive kicked the feet out from under the officer, hit him with the handcuffs dangling from one wrist, and ran off.

Scrambling to his feet, Officer Lee drew his service revolver and gave chase, shooting and calling for his quarry to halt. The suspect eventually stopped and muttered, "I wish you would have killed me." And as Lee took his prisoner in, the young man added, "This case ought to help you make sergeant."

Searching the orange 1972 Volkswagen, police found credit cards and other identity papers in 21 different names, most of them for students. Their suspect could have used any one of a number of student cards he was carrying, but he continued to insist on the identity originally given to Officer Lee. When detectives checked they found the real student, who told them he had lost his identity papers some time over the Christmas holidays.

Next day, Pensacola detective Norman Chapman, puzzling over the riddle of all the credit cards, had an idea. The latest FBI "Most Wanted" list had been circulated only the previous Friday. The detective looked hard at a new name on it: Theodore Robert Bundy.

Chapman phoned the FBI. Agents arrived with wanted posters and fingerprints and an identification of the suspect was quickly made. The man with the stolen Volkswagen Beetle was undoubtedly Theodore Bundy, wanted for questioning in 36 sex assault murders in four Western states, dating back to 1969. He had escaped from prison in Colorado while awaiting trial on one of the murder cases and had been on the run ever since.

Bundy had only one conviction, for the 1974

kidnapping of a 17-year-old girl in Salt Lake City, for which he received a one-to-15-year sentence. While in prison he was arrested for the rape and murder of Carolyn Campbell, a Michigan nurse and sister of a Fort Lauderdale, Florida, police officer. Carolyn's nude, badly bitten body was found in a Colorado snow bank after she vanished on a skiing holiday. Petrol credit card receipts in Bundy's own name placed him in the immediate area at the time of the crime and were among the clues leading to his arrest.

On New Year's Eve, 1977, Bundy squirmed through a ceiling light fixture hole and escaped from prison.

Several of the killings involved bludgeoning, sexual assault and strangulation – a pattern that led Detective Chapman to contact the Tallahassee police team investigating the Chi Omega killings. But yet another possible murder case now loomed large in the minds of the investigating officers. Twelve-year-old Kimberly Leach had disappeared from her school on February 9th. She was currently being sought all over northern Florida and the case was provoking headlines across the state. Was Bundy involved in this, too? When detectives began to question him on Friday, February 17th, they were looking for a lot of answers.

At the same time another team of investigators moved in on the room Bundy had rented since January 7th in a boarding-house only a short distance from Chi Omega. The house was known as The Oaks, because of the mammoth old tree in its front garden. Bundy's fellow boarders there were astonished that the young man they knew as Chris Hagen was a suspect in the horrific student killings.

In a long, rambling all-night interrogation, only part of which was taped, Bundy talked to police about his personality and his "problem." In a later statement, Detective Chapman said that Bundy complained of "fantasies" taking over his life. "He said that in order to keep his fantasies going he had to do acts against society. He said he was a voyeur. He felt like a vampire because he drove many miles in his car at night and could get by on only three hours' sleep."

Asked about the Chi Omega murders, "Bundy dropped his head and in a very sincere tone, with tears in his eyes, he told us, 'The evidence is there. Go find it,'" Chapman said.

While the tape was still running Bundy spoke freely of his New Year's Eve prison escape. He made his way to the University of Michigan and rented a room at the YMCA. But because the Colorado victim was a Michigan girl, he discovered that his name was in all the local papers there, so he set off for Florida.

His goal was the University of Florida, but he was evidently somewhat put out when he bought a map and discovered that it was in Gainesville, in the centre of the state, and not near the sea. "Here's Gainesville, in the middle of nowhere, and I wanted to be by the sea. Isn't it strange? If it had been by Tampa Bay, I may have gone there. Who knows? And so I came to the campus of Florida State University. All this is almost random in a way."

Describing his activities on the run, Bundy said: "I stole things. Towels, you know, some cologne or a racquetball or a pair of shorts. Like going to the supermarket and stuffing my bag full of cans of sardines. I'm not a very good job hunter, and uh, I kinda procrastinate. I was losing sight of my plans to just stick with it, get some identification, get a job, stay inconspicuous. Stealing a car was a shortcut...a stupid shortcut."

In fact he stole a number of cars, although he did remember to wear leather gloves most of the time, thereby avoiding fingerprints. But he sidestepped questions about a stolen white van that witnesses had seen the 12-year-old schoolgirl Kimberly Leach enter. "I really can't talk about it," Bundy said. "We, we'd better not talk about it."

Pressed about the Chi Omega murders, he asked that the tape be turned off and the investigators not take notes. It was then that he rambled on about "uncontrollable fantasies" and "vampire feelings," police said, although he did not admit to any of the murders.

Bundy was ordered by the court to submit to blood and hair samples and teeth impressions. Although hairs are not as unique as fingerprints, and hence, before the developments in DNA analysis, did not provide conclusive proof of identity, still by all the laboratory tests then available, Bundy's hair sample matched the hairs found in the facemask at the crime scene.

A consultant dentist found that transparent overlays of Bundy's teeth impressions "lined up exactly" and "fitted perfectly" on to a police photo close-up of the bite mark on Lisa Levy's buttock. Bite marks, however, presented problems in those days. The soft, yielding, elastic nature of human tissue makes reproduction for comparison difficult. Then space-age technology came to the rescue. A video-computer technique developed in the NASA space programme allowed moon photographs to be read for three-dimensional information. It also allowed depth of bite marks to be determined by computer analysis.

The dental consultant found "30 points of positive comparison" between Bundy's teeth and the bite marks on the victim. It was a double bite, he said. Twice the lower teeth sank into Lisa's flesh with tremendous force, holding the tissue, "while the upper teeth did the scraping."

The consultant added: "It is convincing beyond any discussion whatsoever. There is absolutely no way this can be refuted. His teeth made those marks."

Bundy bit many of his victims and, as we have seen in the case of Neville Heath, severe biting is a trade mark of the degenerate killer, connected as it is in his convoluted mind with love-making. In an American case a man left his victim in a hotel room after incising her body from her neck to her left thigh and dissecting her breasts and vagina. Despite these and other horrendous injuries he inflicted, he said in his statement to the police: "I remember biting her on the nipple. I don't know whether I swallowed it or not. I was beyond remembering anything about it. I was just out of my mind." Just as in the case of Heath and of Bundy, the victim's breasts were a fetish, and it became more important to these perverted killers to use their mouth than to engage in normal intercourse.

The police were now convinced they had the right man in Ted Bundy, and prosecutors agreed. In July, 1978 he was indicted for the Chi Omega murders, signalling the beginning of a long legal drama. It took almost a year of judicial manoeuvring, frequently prompting lurid headlines, before a jury in Miami found him guilty after seven hours of deliberation. The same jury recommended the death penalty.

On Tuesday, July 31st, 1979, Judge Edward Cowart formally sentenced Bundy to the electric chair. He imposed the sentence twice: once for Lisa Levy and once for Margaret Bowman.

Meanwhile, police were assembling evidence linking Bundy to the murder of 12-year-old Kimberly Leach, whose battered and ravished body had at last been found in an abandoned pigsty. She was still missing when Bundy was arrested in Pensacola.

Kimberly disappeared on February 9th, 1978, after leaving school. She had been looking forward to the Saturday night Valentine dance two days later, for which she had already selected her party dress. A classmate told the police she saw Kimberly getting into a white van.

The day before she disappeared, stolen credit cars found on Bundy were used in Jacksonville and a Lake City motel. The white van had been stolen from the Florida University campus, and a man fitting Bundy's general description had signed into the Lake City Holiday Inn using one of the stolen credit cards.

Hundreds of volunteers joined in the search for the missing child, but it was to be 39 days after her disappearance that the hunt came to its grim conclusion. On the afternoon of Friday, April 7th, a state trooper, who was one of about 40 people making a second search of an area about 20 miles west of Lake City, lifted a piece of sheet-metal covering an old lean-to that had formerly sheltered pigs. Stuffed under a mass of debris was a decomposing body clad in the jeans and T-shirt Kimberly was wearing when she was last seen.

The doctor who performed the post-mortem reported "an overwhelming, tearing type of injury" to the child's neck, indicating that she was strangled or hacked about the neck until she died. There was not enough tissue remaining, however, to establish the exact cause of the injury. The body had been in the old pigsty for two months and was positively identified through dental charts.

Bundy was charged with Kimberly's rape and murder, and a parade of police officers testified to finding fibres from Bundy's and Kimberly's clothing in the white van, bloodstains on the van carpet, semen on her knickers, and two footprints made by Bundy's shoes. Again he was found guilty, and given a third death sentence.

Using his impressive knowledge gained as a law student, Bundy conducted his own defence in all the charges against him, a courtroom role he clearly relished. But in the end his performance counted for nothing. He remained on Death Row for almost 10 years, and just putting him there had cost an immense effort. He finally went to the electric chair on January 24th, 1989, when he was 42 years old. He declined the traditional last meal and went to his death with a look of controlled anger. His appeals against the death sentence cost American taxpayers over four million dollars.

The night before his execution, in an attempt to stave off the inevitable, he tearfully confessed to many more murders with full horrific details.

A panel of 42 witnesses saw him die at dawn, a one-minute surge of 2,000 volts passing through his body. They reported that he arched his back against the restraints and clenched his fists as the current hit him. Outside the prison demonstrators cheered and set off fireworks. Many wore T-shirts bearing a picture of the electric chair with the words, "Burn, Bundy, Burn."

The deceptively wholesome-looking man with the engaging smile and film star looks was finally gone. He

Fetishism

had confessed to murdering 23 women and young girls, but police suspected he had killed at least another 15. Even at the end he couldn't bring himself to tell all the truth, but his cockiness was deserting him as he spent his last few days helping detectives from three states to clear their books on unsolved sex killings.

A psychiatrist who saw him the night before his execution said that the only time Bundy felt any remorse for his catalogue of horrific crime was immediately after the first killing. "But then the sex frenzy overcame him and he killed again, and as each crime passed, he grew desensitised. He could not feel any more..."

Bundy himself was embarrassed by his bloody career, at being what one judge called "the most competent serial killer in the USA today." He refused to allow prison guards to overhear him confessing to detectives, and wrote the names of his victims on pieces of paper. One detective said: "From what he's told us I'd say he was the worst mass killer of all time. There's not been another like him."

CHAPTER FOUR

Necrophilia; sadism without aggression; insanity; vampirism
Peter Kurten, Robert Black, David Rulo, Gerald Gallego, Jacques Algarron

Fetishism is closely linked to necrophilia, and the underlying reason for it – fear of women, of a personal sexual encounter with them – is the same. The fear is the result of infantile sexual development. A remarkable number of psychiatrists trace back necrophilia to some abnormality in childhood development.

And necrophilia, or necro-fetishism as it is sometimes called, provokes more interest than might be imagined. Before the Second World War some brothels catered for necrophiliacs, with their prostitutes feigning death and laid out in coffins in a room which had all the atmosphere of a mortuary.

The fetish of the German serial killer Peter Kurten was simply blood. Kurten, who became known as the Monster of Düsseldorf, was born in 1883, the son of a violent drunkard. One of a poor family of thirteen, he was brought up in an atmosphere of over-charged sex. He had to sleep with his sisters, and watch his parents having sex. He claimed that one of his sisters attempted to seduce him, and his father was sentenced to three years in prison for incest with his 13-year daughter.

He also claimed that his sadistic streak was germinated by a dogcatcher who lived in the same house and taught him to masturbate dogs.

Kurten committed his first murder when he was 19. He pushed a boy off a raft in the Rhine and when another boy dived in to help the first one, Kurten pushed him under the raft so that they both drowned.

At the age of 13 he began practising bestiality with sheep, pigs and goats. His first ejaculation coincided with stabbing a sheep while having intercourse with it, and he discovered that the sight of blood gave him intense pleasure. From this moment the link between sex and blood became firmly fixed in his mind.

In such cases the individual is a sadist who exalts in the infliction of violent pain on his victims. This act in itself excites him and thrills him sexually. In these cases too there is usually sexual frustration allied to an inferiority complex, sometimes brought on through organ inferiority.

At 16 Kurten ran away from home and lived with a prostitute with masochistic tendencies, who encouraged him to torture her. Then he was arrested for theft and went to prison for the first time. It was to be the first of 17 sentences totalling 27 years in harsh prisons, incarceration that, Kurten was later to claim, embittered him.

During one interval between prison sentences he lived with a prostitute twice his age who enjoyed being maltreated. This further increased his sadistic streak, confirming his belief that sex and pain were inextricably linked, and that the first could not be enjoyed without the second.

Kurten said he committed his first sexual murder when he was 26, although there is no police record of the incident. He said he strangled a girl while having sex with her in a forest. In his confession he said that while he was in prison, "I got my climax of enjoyment when I imagined something horrible in my cell. The thought of slitting-up someone's stomach was my peculiar lust, and in that way I achieved my ejaculation. If I hadn't had that I would have hanged myself."

Released from prison, he became a professional burglar, although he never lost his ability to pose as a quietly spoken, well-to-do businessman. In 1913 he broke into a house and found 13-year-old Christine Klein asleep there. He strangled the child, cut her throat and penetrated her vagina with his fingers.

In the same year he knocked a man and a woman unconscious with a hatchet and gained sexual excitement from watching them bleed.

He married in 1923 – his wife consenting to the wedding only after he threatened to murder her if she didn't – and two years later moved with her to Düsseldorf, where in the next few years he committed 22 arson attacks. In February, 1929, he attacked a woman, stabbing her in rapid succession 24 times, causing her to bleed profusely. She survived, but several days later Kurten killed eight-year-old Rosa Ohliger, strangling her, then inflicting multiple stab wounds on her body.

Because he changed his killing methods from time to time it was difficult to identify a regular pattern that would help psychiatric investigation, but his killings did reveal all the hallmarks of the archetypical sado-masochist with a fetish instinct. The post-mortem on little Rosa revealed injuries to her genitalia. Ejaculation had not taken place inside her, but Kurten had inserted a finger smeared with semen inside the vagina.

More attacks and murders followed. Those who survived the attacks were able to supply enough information to show that the still unknown assailant was gaining some kind of perverse satisfaction from the act of stabbing.

Those who did not survive filled the city of Düsseldorf with horror. Two girls, aged five and 15, were strangled and stabbed in an allotment near their homes. Their throats were cut in an apparently motiveless act of murder, and neither of them was sexually assaulted.

One Sunday afternoon Kurten took a servant girl for a walk in a wood. He tried to have sexual intercourse with her standing up, but she refused, saying, "I'd rather die."

Kurten replied, "Well, die then!" He stabbed her several times, so violently that the tip of his knife blade broke off inside her spine. She survived, giving police a good description of her attacker, and once again doctors noticed that the stabbing had been in a rapid pattern.

Kurten now changed his killing technique, using a hammer instead of a knife. Three women were bludgeoned to death in September, 1929, and three more hammer attacks occurred the following month. Some of them clearly indicated a sexual motive for the killings.

What was at least predictable about Kurten's behaviour now was its unpredictability. Sadists who need to see blood for their excitement are generally unpredictable as to when they will strike. Because of their feelings of inadequacy and frustration they tend to correct that imbalance, to over-compensate for their acknowledged deficiencies, by performing some feat of derring-do.

On November 7th a five-year-old girl was found dead near a factory yard – she had been strangled and stabbed 36 times. Her knickers were torn and there were injuries to her vagina and anus. A week later police dug up the body of a servant girl, Maria Hahn, who had been dead since August. She was naked and had been stabbed 20 times, suffering, according to the pathologist "coitus per anum."

Kurten was eventually caught when he was identified by one of his victims who survived. Teams of doctors, psychiatrists and psychologists descended on him, all wanting to know, why?

"I was always in a frame of mind when I wanted to kill someone," he explained innocently. "The more people the better. If I had had the means of doing so I would have killed whole masses of people.

"The sex urge was always strong in me, particularly during the last years. But it was increased by the deeds themselves. That was why I had to go out again and again to look for another victim.

"The main thing with me was to see blood...I felt sexually excited." The act of stabbing, he said, brought about an ejaculation. Of one of the children he killed, he said, "I had no satisfaction during the sexual act, only later on during the throttling. I became stiff again, and when, as I stabbed her throat, the blood gushed from the wound, I drank the blood and ejaculated."

Kurten said that after killing and burying Maria Hahn he decided to dig her up. He kissed and fondled the corpse, and then wanted to crucify her body to a tree, "to stir up some excitement," but the body was too heavy. He reburied it, and later frequently visited the grave. He was able to ejaculate simply by fingering the earth over the grave.

Kurten's criminal persona defied all categorisation. He had no modus operandi. Sometimes he robbed his victims, sometimes not. He attacked men, women and children, displayed every sexual aberration, yet lived a normal life as a husband to his wife.

Unlike typical sado-masochists, he was strong-minded, and revealed an incredible memory of crimes committed over two decades. He was a pyromaniac, had delusions of grandeur, megalomania, and sexual mania. He differed from the normal sadist in that he pursued different methods of violence alternatively, had a great ability to lie and deceive, possessed great presence of mind and an ability to bluff.

He blamed his horrific crimes on his 27 years in prison, and his desire for revenge, for "compensatory justice" on society caused by this incarceration. It is customary for the sexual killer to blame someone or something else for his condition, and in Kurten's case this was almost certainly another of his fantasies.

He was best summed up by the prosecutor at his trial: "He butchered his victims only to satisfy his own appetites. He tortured them more and more bestially before he killed them as he became increasingly harder to satisfy."

Much was made of the fact that Kurten only murdered during his leisure hours when he knew he was free from his wife's supervision, and was therefore fully responsible for his actions. But that does not mean that he was insane. It simply means that his sexual craving for blood was so great that his will and intellect were by-passed, totally overcome by his desire.

The jury at his trial would have been unconvinced by that argument. They found him guilty on the nine charges of murder he faced, and he was sentenced to be guillotined. Like Albert Fish, he then described how delighted he would be experience the thrill of being executed.

"It would be the pleasure of all pleasures to hear my

own blood gushing into the basket when my head is cut off," he said.

He must have meant it, too. On the morning of July 2nd, 1931, his execution day, he enjoyed the condemned man's last meal so much – wiener schnitzel, chips and white wine – that he asked for it again.

In the eyes of the law, Dennis Nilsen, Jerry Brudos and Peter Kurten were not insane. So it is important for the psychiatrist to understand what the law regards as sanity, so that he can separate criminals who act in the same way as such men, but whom the law would classify as insane.

At trials in crimes of sexual sadism where there is irrefutable medical evidence supplied by the prosecution that the defendant is sane within the legal meaning of that word, the defence customarily resorts to the argument that he was insane "at the time." The point made is that you can bounce in and out of insanity, which is convenient if you are going about committing crimes.

But what if the defendant is mad anyway, before, during and after he has committed the crime? In that event it is the prosecution, of course, which has to prove its case.

One case – it must surely be the only one – in the criminal history of human vampirism where the vampire was probably not a sadist killer but was simply deranged, was the case of the "Sacramento Vampire" Richard Chase, who murdered six times.

Before he turned murderer, Chase habitually killed rabbits and birds and drank their blood. He would also take buckets of blood from cattle and drink that too. When he became a killer he would shoot his victim, then slit open the abdomen and drink their blood.

There was neither sadism nor sexual gratification in any of these acts – Chase was acting under the delusion that his body was continually running out of blood and the only way he could keep himself alive was to kill and take it from other people.

His condition was caused by massive and chronic

depression, for which he was treated while under arrest with drugs handed out daily. Although clearly insane, he was sentenced to die by lethal gas in San Quentin. At some point, though, he had begun to hoard his drug supply and on December 26th, 1979, he swallowed the whole of his secret cache, lay down on his cell bunk and died.

It is difficult to analyse the mind of a sexual sadist who is already crazy, because one needs to go deeper and find out what made him mad in the first place. Take, for instance the child killer John Straffen. He argued that he killed little girls to show the police that he wasn't mad. It is easy to label such a man as wilfully evil, but it is much more likely that his reasoning faculties simply don't exist, and he is therefore completely insane.

So sadistic child killer John Straffen was mad, and sadistic child killer Robert Black wasn't. Yet there are similarities in the backgrounds of the two that may make us scratch our heads over the meaning of insanity. Black, a Scotsman, killed three little girls and abducted several others. In prison he confessed to indecently assaulting 40 young girls.

His background was a blueprint for future sexual problems. He was illegitimate, fostered out, then put in a children's home, where he indecently assaulted a young girl. He was moved to an all-boys school and for several years was sexually abused by a staff member.

At his trial for the subsequent murder of the three little girls, it was said that he told a policeman he had abducted a child because of "a rush of blood." That could not have been true, because in his van, where he raped his victims before killing them, there was a roll of sticking plaster to use as a gag, black cord to tie up his victim, a cushion cover to put over her head, and what the prosecution described as "a set of revolting probes."

Black was already serving life for child abduction when he was tried in 1994 for the three murders. His list of previous convictions revealed that at the age of 16 he took a seven-year-old girl to an air raid shelter, half strangled her and masturbated over her body, leaving her for dead. A medical report before the court on that occasion described this as an aberration that Black would probably not repeat.

He did repeat it, though. A few years later he indecently assaulted a six-year-old girl and was sent to Borstal. He moved to London after that, got a job at Hornsey Swimming Baths, and was sacked for indecently assaulting a girl swimmer.

Black, already serving life when he was tried, was given three more life sentences and a recommendation that he should not be released for 35 years – he was then 44 years old.

The key to his psyche lies in his depressing upbringing, punctuated by the schoolmaster sexually abusing him. A man who is sexually abused as a boy and then sexually abuses little girls is taking on the role of the abuser, and the girl becomes representative of his weak victim self.

Black grew up to detest his weaker self, and therefore detested the little girls he killed. In the nature versus nurture dialogue, there is a strong argument here for nurture, for surely it is in such cases as that of Robert Black that our society creates its own criminals.

We must, though, accept that there are some potential criminals on the loose out there who were born with mental deficiency, and that they will not be caught until they offend. And then no amount of incarceration will cure them.

David Rulo, for instance. He abducted a woman US army sergeant, Debra Montgomery, at a laundrette where she had gone to do her weekly wash. When he grabbed her she wheeled round and cried, "What the hell is going on?" and slapped him in the face. Rulo, a diminutive drifter who was less than five feet tall, responded by hitting her in the face, stomach, and chest, and knocking her unconscious.

He drove her around for a while in her own car, thinking that after she woke up he would "try to talk some sense into her" about how he had mistaken her for someone else.

"But I decided I couldn't talk sense to her and that I'd better get rid of her," he said. "I knew I would have to kill her or she would tell the police that I hit her."

He drove her to an isolated place, tied her hands, then undressed her. He had intercourse with the still unconscious woman "four or five times," he said. He then drove her to a park "to dump her," but when he heard her groan in the back seat he stopped, took a long nail from his pocket, and stabbed her about 20 times. He also used broken glass to slash her wrists, the inside of her upper legs and her stomach, "trying to cut the veins so that she would bleed to death."

Debra was still alive, so he put a clothes peg on her nose and forced a gag into her mouth to stop her breathing. Then he took a piece of cloth, tied a knot in it, twisted it around her neck and pulled on both ends for about 15 minutes.

The killing of Debra Montgomery bore all the hallmarks of the sexual sadist, but when Rulo confessed that he drove her around with the intention of "trying to talk some sense into her," and "I knew I would have to kill her because she would tell the police I had hit her," he was revealing the infantile reasoning of someone already seriously mentally deficient.

And indeed Rulo was mentally deficient. He was a madman at large. His mental illness began when he was four years old with convulsive seizures. He spent years in and out of mental hospitals, and was on mind-calming drugs in 1972, the year he attacked Debra Montgomery.

At a hearing to evaluate his sanity it was said that he had "a multi-faceted problem, any part of which might create an impaired conscious state."

A psychiatrist said of the pint-size Rulo: "His whole history is one of poor impulse control, hostility and assaultive behaviour. With this there is delusional and grandiose idealism, indicating schizophrenic process of long standing.

"He has brain damage as indicated by a convulsive disorder and abnormal electro-encephalogram. The combination of these pathological processes makes him a very sick and dangerous man. He may appear normal to those around him, but his behaviour is unpredictable and explosive. If he is turned loose, he will kill again."

Rulo was not turned loose, but sent to a maximum-security mental hospital. He leaves us with the impression that a sexual sadist killer is bad enough, but a sexual sadist killer who is also insane is horrific.

Another sexual sadist killer who was probably made in the womb was Gerald Gallego, whose killing spree spanned a two-year period between September 1978 and November 1980. Criminologists were fascinated when they discovered that Gallego's father, also named Gerald, was the first man to be executed in Mississippi's new gas chamber on March 3rd, 1955, for three murders. Typical of the father's psychopathic violence was the fact that during one jail escape he blinded a warder with acid, pausing long enough to kick the blinded man to death.

He was 28 when he was executed, and his son, born in July, 1946, was then eight years old.

At 10 Gerald Gallego, junior, was a burglar; at 12 he was sent to reform school for forcing sex on to a six-year-old girl. By the time he was 16 he had served another five-year stretch for burglary.

His uncle and three cousins were serving life for murder in various Californian jails, and most of his male relatives had violent criminal records. His half-brother was serving life for shooting a liquor store assistant. The entire family was so contaminated with evil that psychiatrists were convinced that Gallego's forthcoming sexual-sadist killing spree was written in his genes.

This began after he married his slim, petite, blonde "wife" Charlene, who incredibly turned out to be the ideal sadistic killing partner for him. Although they had gone through a marriage ceremony, she was his seventh "wife," for he did not bother to get divorced before re-marrying.

They first picked up two young girls, whose bodies were later found on a Californian highway. The younger, aged 16, had semen deposits in her mouth and anus. Sticky residue on her wrists and ankles suggested she had been taped to restrain her, after which she had been shot.

A deep bite mark on her left breast had almost severed the nipple. Later it was established that while he sodomised the girl, Charlene got her kicks by biting her breasts.

The older girl, aged 17, had semen in her mouth, anus and left ear, and there was a deep bite on her buttock. The nipple on her right breast had been almost chewed off. She had also been taped and later shot.

Gallego, it seemed, was a poor sex performer unless the agenda included anal sex, which Charlene hated. It was she who suggested that they should kidnap teenage "sex slaves," to restore his waning libido. When he demurred on the grounds that they might report him, Charlene pointed out that dead girls don't talk.

After the first kidnapping they picked up two runaways, aged 13 and 14. They were driven to a lonely spot, where they were taped. Charlene was furious when Gallego started to have sex with them without waiting for her to undress and join in, and she insisted on having 20 minutes with the girls alone. She bit off their nipples.

Between times Gallego committed incest with his daughter on a number of occasions while Charlene was present. As a result, the girl, then aged 14, was said to have "ambivalent" feelings towards her father.

They next picked up two 17-year-old hitchhikers who were hoping to get into porn movies. The two girls willingly got into Gallego's van. Again he drove them to a lonely spot, where he and Charlene tortured them for hours before killing them with a hammer and burying them.

A few days later they picked up a heavily pregnant woman. Both abused her sexually before hitting her with a hammer and burying her while she was still alive.

In July 1980 the couple went looking for a new victim

to celebrate Gallego's birthday. They kidnapped a barmaid as she left work and took her to their home.

While she was fully conscious, the barmaid was whipped, sodomised by Charlene using a thick black rubber dildo, hung up by her wrists from a nail in the wall and whipped again. She was forced to perform oral sex on both her abductors, and her nipples were almost chewed off.

Gallego sodomised her three times during which she was compelled to perform oral sex on Charlene. The couple openly consulted an illustrated paperback book on S and M as a guide to their activities.

The hysterical woman begged to be killed, and Gallego obligingly strangled her. He put her body in his van and drove to a local river, where he dumped it, hoping it would be carried down to the sea. Three months later the woman's skeleton was found on a sandbank, its hands still tied behind its back.

Gerald and Charlene Gallego killed another couple before they were caught. Charlene worked out a plea-bargain, exchanging 16 years in jail for her testimony against her "husband." He questioned her for six days at their trial, but that didn't save him. He was executed by lethal injection.

What, one indeed may ask, was at the root of Gallego's astonishing depravity, if there were any other reason than that written in his genes? It might have been a symptom of his rage against his mother, whom he hated, his fears about his masculinity, which Charlene was well aware of, and his need for total control over others.

Although Charlene was someone he could dominate, she was also a dominant person herself, so she turned out to be someone upon whom he could lean. He had a problem he couldn't dominate, however – a superstitious fear of phantoms. He used to exorcise his van to get rid of the ghosts of his victims. And, a doctor testified, "he feels that he has his father inside him."

Necrophilia; sadism without aggression; insanity; vampirism

We have dealt at length with sadistic behaviour accompanied by sexual aggression. But sadistic torture and masochistic suffering are not limited to physical preparation for the sex act – they can also reach deep into the psyche of the individual. We have also heard a lot about sadism but rather less about masochism, with which it is often linked.

One case that occurred in France in the 1950s combined both these elements – sadism without physical aggression, and masochism. It happened when Jacques Algarron, an army second lieutenant freshly graduated from St. Cyr military academy, met Denise Labbé, the single mother of a young child.

Despite having had a number of lovers and generally possessing rather elastic morals, Denise was an excellent mother to her daughter Cathy. But she was doomed to be dominated, by an agonising wish to suffer pain. And it so happened that Jacques Algarron had an overwhelming desire to dominate.

The young lieutenant's favourite author was André Gide, who wrote that since God did not exist, man was faced by a blank and uncaring universe. This entitled the superior being (the role in which Algarron saw himself) to commit violent acts simply from the need to assert his individuality.

By one of those amazing tricks of fortune, like Neville Heath with Margery Gardner, this supreme male sadist was thrown into the arms of a copybook female masochist. They made love violently, during which he scratched her back so deeply as to leave deep scars on her. One day gazing intently at her with his cruel green eyes, he said tensely, "If I asked you to murder your daughter, would you do it for me?"

Denise tried to tear her gaze away from his eyes but could not. "Yes," she replied weakly.

Over the next few weeks, goaded by her lover, she tried four times to kill little Cathy, each time shrinking back in dread from the screaming child. Each time she failed Algarron prepared to leave her – once he even turned up with a new girl friend to show his contempt for her.

Denise protested, pleaded. "We have not the right to do it," she said. Algarron replied, "One has the right to do as one likes. It is above all because one has not the right to commit a certain act that this act assumes a special value."

The special value, he assured her, was that it would bond their relationship together for eternity. They would be married and they would be as one.

We all know, of course, that the direction in which we point our ego is based on what is good or bad, or what is pleasing to our ego. It follows that someone with a character deficiency has an over or under amount of ego-appreciation – and in Algarron's case this was over-ego-appreciation, by which he determined all his actions.

Algarron was to argue that by breaking free of his subconscious mind, where through the facilities of reason and judgement rational conclusions are reached, he was able to exercise free will, a product of the individual and responsible to himself alone. This, it need hardly be said, is a very dangerous condition.

On the afternoon of November 8th, 1954, Denise Labbé was in the yard at her mother's home, doing the washing. Her mother and sister had gone out shopping. Steeling herself, Denise seized her two-and-a-half-year-old child and plunged her head-first into the washing basin, holding her under until her last struggles ceased and no more bubbles broke the surface.

At that moment the front doorbell rang. It was Denise's mother, who had forgotten to take her key. Weeping and shaking, Denise let her in, crying hysterically that she had just discovered Cathy accidentally drowned in the washing basin.

Police suspected that something was not quite right when they arrived and found the child's body still floating in the basin. The mother had made no attempt to remove it. Aware that she might be suspected, Denise sent a coded telegram to Algarron indicating that she had succeeded.

Necrophilia; sadism without aggression; insanity; vampirism

But later, when they met, Algarron shrugged his shoulders. "I find it all very disappointing," he said dismissively. "It means nothing at all to me now."

Although they spent the next three days in bed together it was evident to Denise that Algarron had no intention of making her his wife. So she went to the police and made a statement implicating her lover and admitting manslaughter.

The courtroom battle was virulent and bitter, for the case against Algarron required a great deal of proof. That they were a sado-masochistic couple was soon evident from cross-examination. Algarron was asked: "What about those famous practices of yours, the scratch marks?"

He replied: "She asked me to hurt her because she likes suffering."

He was accused by Denise's counsel of experimenting on her like a guinea pig. "It was not an operation with the knife and scalpel, but with the mind, and you performed it to obtain a profound intellectual orgasm."

The jury found them both guilty. Denise Labbé was sentenced to penal servitude for life, and Algarron was given 20 years' hard labour.

•

Men have tortured women in the name of sex – and some women have enjoyed it – for centuries. In the 14th century, for instance, an English army led by Sir John Talbot was unable to proceed from its Channel port to make war in France because of bad weather.

With nothing to do on shore, the soldiers discovered a nunnery in Hampshire and whiled away their time gang-raping and sadistically abusing the nuns until the weather improved. There was no inquiry, no charges brought. The authorities shrugged their shoulders metaphorically, and dismissed the affair as the sort of thing soldiers do.

Fortunately we take a graver view of such events today.

We know that criminal sadists are socially immature because they have failed to adapt to the rules of society, they have failed to be conditioned. For Nietzsche, a criminal was "a strong man made weak...by a tame society," but that is taking the idea to an unsatisfactory extreme. The criminal sadist has simply failed to grow up – he has remained sexually infantile. Freud said that a baby, if it had the power, would destroy the world from the frustration of its infantile desires. Peter Kurten, Dennis Nilsen, Jacques Algarron, Gerald Gallego and others like them were probably living proof that Freud was right.

For most of us, the psychopathic criminal sadist is an enigma wrapped up inside a conundrum. He is a permanent stranger among us. And however much empathy we bring to bear, we cannot enter into his mind just by an act of will. His is a very secret hell, a landscape of private devils and cruel lusts.

CHAPTER FIVE

SEXUAL MYTHS: PORNOGRAPHY; CASTRATION,
REHABILITATION; LUNAR KILLING
The death of Jane Longhurst; Paul Beart, Bobby Long

There are several myths, some of them alarmingly erroneous, surrounding sexual crimes. One is that they are often triggered by pornography, the whipping boy of feminists, the *bête noire* of puritans, and sometimes, even for the uncommitted, the reason for all evil.

Pornography, like flagellation, is rooted in history. The Greeks and the Etruscans decorated their vases with men holding larger-than-life erections, and 2,500 years later the Victorians read banned erotic books published in Paris (with copious typographical errors) and smuggled across the Channel. The favourite of all was *My Secret Life* by an author who styled himself simply as Walter, and who seems to have spent his entire life assuaging his lust. Here he typically describes one of the countless women he seduced:

"My fair friend, whom I shall name Vanity, (the only fitting name for her!) was in a voluptuous state of sexual surrender when, drawing my fingers from her quim, and rising with horn-like pego, I was able to lead her gently, unresisting, to the bedroom. "Don't now – don't!' she was still moaning as I threw up her clothes, kissed her between her thighs for an instant only, until they opened more, then briefly ran my fingers between the moist lips and, in a second with one lunge, I was up her. 'Don't! — aherr!' was all she said, then lay silent with eyes closed, while I remained embedded in her, motionless, my pego throbbing and enjoying its possession."

There is no evidence that such explicit pornography led its readers to sexual crime in the Victorian century, a period saturated with pornography. We can safely assume that Jack the Riper was not inspired by reading Walter before he set off on his prostitute-killing rampage in Whitechapel.

My Secret Life has other dimensions besides pornography. Water is an explorer, an adventurer, a social commentator, and he is also didactic in the sense that for his drooling male audience he was able to explain with remarkable insight the woman's view of sex. Of one woman's sexual response he writes: "When spending, she showed it plainly and did not attempt to hide it, as some do. Indeed, she could not have done so, if she had wanted to, for her vagina would close so strongly that there was no mistaking it. Besides that, her face first went scarlet, perfectly scarlet, a minute afterwards perfectly white, and then gradually recovered its natural colour; I have never seen that sort of change in any other woman's face. She always kept me up her as long as she could – twining her long legs around me to hold me there, while her long arms held me firmly around my buttocks, as she lay perfectly quiet with her eyes closed."

Interestingly, it was at about the time that this was written that a popular London doctor named Acton was opining: "To suggest that a woman enjoys the sexual act is a vile aspersion."

Rampant though Walter was, he was not a man who might be clinically defined as a Don Juan type. Psychiatry usually understands by Don Juanism a male who is driven into sexual contacts by a collection of factors, such as latent homosexuality, incestuous mother-fixation, fear of impotence (castration anxiety) and sex hostility. He may suffer from arrested psychosexual development, or infantilism, searching for his mother in all women, without being able to find her. Because of this he is condemned forever to disappointment in his partners and is never able to achieve true physical and emotional satisfaction.

Walter, by contrast, is simply a sexually active male, an individual for whom psychiatry has no name, because a person who is constantly sexually active is not necessarily perverted or disturbed. The psychiatric team of Drs. Eberhard and Phyllis Kronhausen who studied *My Secret Life* and became acquainted with the author's personality, reported: "Most great lovers in history, from Casanova to Frank Harris and Henry Miller, have…been Walter and not Don Juan types. So are many individuals to whom psychiatric literature refers as 'Don Juan' and nymphomaniacs. Not that there are no cases of sexual hyper-activity due to all kinds of neurotic reasons, but it is our impression that conservative clinicians tend gleefully to label patients with a stronger sex drive than they are familiar with as so many cases of 'satyriasis' and 'nymphomania,' although nobody seems to know just what is really meant by these terms."

The sexually active male of the Walter type demonstrates a compelling need for variety. Walter wanted more than just sex, he wanted physical contact with women. He writes: "Exceedingly nice women [they were in fact prostitutes] were to be met in the Quadrant from eleven to one in the morning, and three to five in the afternoon. I would have one before luncheon, get another after luncheon, dine, and have a third girl." Excessive, perhaps, but not abnormal, and certainly not criminal. Among other things, Walter was demonstrating in the 19th century a need for prostitution, a need still much in evidence today.

Advances in technology have meant that pornography has become visual since Walter's time. What was in books in Victorian England is today easily available in explicit video and film, ready for private viewing in the drawing-room. Raw sexuality is rampant in the mass media and porn is chic among the liberal intelligentsia. Whether that is the sort of society we should be nurturing is not for debate here. But we can attempt to answer the much-debated question: does pornography cause rape and sexual murder? For the evidence is that it is no more connected to sexual murder in our time than it was in Walter's.

That doesn't stop those opposed to its very existence getting heated, all the way up to the House of Commons, where a law clamping down on some internet access has been proposed. The minister who made the announcement said that violent sexual pornography was extremely offensive to the vast majority of people, and that it had no place in our society.

A Home Office announcement elaborated: "The fact that it is available over the internet should in no way legitimise it. These forms of violent and abusive pornography go far beyond what we now allow to be shown in films or even sold in licensed sex shops in the UK, so they should not be available online either."

Under the proposals, possessing "violent and extreme pornography" would carry a sentence of up to three years in jail.

The ban would embrace possession of porn depicting "scenes of extreme sexual-violence" and other obscene material such as bestiality and necrophilia. It would cover violence that is or appears to be life-threatening or is likely to result in "serious and disabling injury."

It needs to be stressed again that all the categories of material proposed for banning are already illegal to publish in the UK. However, the global nature of the internet means that obscene material can now be published electronically in the UK from abroad. Campaigners hoped that the creation of a new offence of possessing violent and abusive pornography would reduce demand for it.

The move to clamp down on violent internet porn was driven by 74-year-old Liz Longhurst, who had fought for a ban since her daughter Jane, a Brighton schoolteacher and musician, was strangled by a pervert obsessed with sickening internet images. She said: "It will be Jane's memorial. These horrific sites fuelled her killer's dangerous fantasies."

Jane's killer, Graham Coutts, kept her body for some weeks in a crate that he left in a storage company, re-visiting it from time to time, before removing it and attempting to burn it near woodland at Pulborough in West Sussex.

According to the medical evidence, Jane had suffered a painful and uncomfortable death, probably taking two or three minutes to die as her killer strangled her with a pair of tights. Before passing out she had probably struggled and made choking sounds. The tights – still around her neck when her naked body was found – had been tied so tightly they were difficult to cut off.

The computer memory belonging to Coutts was found to contain 809 pornographic images. Of these, 699 were categorised as asphyxiation and strangulation, rape, torture and violent sex, or dead bodies. The records showed that he had visited websites including "Necrobabes," "Rapepassion," "Hangingbitches," "Deathbyasphyxia," and "Violentpleasure," and the day before Jane's disappearance there was "a great deal of activity on the sites." The visits to the sites ceased after Jane's murder – she was killed in March, 2003 – until the following month, April, when they were revisited in the days preceding the dumping of her body.

At Coutts's trial the prosecutor said, "The murder was the manifestation of the defendant's fixation with helpless and strangled women in a sexual context. He acted out for real on the unfortunate Jane the fantasies that he had filed on his computer – the strangling, killing and raping of her.

"He subsequently kept and visited his 'trophy' until the smell forced him to dispose of the body. Death was not only intended but was perversely desired. There is an obvious parallel between the images he chose to access and the scene that must have confronted him whenever he visited the storage company where he kept her body.

"These images accessed by the defendant after the death of Jane, when he alone had access to her body in the storage unit, graphically show the fantasies he enjoyed."

Two of Coutts's former girl friends claimed in court that he liked to throttle them during sex. Testifying from behind a screen, one of them said that at first her sex life with him was normal, "but then it became more adventurous. He would tie me up, tie up my hands with stockings or the cord of a dressing gown. He liked to stroke my neck and he wanted me to put my hands around his neck. It was his suggestion. He wanted me to press harder and harder when it got near the end, hopefully with a view to making him pass out.

"He also wanted to put his hands round my neck. Over time I let him. He wanted to make me black out, to become unconscious; he wanted me to try it. He said it would be a very good orgasm before I was unconscious."

The second woman also said that at first sex with him was normal, but later "he began to want to do different things. A lot of it was me being upset or distressed, upset about other things. It turned him on."

Once she cried when she was telling him about a family problem. "I was asking him for advice. I was upset. He said, 'I'm getting turned on, baby.' He wanted to have sex and I didn't. He masturbated in front of me." Later in their relationship he would put his hands around her neck, saying it would "heighten the feeling of orgasm." He would also feign strangling her with knickers or tights.

"He would sometimes cross them or loop them. Sometimes the two legs of the tights would be tied around together. Then he'd hold them. Sometimes he would want me to struggle, sometimes he would want me to be quiet, to act as if I were unconscious."

He would also tie her hands behind her back, put a pillow over her head and masturbate.

Coutts told the court that from the age of 15 he developed an obsession with the idea of strangling a woman with a ligature. Using the internet, he discovered that he was not the only one to harbour such a fantasy. He had feared his obsession might "lead me to do something bad," and that someone might die. But this worry abated when he began a relationship with a woman who enjoyed sexual asphyxiation.

He admitted that he was such a porn addict that he had asked his girl friend to put a password on their computer to prevent him from using the internet.

He claimed that Jane's death was an accident during consensual sex – "a tragic and totally unforeseen blunder," he called it – but after nine hours' deliberation the jury found him guilty and he was jailed for 30 years. Immediately Jane's family said they would begin to put pressure on internet service providers to block sites catering for people obsessed with harming women. The murder conviction was later thrown out, the appeal court ruling that the jury should have been given the chance to consider a manslaughter charge. A new trial allowing for manslaughter to be considered began in June 2007 where Coutts was again found guilty.

Liz Longhurst subsequently organised a 50,000-signature petition demanding the law be changed. She was backed by two MPs. She claimed: "The internet normalised things for my daughter's killer." Jane's sister said: "These [violent] sites led to Jane losing her life."

But not everyone is happy with all this — in fact, sado-masochists who have consensual violent sex were outraged. The Spanner Trust, named after an infamous S and M trial, said: "We fear people will be criminalised. You can't distinguish between consensual play and real sexual brutality."

Some years ago when farmer Tony Martin of Norfolk shot and killed a burglar at his farmhouse there was considerable debate about the sufficiency of the law in such cases, which allows only "reasonable force" to be used by a homeowner to defend himself against an intruder. The problem homeowners had — and still have — was how exactly do you define "reasonable force?" The same kind of problem arises with internet pornography: how does anyone define "violent sexual content?" A summary of the government proposals revealed fears by some people that their consensual sexual practices would be targeted.

One group into bondage and sado-masochism wrote: "The theory that people should be punished for viewing an image that simply involves the idea of sexuality with violence shows that the proposal being made is to introduce a form of thought crime."

Many people seem to agree with that, because in a recent survey, 241 respondents said the law should not be changed and 143 said it should. Wendy McElroy, author of *XXX: A Woman's Right to Pornography*, says: "Images and words do not rape; human beings do. Censorship removes avenues for catharsis and drives discussion/freedom of speech into the shadows. The crusader has made society less safe and less free."

And Shaun Gabb, Director of the anti-censorship organisation the Libertarian Alliance, said: "If you are criminalising possession then you are giving police inquisitorial powers to come into your home and see what you've got. This is something we never had in the past."

The newspaper columnist Carol Sarler expressed her concern about the proposed legislation in the *Observer*: "Mrs. Longhurst's passion is as understandable as it is forgivable. The only understanding that one might afford the Home Office, however, is that it proves itself once more unable to pass by an opportunity for vote-grabbing legislation based on little more than the politics of 'obvious, innit?' It's horrid, ergo, we ban it.

"Actually, it's not obvious at all. For a start, nobody has offered proof beyond the circumstantial that there is any cause and effect to lay at the feet of these websites... Mrs. Longhurst has said, 'If the furniture of people's minds is polluted with this stuff, they can become very dangerous.' Yet she then admits: 'I don't think we can ever prove that 100 per cent.'"

Ms. Sarler thinks that the weirdo may be drawn to the internet images just because he is a weirdo. "I even wonder, sometimes, whether the wretched images help keep the sad bastards sated and, thus, the rest of us out of harm's way."

This is, however, a debate where the two sides are polarised. A pro-ban journalist said she Googled the words "violent," "porn," and "fetish" and got 1.47 million results, most of them promising images of bondage, torture and "extreme forced sex," and a proportion of them were free to view. "The smorgasbord of hardcore images highlights the enormous demand for it, which in turn normalises the desire for it. If 1.47 million sites exist to cater for the consumers of violent porn then an

Neville Heath the sexual sadist. He launched a frenzied attack on his victim leaving her a mass of torn flesh on the blood-soaked hotel bed

Sado-masochism; history and sexual implications of flogging; "spanking;" bondage (Chapter 1)

Ben Fawley, an amateur photographer with a bi-polar disorder, had a history of violent assaults on women when they tried to break off relationships

Graham Young poisoned his pets, his family and then his friends at work

Sado-masochism; history and sexual implications of flogging; "spanking;" bondage (Chapter 1)

Homosexual serial killer Dennis Nilsen and some of the household objects that became instruments of death and dismemberment: a necktie, knife, chopping-board, headphone cable – and a pot for boiling heads

Steven Bailey created a torture chamber in his bedroom, equipping it with a harness and accessories such as handcuffs, ropes and similar bondage gear to restrain a person during sex

Homosexual sadism; mythomania; torture (Chapter 2)

Ted Bundy. He claimed that his addiction to hardcore porn fuelled his lust for murder

Jerry Brudos was a shoe fetishist, serial killer, rapist, torturer and necrophiliac who stalked women

Fetishism (Chapter 3)

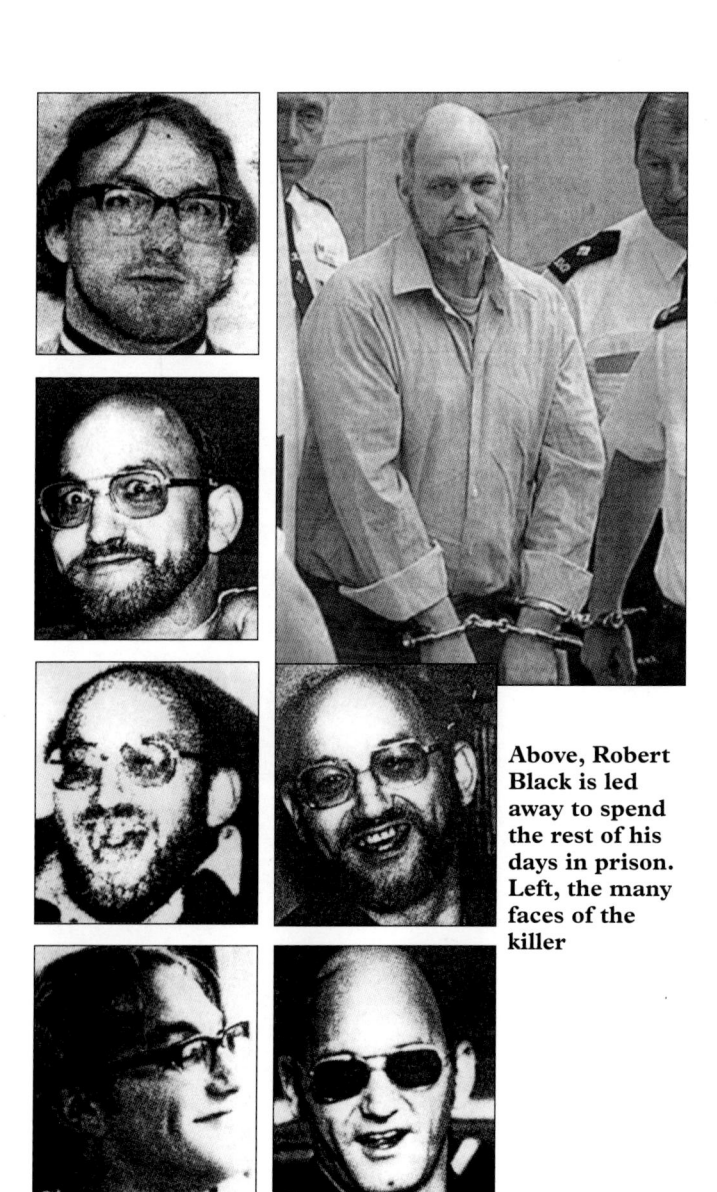

Above, Robert Black is led away to spend the rest of his days in prison. Left, the many faces of the killer

Necrophilia; sadism without aggression; insanity; vampirism
(Chapter 4)

Jane Longhurst and her sadistic killer Graham Coutts

Sexual myths: pornography, castration, rehabilitation, luna killing
(Chapter 5)

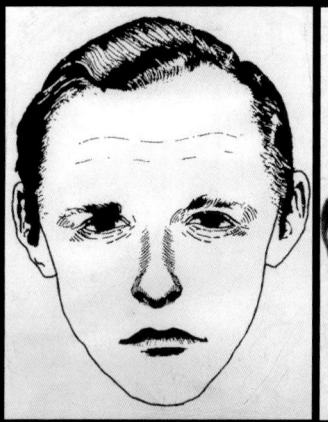

Jack the Stripper. Identikit pictures released to the press, made up from the descriptions of two suspects. They were never traced

In 1888, the murder of at least five prostitutes in London brought terror to the streets. The true identity of Jack the Ripper is still not known to this day

Mutilation for sexual satisfaction; symbolic sadism; prostitution; erotomania (Chapter 6)

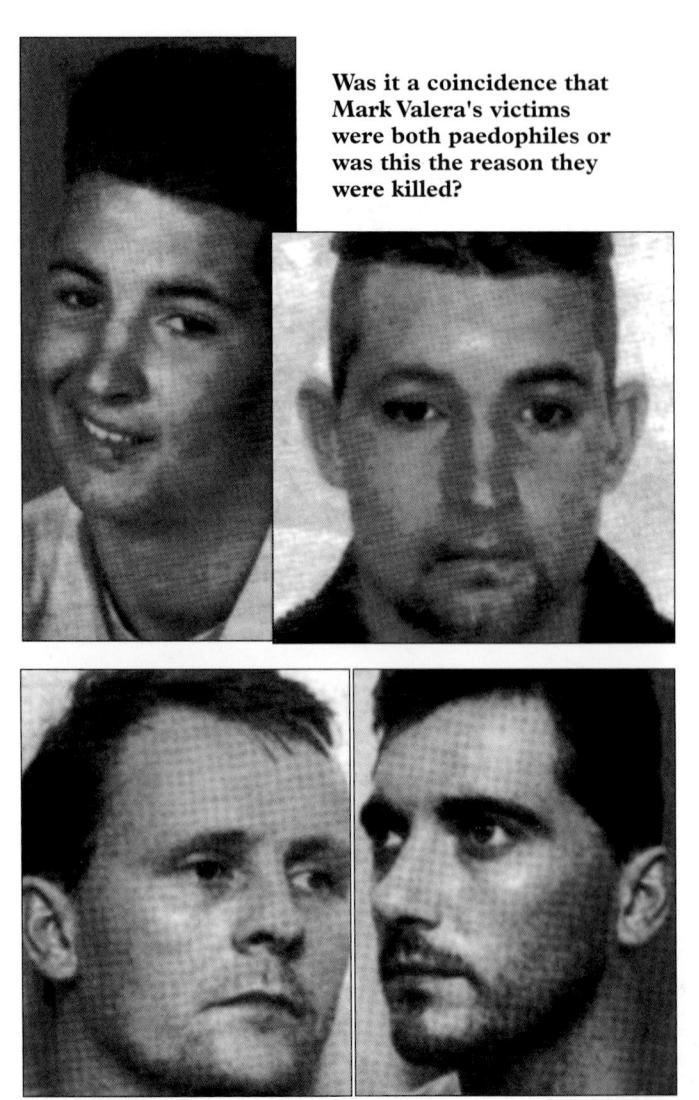

Was it a coincidence that Mark Valera's victims were both paedophiles or was this the reason they were killed?

Timothy Morss and Brett Tyler became lovers in prison

Paedophilia; child abuse (Chapter 7)

attraction to it can cease to seem aberrant."

In studies which involved showing men massive amounts of violent and misogynistic pornography, researchers Edward Donnerstein and Neil Malamuth found that regular viewing of violent sexual content makes men sexually aroused and more aggressive, and desensitises them to the effects of violence on victims. Their first finding is fairly obvious, their second is questionable (it must surely depend upon the individual), and what could have been an important third finding, that violent sexual pornography causes rape, is noteworthy by its absence.

But the researchers found that education, not censorship, is the best way to counteract any negative effects of violent pornography on adults. They conclude: "Censorship is not the solution. Education, however, is a viable alternative."

There is of course a third solution – which is for the government to crack down on the suppliers of internet porn rather than the viewers, in the same way that the drug problem is tackled through the pushers more than the users. That means that internet service providers must develop systems to scrutinise sites from which they are making handsome profits.

Although there is no evidence of a direct link between viewing violent images and committing violent acts, the British Psychological Society came out in favour of the proposals, citing developing research that individuals who were predisposed to commit violent or other sexual offences might become more likely to do so when exposed to such material. Some BPS members, however, disagreed.

Curiously, while anti-porn campaigners argue that porn degrades and brutalises women, the protection and proliferation of the porn and sex industry is significantly led by women. The Playboy empire is now run by Christie Hefner, founder Hugh Hefner's daughter, and a recent report in Britain revealed that the number of women downloading internet porn has soared by 30 per cent in the last 12 months.

With no believable statistics to back their case, anti-pornography campaigners frequently resort to anecdotal evidence that suggests that any obsession with sexual violence images may feed a pre-existing tendency towards sexual violence. One of the anecdotes they frequently cite concerns Ted Bundy, whose case we have examined in Chapter 3.

Shortly before his execution Bundy called for a psychologist and head of a right-wing Christian organisation, James Dobson, to visit him in the death cell so that he could make a final statement. He wanted to warn the world that every one of his killings was fuelled by a combination of violent porn and alcohol. He had been addicted to porn since he was 13, his tastes growing progressively more hardcore, he claimed, until images alone were not enough to satisfy his desire. This material gripped him, and it had fuelled his lustful crimes. Pornography "brought out a hatred that is just too terrible to describe."

Bundy said that his addiction happened in stages. As a young teenager he encountered soft-core porn in local shops. "I want to emphasise that this is the most damaging type of pornography, and I am talking from personal experience. I committed my first assault a couple of years after encountering pornography for the first time. My last vestiges of restraint, the barriers to actually doing something, were being tested and constantly assailed through the kind of fantasy life that was being fuelled by pornography."

He also claimed that alcohol had a strong effect on him, and this, in conjunction with pornography, eroded all his inhibitions.

Psychiatrists recognised plenty that was dubious about this confession. First, Bundy was a highly intelligent young man who knew how to use words and argument. Second, he was talking to a known anti-pornographer. Third, he had nothing to lose. He was a few hours from death and could not be held accountable for his words. Most important of all, he was in a position where a man might say anything to deflect his guilt in order to avoid accountability for his actions.

Despite his having become a rallying cry for the antis, Bundy and his "confession" have long been discredited. The confession is spurious because he was a proven liar and a psychopath, a proven spotlight-seeker and a proven braggart, and because he had years in custody to make his addiction claim and never once mentioned it until he was within inches of his execution.

It is also spurious because it applies only to Bundy and, of course, to a few other criminal perverts, but tells us nothing about the rest of mankind. Its proclaimed message is that we are all potential perverts. In fact, the only message it sends out is one we already knew – that Bundy had a sick mind.

The truth is that there isn't a single argument on the side of the anti-violent porn people that would stand up to reasonable scrutiny, and no case at all if free speech is considered as part of the equation. As is the case with so much of the "let's ban everything" lobby these days, the argument is heavily laced with emotion.

There is a parallel here with those people who can't take an alcoholic drink without becoming violently aggressive. Is this a problem about alcohol, or a problem about certain people who drink it? If the answer is it's about alcohol, then we should ban all alcohol.

We could go further. If we banned all news reporting, on TV, in newspapers, on the radio and the internet, there would be such a void of information that there would probably be a marked reduction, if not a cessation, in all terrorism.

These examples seem ridiculous because they are so huge. Liz Longhurst's crusade is small by comparison – but that doesn't make it any the less ridiculous.

Nor is the issue about the ease with which someone may intentionally find such material on the internet. The internet does make things easy for the searcher, but it does not force anything on anyone. You have the choice to view or not to view.

Was Jane Longhurst's killer likely to kill anyway, regardless of the internet? At his trial in 2004 he was

35. He claimed that he had wanted to strangle a woman since he was 15 years old. But when he was 15, in 1984, there was no violent sexual porn on the internet. So the desire to kill was within him long before he logged on to anything.

The complexity of the role that violent pornography plays in the execution of a sexual crime has long been debated. The question is not whether it should or should not exist, but whether its non-existence would reduce the incidences of sexual crime. Researchers have already come to the conclusions censorship is not the answer.

In any event, the government's proposals were inherently flawed. They covered faked acts with consenting actors. They even covered private images of consenting adults' private sex lives. There are two points of view about bondage and sado-masochism – some believe it is aberrant, and some believe it is not. The first point of view surely cannot be a reason for jailing for three years – that is the suggested sentence – people holding the second point of view.

The anti-porn campaigners behind the proposed legislation stuck to anecdotal evidence because there was no other evidence. There have in fact been innumerable studies over the past half-century seeking a link between viewing pornography and violent crime. Not one of them has found any conclusive evidence to support such a link.

If there were a link, it would be feasible to suppose that there would be an upsurge in copycat killings similar to the death of Jane Longhurst by visitors to the hundreds of thousands of porn-based internet sites. No such upsurge has happened.

By far the greatest influence on Ted Bundy must have been his early upbringing, which occurred long before he was exposed to pornography. But other sex offenders have blamed their problems on pornography, probably for the same reasons. They include Ian Brady and his accomplice Myra Hindley.

It has been shown that pornography is used by around

85 per cent of sex offenders. Significantly, what has not been shown is what percentage of non-sex offenders use it.

For some people, pornography is merely a sexual stimulus with a partner, a harmless release for sexual excitement. For others it fulfils a need. In this second category are generally people with empty or immature emotional lives. They mistake the sex they see in pornography for love.

In some countries that have relaxed censorship laws there has even been a decrease in sex crimes. Compared with Britain, the liberal-minded Scandinavian countries are awash with pornography, but they have dramatically less sex crime than we have in Britain. Until 1969 Denmark had about 85 cases of sexual crime per 100,000 of the population. In that year the Danish government repealed the law censoring pictorial sex, and sexual crimes dropped to less than half the pre-1969 figure.

•

A far more sinister role is played by pornography when it is produced by paedophiles and involves children. This is an area of highly organised crime which is difficult to crush.

The videos are made by experts and circulated among tight-knit rings of paedophiles operating globally. One was known to be on sale a few years ago for £4,000. It showed a boy of probably eight years of age being tortured and sexually abused by two men. Because of the internationalism of the participants, those responsible are difficult to trace. European police forces generally have enough national problems on their hands without getting too involved in cross-border crime. They are also hampered by differences in national laws. Until recently, for instance, the penalty for producing child pornography in the Netherlands was a mere three months' imprisonment. Now, although it can be a maximum of six years, it is still far behind the British penalty.

In 1995 Interpol revealed that as many as 30,000 paedophile pornographers were operating across Europe. No national police force took any action on this warning.

The journalist Nick Davies wrote in *The Guardian* of his experience while sitting in the Blue Boy Club in Amsterdam's Spuistraat. "I...flicked though the catalogue on the bar, offering 'truly the best boys in town,' and watched a Japanese businessman make his purchase."

In Berlin, Davies reported, a social worker told him there were some 700 east European boys, aged from 11 to 17, who had ended up in the sex industry in the city.

In the course of his investigations Davies met an exiled British paedophile who described to him how fellow-paedophiles commercialised their sexual obsession.

"They were trafficking boys from other countries, running legitimate gay brothels and selling under-age boys 'under the counter;' they had branched out into the production of child pornography. And they had killed some of them. One boy had simply been shot through the head; he had been causing trouble and had been executed in front of several paedophiles. Another, he [the informant] believed, had been thrown into one of the canals.

"But the one about whom he spoke the most was a boy who had been tortured and killed in the most painful fashion in the course of producing a pornographic video." Davies's informant had seen most of the video himself and had vomited before he could reach the end.

This is a kind of sexual sadism that is a sickness as well as a crime. And because of the covert nature of its participants, and the flood of nameless victims coming from broken homes and even broken countries, it looks like a crime that is here to stay.

•

Sexual myths: pornography, castration, rehabilitation, lunar killing

Another myth about sexual killers, promulgated in such cases by the liberal intelligentsia, is that they can somehow be reformed. As a case study let us consider Paul Beart, who was sent to prison for five years for a savage, three-hour sexual attack on a friend of his family. After serving only three years he was released on licence at the age of 26, having duped prison officials into believing he was no longer a risk to women. He had "successfully" completed a rehabilitation course and a "relapse prevention" scheme.

Almost immediately Beart broke his parole terms by leaving his home territory of Boston, Lincolnshire, and travelling to Newquay in Cornwall. There he began stalking three women, then unsuccessfully tried to hire a girl from an escort agency. On the night of April 26th, 2001, he attacked two teenage girls, who managed to escape. He then hid beside a pathway and pounced on restaurant manageress Deborah O'Sullivan, 36, as she walked home from a Newquay nightclub. He stripped her, even wrenching the pierced rings from her ears and navel. He twisted her arms so severely that they were broken; he tore an eight-inch gash in her stomach with his bare hands; he burned her body with a cigarette lighter; he bit her face so savagely that she was unrecognisable and he brutally battered her while raping her.

Before Deborah lost consciousness, pleading with her attacker through her swollen lips not to hurt her any more, Beart said, "You know I'm going to kill you, don't you?" Deborah, who had never met her murderer, was unable to reply. Beart was to say afterwards that her eyelids slowly closed, her chin dropped and she nodded her head twice in defeat. Then he beat her unconscious with an iron refuse can.

Deborah was taken to a Plymouth hospital in a coma. She died there three days later, on April 29th, 2001, from the multiple injuries he inflicted upon her.

The case of Paul Beart focuses on his so-called "rehabilitation" scheme while in prison, for despite the well-known fact that men who carry out violent sexual crimes will usually do so again if they are allowed to do so, society remains unrealistically optimistic about such criminals. Having manipulated his early release, Beart was placed in the care of the probation service which immediately assessed him as possessing "a high risk of re-offending;" he was, they thought, a danger to the public. Even so, when he broke the conditions of his licence by going off from Boston to Newquay and failing to report to probation officers, they did not inform the police; instead, they sent him a letter, which is standard probationary service procedure.

Beart, who gave himself up after murdering Deborah O'Sullivan, was tried at Bristol Crown Court and smirked as he was sentenced to life imprisonment. After that, the probation service conducted an official internal inquiry into why a man with such a history of violence was treated so leniently, and was allowed to roam around the country looking for victims, and concluded that the behaviour of the officers involved was "appropriate."

Now classified as "an untreatable sexual sadist," Beart will almost certainly be given some sort of psychiatric treatment in prison, with the object of determining whether he will pose a danger to women in the future. But doubtless he will continue to sneer silently, for he has decided to use his intellect to take on the system. He has four A levels, and dropped out of a university course when he was doing well. In prison after attacking his family friend, he went along with everything that he was told, manipulating his counsellors into believing that he was a reformed character when, all the time, he was laughing up his sleeve. Even during the five months he was on probation he never missed an appointment with his probation officer, for it was part of his plan to lull the authorities into believing he was squeaky-clean.

•

So is early release from prison and a spell on probation

the right way to treat sexual criminals? The Home Office insists that probation does work. In fact, it doesn't work. According to a study covering the two years between 1997 and 1999 at least 900 serious offences – including murder, rape, kidnapping and arson – were committed by criminals while they were being supervised by the probation service after early release from prison sentences. About 70 per cent of repeat offenders who are given probation commit further crimes, according to figures produced by the Home Office itself. These include a fair sprinkling of callous sadists like Paul Beart, prowling at night for their next unsuspecting victim. This price is much too high to pay, as Deborah O'Sullivan would have testified had she still been alive.

That serious efforts are made in Britain to rehabilitate sexual criminals is another myth. A lot of people who are likely to commit sex crimes are already in prison, so it's worth taking a look at what sort of people they are. According to the Office for National Statistics, more than three-quarters of male remand prisoners suffer from a personality disorder. One in 10 have a functional psychosis and more than half experience depression. The majority of men in prison aged 60 and over (57 per cent) have committed sex offences.

The government's five-year plan to reduce re-offending, published in 2005, stated: "We continue to imprison too many people with mental health problems. Dangerous people with mental health problems must be kept secure, and treatment is available for severe personality disorders in prison. Those with the most serious problems can also be transferred to a secure hospital place."

Some prisoners have more than one mental health problem. Nearly three-quarters of sentenced prisoner suffer from two or more mental disorders, and one in five has four of the five major mental disorders. Neurotic and personality disorders are particularly prevalent – 40 per cent of male and 63 per cent of female sentenced prisoners have a neurotic disorder, over three times the level of the general population. Sixty-four per cent of male and 50 per cent of female sentenced prisoners have a personality disorder.

Mental health problems among prisoners are often linked to previous experiences of violence at home and sexual abuse. About half of women and about a quarter of men in prison have suffered from violence at home while about one in three women report having suffered sexual abuse, compared with just under one in 10 men.

Prison regimes do little to address the mental health needs of prisoners. Research has found that 28 per cent of male sentenced prisoners with evidence of psychosis are reported spending 23 or more hours a day in their cells – over twice the proportion of those without mental health problems.

•

You will not too often come across brutes like Paul Beart before someone cries out, "Castrate them!" This is a cure-all apparently inextricably interwoven in most discussions about sexual killers, and as such it is another myth.

Castration is a supposed remedy based more on militancy than biology, for it pre-supposes than men castrated after puberty cannot indulge in sexual intercourse. They can, of course. Castration means the removal of the testicles, not the penis, and while the penis is there so is the driving force. All that castration prevents is procreation.

A man who has been castrated does not lose his sexual appetite. Many men castrated after puberty can still have intercourse and can ejaculate from the prostate gland – the centre of erection is not testicular but in the spinal cord. The Chinese were aware of this when they created their eunuchs by castrating them before puberty. If it was necessary to castrate after puberty they removed the penis as well as the testicles. As adults, Oriental eunuchs revealed degenerative changes, notably a loss of mental capacity. After post-puberty castration the memory of sexual feeling remains for perhaps as long as seven years, so that if a sexual killer were castrated he would have to be kept away from women for at least that period. The American psychiatrist Dr. J. Paul de River, dismissing castration for sexual offenders as turning back the clock to medieval times, wrote: "In the act of coitus we are dealing with a complex mechanism in which the psyche, the spinal and the sympathetic nervous systems are involved."

In any event, some psychiatrists understand that rape committed on an unknown woman is not the act of a man whose sexual impulses are out of control. Poor sexual performance during rape is high, suggesting that sex is not the prime motive for rape. This raises the question: would a castrated man continue to attack women, and perhaps kill more of them in revenge for his obvious lack of performance?

Other observers, it should be said, don't accept the mantra that sex is not the prime motive for rape. This point is made by Professor Steven Pinker of Harvard University in his book *The Blank Slate* (published by Penguin Books). First he quotes gender feminist Susan Brownmiller, who wrote:

"Man's discovery that his genitalia could serve as a weapon to generate fear must rank as one of the most important discoveries of prehistoric times, along with the use of fire and the first crude stone axe. From prehistoric times to the present, I believe, rape has played a critical function...it is nothing more or less than a conscious process of intimidation by which all men keep all women in a state of fear."

This, says Professor Pinker, grew into the modern catechism: rape-is-not-about-sex...our culture glorifies violence against women. "But the fact that rape has something to do with violence does not mean it has nothing to do with sex, any more than the fact that armed robbery has something to do with violence means it has nothing to do with greed. Evil men may use violence to get sex, just as they use violence to get other things they want."

Another myth involves the "full moon killer."

Many sexual serial killers evolve a discernible pattern of killing. One such was Bobby Joe Long, who killed on Sundays, and preferably when the moon was full. "I knew I was sick," he confessed after he was sent to Death Row for nine rape-murders. "But there was nothing I could do about it." He claimed that he couldn't sit still when the moon was full, that even the smallest thing set him off. "And I'm not the only one, either. All over Death Row you can tell when it's the full moon."

Long, a Florida X-ray assistant who was convicted in July, 1986, blamed incidents that happened in his life for turning him into a sexual killer, and at first glance they would appear to merit some analysis. When he was 11 he began to grow breasts. His whole body became feminine, but this didn't come as a total surprise to his family. He had a hereditary congenital disorder that had afflicted other male relatives, and his doctor advised surgery. Consequently six pounds of tissue was removed from his chest. But it didn't solve another problem that was invisible. He claimed he was fated to experience a lunar "menstrual" cycle that would remain with him for the rest of his days.

At 19 he suffered a severe head injury in a motorcycle accident. It was not the first head trauma he had suffered. As a child he was knocked unconscious four times in various accidents The cumulative effect of these mishaps and his motorbike accident was that he had significant brain damage, which left him with a permanent limp and numbness on one side of his face. As we have seen in other such cases, the brain damage had an affect on his temper. He had a short fuse, and it took little or nothing to provoke him to violence.

Added to this cocktail of disadvantages, Long developed an insatiable sexual appetite. He wasn't satisfied with sex two or three times a day with his wife

Sexual myths: pornography, castration, rehabilitation, lunar killing

– he masturbated at least five times a day as well, and lusted after every woman he set eyes on, including his wife's sister and her friends. The addiction to sex, he claimed, began while he was in hospital recovering from his motorbike accident. He would lie in his hospital bed having lurid fantasies of group sex and raping women.

His marriage didn't last, but friends claimed that not all the faults were on his side. Like his mother, his wife was domineering and manipulative, and between them they formed his resentful view of women as exploiters who needed to be taught a lesson. Prostitutes, he decided, were the worst of all, exploiting the need for sex in men, particularly men like himself, who were ruinously addicted to it. So prostitutes made up the bulk of his murder victims. One girl he spared and who was not a prostitute was Lisa McVey, 17, of Tampa. Lusting after her, he pulled her off her bicycle as she was riding home in the middle of the night.

Long gagged, bound and blindfolded her. Telling her he did not intend to hurt her, he then raped her. Lisa told police: "He said that women were always walking all over him and this was his revenge."

Long was later to say that he tried to tell doctors that there was something wrong with him when he was about to be discharged from hospital. Half his face felt dead and he could think of nothing but sex. He was aware of his short temper. These outbursts would erupt without warning, passing as quickly as they came and leaving him with no memory of them. On one occasion his mother angered him by saying she was taking his car to go shopping. He grabbed her, put her across his knee and beat her. Then he stormed out, and when he came back he had no recollection of what had happened.

It was much the same when his murder spree escalated to one murder after another. After each killing he would return to his flat and sleep soundly for as long as 12 hours. On waking he wondered if he had dreamt the murder or had actually committed it. To find out he would buy a newspaper and read in it that the killing really did happen. But that didn't stop him.

During a two-year spell Long raped 50 women, contacting them when they advertised something in the "For Sale" ads in the local newspaper. Sensing that something was wrong with him, he made an appointment with a doctor, but walked out without seeing him when he realised that the doctor would report him to the police.

He lost one job after another as an X-ray technician through the advances he made to women patients, most of whom he unnecessarily made to undress before X-raying them. Aware that his obsession with women was ruining his life, he hated them for it. His killings finally came to an end after his arrest for the abduction and rape of Lisa McVey.

On the face of it Long had a plausible case for being considered as a disturbed person. But when you begin to peel back the layers of his complaints some of them do not stand up. A serial murder-rapist cannot legitimately claim that he is so obsessed with sex that women must be to blame, and he is obliged to kill them in revenge. On his own admission he knew he had a medical problem, but he didn't know what it was. He said that if he had had any idea that it was neurological he would have gone to a neurologist. But when he found he couldn't stop killing he could have given himself up. He killed again after letting Lisa McVey go – stripping his victim and driving around in his car for two hours with her nude body beside him before dumping her from an overpass – so would there have been even more killings if the police hadn't caught him?

As for the lunar menstrual cycle and the regular full moon brouhaha on Death Row, there is no scientific validity in the idea that the moon influences a man to kill or commit sex crimes. This is a myth handed down from our pagan ancestors, to whom it rightfully still belongs.

The jury at Long's trial were unimpressed by his claim that he was brain-damaged, and found him guilty of first-degree murder. They found that he knew what he had done and he knew it was wrong. Doctors giving evidence against him testified that he had made a good recovery from his motorbike accident and had no lasting cerebral impairment. This, it should be said, was later challenged by a psychologist, who thought that Long's pre-trial examination had been superficial. The EEG evaluations had not spanned the full 36 hours needed to determine a deep cerebral dysfunction and the neurological reflex tests were flawed because Long was shackled when they were carried out. In addition, according to the psychologist, the doctors had not sufficiently considered the psychological and physiological effects of the hormonal disorder that made him grow breasts.

•

A final myth many of us like to believe is that age is a deterrent to sexual deviation. That was not the case for 75-year-old Anthony Shelley.

Estranged from his wife, he spent much of his time at home in Stafford on the phone calling sex chat lines. He made 130 calls to Faye Thorneycroft, 19, a local prostitute; then in December, 2000, hired her to have sex sessions with him at his flat. She tied him up, handcuffed and gagged him, forcing him to drink a stupefiant before making off with his cheques. When she left, Shelley died. In June, 2002, Faye Thorneycroft was given a life sentence for his murder.

CHAPTER SIX

MUTILATION FOR SEXUAL SATISFACTION; SYMBOLIC
SADISM; PROSTITUTION, EROTOMANIA
*Jack the Ripper, "Jack the Stripper," Robert Hoskins,
Arthur Jackson*

The murder of prostitutes by a killer who believes he is on a divinely inspired mission against vice is familiar to all of us. Peter Sutcliffe, the Yorkshire Ripper, claimed that he killed street girls after hearing voices from God. Certified as insane, Sutcliffe was sent to Broadmoor.

Britain's oldest, most written-about serial killing, the murder by Jack the Ripper of five prostitutes, or maybe more, in Whitechapel in 1888, may also have had religious undertones. In a recent book, *Prisoner 1167, the Madman who was Jack the Ripper*, the author James Tully points the finger of suspicion at a man named James Kelly, who, interestingly, was a Broadmoor inmate before he escaped. Kelly, who was uncompromisingly religious, frequented prostitutes, and bore a grudge against his mother for abandoning him as a baby. He had been judged insane after stabbing his young wife Sarah to death in 1883.

After his escape from Broadmoor, says Tully, he became the Ripper, starting his grim work in August, 1888. By a majority of votes among a century of researchers, the Ripper's first victim was prostitute Martha Tabram, and, says author Tully, Kelly "needed to mutilate the vagina, the breasts and the abdomen in the outpouring of rage against those parts of the female body which he associated with his mother, his wife and the prostitutes for whom he felt so much contempt." This kind of mutilation is called symbolic sadism, the term used for the condition in which the subject expresses his sadistic impulse by acts of mutilation of some symbol that has specific meaning for him.

Eight days later the Ripper murdered Annie Chapman, another prostitute, with whom "he experienced for the first time the ultimate sexual gratification of plunging his hands deeply into the warm entrails of his victim's corpse, and then removing the identifiable womb – which exemplified all the hatred he felt for his mother."

A Dr. Edgar Sheppard wrote a letter published in *The Times* in which he said that the murders all pointed to one individual, "and that individual insane. Not necessarily an escaped, or even as yet recognised, lunartic." There were many lunartics in the asylums, he went on, with a delusion that they had a mission to destroy vice, and that was why the killer was selecting prostitutes as his victims.

Dr. Forbes Winslow, another doctor who wrote to *The Times* at the time of the Whitechapel murders, described himself as "an expert on lunartics" and claimed that the killings were "the work of a homicidal lunatic who between the murders was in a 'lucid interval,' and the murders would recommence directly this state had passed away.

"The murderer is one and the same person, a lunatic suffering from homicidal monomania who during the lucid intervals is calm and forgetful of what he has been doing the midst of his attack."

In November of the "Ripper year" came the murder of Mary Kelly, who many regard as the Ripper's last victim. Two authors, James Tully and John Morrison, have posited that there was a connection between Mary Kelly and James Kelly – Morrison claims that she was Kelly's girl friend and had changed her name to Kelly in hopes that he would marry her. He didn't, says Morrison, and she went on the streets, abandoning the baby she had by Kelly, who then set out to get his revenge, killing other prostitutes on the way. Whether or not you believe that, you have to believe that the Ripper went ballistic when he cornered Mary Kelly in her squalid tenement room in Miller's Court, Dorset Street, Whitechapel,

After killing her he removed the whole of the surface of her abdomen and thighs and emptied her abdominal cavity of its viscera. He cut off her breasts, mutilated her arms, hacked her face and severed the neck all round down to the bone.

He skinned the right thigh to the bone and skinned and removed the muscles of the left thigh right down to the knee.

He placed the viscera in odd places, e.g., the uterus and kidneys and one breast were placed under her head and the other breast by her right foot, her liver between her feet, the intestines by the right side and the spleen by the left side of her body. Pieces of skin and muscle were scattered on the table.

All that remained of Mary Kelly, attacked much more frenziedly than any of the other victims, was a heap of bloody flesh scarcely recognisable as once having been a human being.

Dr. Edward Bond, who conducted the post-mortem on Mary Kelly and had studied the notes on the injuries of the other Ripper victims, was asked to make a report to the Metropolitan Police on the killings, and very early on he dispensed with the popular idea that the killer might have been a doctor:

"In each case the mutilation was inflicted by a person who had no scientific or anatomical knowledge. He does not even possess the technical knowledge of a butcher or a horse slaughterer, or any person accustomed to cut up dead animals."

In a 19th century attempt at criminal profiling, he said of the Ripper: "He must be a man subject to periodical attacks of erotic mania. The character of the mutilations indicates that the man may be in a condition sexually, that may be called satyriasis. It is possible that the homicidal impulse may have developed from a revengeful or brooding condition of the mind, or that religious mania may have been the original disease."

Satyriasis is abnormal sex craving on the part of the male – its opposite in the female is nymphomania. Since it usually embraces perversion, it is an extreme form of sex-dominated hypaesthesia (reduced sensibility to touch). In satyriasis the individual's perversions tend to take control of his mind until his eroticism can only really be satisfied by his perversions.

The problem with the conditions of satyriasis and sex-dominated hypaesthesia is that individuals may differ widely in the degree to which the conditions dominate their personalities. They may manifest themselves both in a Casanova type who is seen as just one of the lads with a healthy sexual appetite, and in a brutal rapist. Whether a man will emerge as one or the other will depend on a very considerable variety of background and environmental factors.

Consider for example armies of soldiers on the march, raping, looting, pillaging as they go, acting completely out of character from what they would otherwise be as civilian individuals. Several such Russian armies attacked the eastern frontier of greater Germany in January, 1945, and captured Berlin five months later, bringing the European sector of the Second World War to an end. During their path to victory it is estimated that the Russian soldiers raped about two million German women, more than 100,000 in Berlin alone.

What turned these men from human to animal behaviour was a variety of environmental factors which before their enlistment would have been alien to most of them. The push to Berlin was deliberately speeded up on orders from Stalin, at the cost of far more lives than was necessary, so the soldiers saw their comrades dying around them in thousands, the wounded left to succumb in agony, simply because their officers wanted the advance quickened. This in turn led to gunnery inefficiency, lack of disciplinary control, and a consequential deterioration in the soldiers' living standards. The result of these environmental situations was that the soldiers became brutalised. And as a backdrop to this they remembered what the Germans had done to their own women when they invaded Russia three years earlier, so another environmental factor was revenge.

Systematically anaesthetised of all human emotion by the life they were being forced to lead, groups of Russian soldiers gang-raped any woman they could find – girls, mothers, grandmothers, and sometimes all three generations in a single family. Being themselves scarcely human at this point, it was easy for them to regard foreign women as scarcely human too. Sometimes the women begged to be killed. That astonished the Russians, who apparently hadn't entirely departed from the human code of honour. "German soldiers kill women, Russian soldiers don't," they replied. But this was still murder at remove because hundreds of thousands of the violated women killed themselves from shame. Armies of Russians were thereby turned into sexual killers because of the environmental factors engulfing them. All men are rapists, say some misguided militant feminists, but fortunately this proved to be not quite so. There is documentary evidence to show that a large minority of soldiers behaved impeccably and one document reveals that a soldier who was about to commit rape was shot dead by a comrade.

•

In his report on Jack the Ripper, Dr. Bond thought that the murderer would be an inoffensive-looking man, probably smartly dressed. If that were so, he would be solitary and eccentric in his habits. He was most likely to be a man without regular occupation, but with some small income or pension.

"He is probably living among respectable persons who have some knowledge of his character and habits and who may have grounds for suspicion that he isn't quite right in his mind at times."

All this, it has to be said, fitted the Broadmoor escapee James Kelly to a tee – although it also needs to be said that the number of candidates for the title of Jack the Ripper would fill this book. Kelly was vengeful, brooding, solitary, eccentric, an upholsterer by trade but with no regular job, had religious pretensions and received a small income from a legacy. Some of his acquaintances were certain that he had mental problems. But setting Kelly aside, we can see that emotional extremes, coupled with melancholia, satyriasis and the sense of a divine mission, are factors likely to be present when the Ripper, whoever he may be, sets out to kill for sexual gratification. With such a person an analysis of his mind is difficult, even impossible, because he is mad, and the mind of a madman is chaos.

•

Another London prostitute killer surfaced three-quarters of a century after Jack the Ripper and he too was never caught. He was known as Jack the Stripper, after his predilection for leaving his victims' nude corpses hidden in places near the River Thames, and no doubt he too was in the condition of satyriasis.

It was reasoned that the killer, who terrorised the twilight world of London vice in the mid-1960s, was a strong, virile man who, left unsatisfied by normal intercourse, penetrated his victims anally and at that same time held them in a tight grip, probably around the neck. All the victims had slight marks on their necks apparently made by fingernails, either their own in self-defence or their killer's. Other marks indicated that pressure had been applied in the nose and mouth areas. All the victims died very quickly.

Detective Assistant Commissioner John Du Rose, of Scotland Yard, who led the hunt for the serial killer, said, "He knew that his prostitute victims set no limits to the sexual acts in which they would allow their clients to indulge. In obtaining satisfaction he became utterly frenzied and, at the moment of his orgasm, the girls died."

Du Rose thought that when the killer was with his first victim he might not have realised that she was dead and for that reason pushed a gag into her mouth. With his subsequent victims he knew that they had died so he made no attempt to gag them.

"One could postulate a theory that had this man been caught after the death of the first prostitute, and the circumstances of the sexual act had been revealed in court, the jury might have brought in a verdict of manslaughter or even accidental death," Du Rose said. "But when he continued to indulge in his particular perversion, well knowing that the girl concerned would die, then he must have recognised that he was fulfilling himself as a murderer."

The hunt for Jack the Stripper was wound down after the chief suspect committed suicide in his garage. He was never named.

•

Fear of women, rather than hatred of them, is most often the underlying motive for attacks on prostitutes – the prostitute is seen as an easy, accessible target on which the assailant can wreak his vengeance.

Sadly, men don't talk about prostitution. Male journalists, equally regrettably, don't defend prostitution. They leave it to their journalist sisters to ride roughshod all over them. This is a pity, because if they did defend it they would be able to explain something that many women don't understand – that prostitution exists because it is necessary for men, because it has a vital place in the human condition.

There are several reasons for this. The first is that the biology of men is driven by sex in a way that most women cannot begin to imagine. Men need more sex than women. Partner variation is an integral part of the psyche of male sex. So too is non-emotional involvement. Men have no difficulty in compartmentalising their love lives – which is why a man will become violent to anyone who seduces his wife, whom he loves, yet will, if he can, go to bed with any number of other wives – the so-called double standard.

Normally, sexual problems in the human male largely disappear when sex is available. They surface, sometimes dangerously, when sex is not available. At worst, this can lead to violence, at best, to listlessness and attention deficit. If you don't believe that, talk to any woman university lecturer about the problems she has with male students, which she does not have with female students.

Despite recent affirmation by a woman newspaper journalist that consensual sex has never been so easily obtained as in our time, many men do not have the social graces, the persona, the courage, or perhaps even the looks to get as much free sex as they want. So they go out and buy it. That they can do so effectively caps to a large extent the explosive volcano of their testosterone.

Many women who can grasp the male need for regular and different sex, nevertheless have some difficulty in accepting it. There are certain truisms in human gender relationships that men don't like saying and women don't like hearing, and one of them is that some women in a permanent relationship can't or won't satisfy their partners sexually. Another is that man is by and large not ideally suited to monogamy. Sometimes some men need change, excitement, greater interest, and more thrills, which some women can't give them. This is not all masculine self-indulgence, as some feminists would have you believe; it is a biological fact supported by tons of thumping testosterone.

When I worked in investigative journalism in Fleet Street my newspaper ran a sex quiz which *inter alia* asked those readers aged between 18 and 24 how many times a week they had sex. An interesting number of young men said three times a day, or 21 times a week. One male respondent said seven times a day. He did not say how many days he could sustain this feat, but I have yet to meet any woman who, for free, desires to match any of these performances.

Where, one wonders, would all this excessive male energy be channelled if the recent unhinged suggestion in a respectable newspaper were to be adopted – that prostitution should somehow be stopped entirely? How much misery would be visited upon innocent women by predatory males? How much misery would indeed be visited on millions of the male population?

Yes, millions. There are apparently 80,000 known prostitutes in the UK. If their customers are aged 16 to

Mutilation for sexual satisfaction; symbolic sadism;
prostitution; erotomania

60, that would suggest a market of around 20 million men. According to research, one in four men in the UK has paid for sex – that is, possibly around five million men. Interestingly this is a figure that one woman MP found "pretty staggering" – a statement that, coming from an MP, is in itself pretty staggering, and further proof, if any is needed, that many women don't begin to understand the need for prostitution.

If the 80,000 prostitutes have a customer repeat frequency of 14 days it would mean that they entertain round 25 customers a week. Even if these figures are shaky, one thing is for sure, a lot of men are paying a great deal of money to the 80,000 ladies, who can't be living on thin air. The fact that these figures are in such biblical numbers adds numerical weight to the submission that men need prostitution.

It is as biologically natural for a young man to seek out sex as it is for a young woman to become a mother. Neither the one nor the other can be prevented without enormous damage to humankind. This is a fact of nature. The attempted enforcement of changes by one gender upon the other gender that conflict with the nature of things is therefore both cruel and barbaric. It is a great shame that men have not answered back, in anything like sufficient numbers, the avalanche of emasculation that has been heaped upon them in the last 50 years, and an even greater shame that so many of them have acquiesced in it. Is this part of the reason, one wonders, why so many of them are afraid of women and seek vengeance in violence against them?

The increased incidence of sexual crime is linked to a change in attitudes towards sex during the last dozen years, which in itself has led to a rise in promiscuity, an increase in the use of prostitutes and inevitably a surge in sexually transmitted diseases among young people.

A study on sexual behaviour published in November, 2001 (National Survey of Sexual Attitudes and Lifestyles, which questioned 11,161 people aged 16 to 44), revealed that in the previous 10 years the number of men who had paid for sex had more than doubled, from one in 48 in 1990 to one in 23 in the year 2000. For men in London the figure was one in 11.

The report found that Britons increasingly prefer to have a number of sexual relationships rather than marry, with one in 12 men and one in 28 women saying that they have slept with more than 10 different people in the previous 10 years.

Among people aged 25 to 34, more than four in 10 men and one in five women say that they have had sex with more than 10 different people in their lifetime. For many, staying faithful was no longer important. One in seven men and one in 11 women say that they had overlapping sexual relationships in the past year. But despite the shedding of Britain's sexual inhibitions, the report shows that people on average have sex only once a week.

The same report disclosed that the number of men who reported ever having a homosexual encounter rose from one in 28 in 1990 to one in 19 in the year 2000. For women, the incidence almost tripled, from one in 56 in 1990 to one in 20 in the year 2000.

•

One of the things women don't like about prostitution is the idea that sex, the secret weapon in their armoury, can be bought. A prostitute, however, sees sex as a straight trade-off. Some can apparently earn around £2,000 a week, presumably tax-free. Others can earn £2,000 a night, also tax-free. For those who can and choose to do so, this sort of financial return must be at least attractive.

But a recent newspaper feature dismissed this idea. It opined: "Many women who work in the supposedly 'safe' part of the industry – saunas, massage parlours and flats – are in effect, sex slaves." It offered no evidence, statistical or anecdotal, to support this sweeping assertion, giving credibility to the thought that the idea that women are forced into the sex-for-sale industry is one of the great myths of the anti-prostitution lobby.

Mutilation for sexual satisfaction; symbolic sadism; prostitution; erotomania

A woman may be hard up, she may be on drugs, she may have low self-esteem, she may have 10 kids and no money, she may have come lately from Eastern Europe, she may not speak good English, she may be indolent, or a boozer, or all the other options may be unpleasant for her, but she isn't forced to sell her body. She chooses to do so. Conditions for a slave trade no longer exist in third-millennium welfare Britain. Many prostitutes may not like being prostitutes, just as many clerks may not like being clerks. But the facility to walk away from it is open to the vast majority of clerks as well as prostitutes.

Women politicians and writers who argue the case against prostitution do so because it fits their agenda of personal prejudice, an agenda based on deep-rooted angst. But women have much more to fear from street working than from a properly organised system of brothels. For it is these so-called street workers who are almost always the victims of male violence.

Street working, as distinct from traditional prostitution, only exists in the first place because no government has ever had the courage to promote a more decent alternative. It has become a dirty, shady business run by pimps, exploiting women, closely entwined with trafficking, only because successive governments refuse to come to grips with a basic human condition.

If it has been infiltrated by illegal immigrants, that should not be seen as a condemnation of prostitution, rather as a condemnation of inept government. No one wants it, of course, and it should be and can be swept off the streets. The best way to do that is to make traditional prostitution more accessible, so that for the customers it becomes a more attractive alternative to approaching street girls.

Is there any visionary in government ready to grasp this nettle? Step forward former Home Office minister Fiona Mactaggart, who, at the beginning of 2006, came up with a plan to allow two women and a maid to work together in mini-brothels, her argument being that it would protect them from violence and exploitation.

Months later, at the time of a case involving the murders of five Suffolk street workers, Ms. Mactaggart, now a backbench MP, re-stated her plan. The murders, she said, demonstrated the need to implement the idea. It is perhaps a sad marginal note that the motivation of the Mactaggart plan appears to be only to protect women and not to address the needs of men.

Were we getting there? Not really. For from the same government, almost in the same breath, Harriet Harman, the Constitutional Affairs minister, was proclaimed as the first government minister to call for men to be prosecuted for paying for sex. She cites "a radical experiment in Sweden, where the government has decriminalised the sale of safe sex and started prosecuting men who buy it."

In fact we already have an even more pernicious form of torture right here on our own doorstep. This is the sinister habit, promulgated in law enforcement circles, of arresting the customers of prostitutes and then subjecting them to a term of repentance and humiliation in front of fellow-victims and a steely-faced "counsellor."

It is hard to understand why men arrested for approaching a prostitute should allow themselves to be subjected to this kind of barbaric emasculation, which, if nothing else, must be a gross state-sponsored infringement of their human rights. Part of the answer must be that in the continuous move towards gender equality in this current social revolution men are being so brainwashed – by some of their own gender as well as by women – for the "sins" of the past, that they actually feel guilty about wanting sex, and in that sense they welcome the public hair-shirting.

All revolutions are driven by minorities – extremists who impose their will upon others. The current social revolution is a magnet for liberal, influential feminine bleeding hearts, extremists who are only too delighted to champion the cause of their downtrodden sisters "forced" to sell their bodies for sex. It is hard to escape the conclusion that, revelling in men's sense of guilt, these women are vicariously enjoying a sense of revenge. Because British men are essentially emotionally immature, they can easily be made to feel guilty about paying for sex. And any woman who enjoys a bit of *Schadenfreude* at the expense of the opposite sex is going to have a field day in this situation.

But differences of gender opinion which are revenge-based on both sides are not going to get anyone anywhere. The place of prostitution in society – and it must have a place – must be properly addressed if women who choose to be in it are to be protected from violent men.

•

A man who won't go to a prostitute but nevertheless fills his mind with sexual images may become a stalker. A French doctor, Jacques Ferrand, first coined the term erotomania in 1640. It has now become one of the symptoms of stalkers – although not all stalkers are necessarily erotomaniacs.

"Erotomania," he said somewhat wordily, "is a state of the most unbridled excitement, filling the mind with a crowd of voluptuous images, and ever hurrying its victims to the acts of the grossest licentiousness in the absence of any intellectual powers."

Today erotomania is recognised as an illness, a form of schizophrenia that has less to do with sex and more to do with a deadly delusion – the false belief that someone loves you.

Erotomaniacs are generally resourceful and intelligent people, and their delusion is such that a lack of response dos not deter them. Instead it drives them on to threaten and even kill their victims – all in the name of love. It is a crime that has been increasing at an alarming rate over the past 25 years. Because of the phenomenon of the celebrity stalker – the TV personality Jill Dando was killed by a stalker – it has also received increasing media coverage.

Probably the most famous victim of a celebrity stalker

is the actress-singer Madonna. In January, 1996, she went to court in Los Angeles to face a 38-year-old drifter accused of stalking and threatening to kill her.

"He told my secretary he was there to take me away," she testified. "He told me that if he couldn't have me he would slit my throat from ear to ear."

It had begun, the court was told, when the stalker, Robert Dewey Hoskins, was first seen hanging around the star's Hollywood Hills estate. Hoskins jumped a security wall and was speedily ejected by a private guard. He continued to confront Madonna at the gates, leaving her a note that said: "I love you. You will be my wife for keeps."

He disturbed her so much that she sold her estate. Seven weeks later she was at another of her homes in Florida when Hoskins turned up again, this time carrying a wooden heart inscribed, *Love to my wife Madonna*. He jumped the protective fence again and lunged at security guard Basil Stephens. The guard shot him twice, wounding him in the arm and the abdomen.

Los Angeles detective Andrew Purdy said, "We believe that under the circumstances the guard had every right to shoot the intruder."

Hoskins, who had served time for burglary and parole violation, and had suffered for years from drug and alcohol abuse, boasted to acquaintances that he had married Madonna after she picked him up off the street in her stretch limousine.

Such is the weird world of stalking that at first Madonna refused to testify, claiming that it would be too traumatic. She reluctantly changed her mind after the judge threatened to have her arrested if she didn't appear. Hoskins's obsessions, she said, had caused her to have nightmares, and she dreaded facing him even in the security of a court of law.

"I don't want to be in the same room as him," she told the jury. "I feel sick in the stomach. I still have terrible thoughts that he might be in my house, chasing after me."

*Mutilation for sexual satisfaction; symbolic sadism;
prostitution; erotomania*

Hoskins was jailed for two years and sent to a psychiatric institution for evaluation.

Similar case histories reinforce the medical view that erotomania is one of the most tenacious, chronic and difficult illnesses to treat because the delusions are so profound that they are virtually unresponsive to medication.

An erotomaniac does not at first have any intention of harming his or her victim and indeed does not even understand the hurt being caused, which makes it difficult to prove intent in a court of law. The onus is on the victim to prove that he or she is being stalked, and in Britain there is little to distinguish a stalker from a thwarted lover who cannot accept that the affair is over.

This means that it is often not until the situation is completely out of control that the victim will seek help or protection. Even then, as in the case of Sergeant Ray Dunning, an Australian soldier, the necessary protection may not be forthcoming. After several sexual encounters with 40-year-old Diane Robinson, Sergeant Dunning made what he thought was a clean break.

He told her that he was about to be posted to Townsville, Queensland, where his wife Veronica would join him with their three young children. As a result, the affair was now over.

But Diane Robinson was an erotomaniac and no amount of rational argument would stop her from stalking Dunning and his family around Townsville – which she proceeded to do for the next six years. During that time Dunning did everything in his power to lose her. He wrote to the Australian Prime Minister, the attorney general, the solicitor general. He moved army base, took out a restraining order after she bumped into his car at a petrol station, and ignored her constant phone calls, letters and messages.

After four years Veronica Dunning packed her bags and left with the three children. She was scared – with good reason. Dunning then decided to confront his stalker. He wrote in his dairy: *"I pleaded with her...She said she would never get out of my life, and if she couldn't have me then no one else could. All the time she was taunting me, demanding sex. Despite my military training something snapped and suddenly I was so wound up I started hitting her. All of a sudden she was lying on the floor and my hands were wrapped tightly around her throat. She was making this gurgling sound and her face turned blue..."*

Ray Dunning pleaded guilty to manslaughter and was jailed for six years. In an interview from prison he said, "It is ironic that the law could not help me in my need in all those years of hell, but it had no trouble awarding me one year in jail for every year of hell she gave me. I have lost everything, my family, my career, my freedom, all because no one could stop this woman."

At some point the passion initially felt by the erotomaniac turns into a passionate anger, and an intent develops in his or her mind, albeit subconsciously, to bring the continuous chase to an end, to resolve the mystery of the elusive lover.

The American actress Theresa Saldana, who starred with Robert de Niro in *Raging Bull* and who was stalked by a man named Arthur Jackson, is a case in point. Jackson wrote in his diary: "Theresa Saldana is the countess of Heaven in my heart and the angel of America in my dreams. She is a soul mate to me. I have psychedelic fantasies of romance about her in springtime, enchanting visions of our walking together through the gardens of magnificent palaces in Heaven."

Jackson, a paranoid schizophrenic who developed erotomania towards the actress, flew from Scotland to America and travelled around the country stalking Theresa with the express purpose of murdering her so that they could be united in Heaven. In 1982 he stabbed her 10 times in the back outside her Sunset Boulevard apartment. She underwent a four-hour operation to repair a punctured lung.

Jackson was sentenced to 15 years for attempted murder, but even from prison he continued to write threatening letters to Theresa, believing that she had bewitched him. He was eventually extradited to Britain in June, 1996, after confessing to killing a man in London 30 years previously. He pleaded guilty to manslaughter on the grounds of diminished responsibility and was sentenced to life imprisonment.

Arthur Jackson is an example of severe erotomania, where the disease has progressed so far that the stalker resorts to violence against his victim. Emotional unconcern is one of the main characteristics of the erotomaniac; victims find it hard to believe that the stalker is unable to see how much pain he is inflicting.

Erotomaniacs develop their obsessions much as an ordinary person develops a crush. Once they have been rejected they cross a psychological boundary which, to most of us, is downright bizarre. To the normal person rejection in love leads to hurt and perhaps anger at the person who has thwarted us, but we control our grieving and then move on. Erotomaniacs, however, follow a different path. They move from the initial contact, placing the love object on a pedestal, to being rejected, and then to projecting their own feelings on to the object. In other words, because they cannot bear the pain of rejection, they convince themselves that the victim really does love them.

A forensic psychiatrist, Dr. Reid Meloy, believes the erotomaniac defends his shame at being rejected with very intense anger, and the anger fuels the pursuit of the victim to rectify the situation. The pursuit itself can be motivated by a desire to injure, to control, to dominate, or in some cases to kill the victim. If the erotomaniac is successful, his narcissistic fantasy is restored. Or if the two are united in death or disaster, then in the mind of the erotomaniac they are together as they should be.

One stalker whose pursuit ended in death was Mark Chapman, whose victim was the superstar ex-Beatle John Lennon, gunned down outside his New York apartment in December, 1980. The trial of Texan-born Chapman revealed him as an erotomaniac in whom the disease was so advanced that he thought he could take over the persona of his idol if he could get rid of him. The court was told he was not so much obsessed with

Lennon as believing that he actually was Lennon. He had been stalking his victim for about a week, walking around New York wearing badges proclaiming himself to be John Lennon.

He pleaded guilty, he said, because he had spoken to God, who had instructed him to confess to the murder. He was sentenced to 20 years to life for second-degree murder.

Unanswered questions abound in many stalking cases. A psychiatrist, Dr. Doreen Orion, compares stalking to terrorism: "A terrorist targets a country, a stalker targets a single victim. Terrorist activities are always taken seriously by the authorities, but the violation of a restraining order by a stalker is routinely assigned as low priority. Stalking has become the most common form of social terrorism."

After extensive research into erotomania Dr. Orion believes that incarceration is not enough. She suggests group therapy and mandated treatment as essentials after the erotomaniac has been legally punished.

CHAPTER SEVEN

Paedophilia; child abuse
Morss and Tyler, Mark Valera

The term paedophilia refers to a perversion that requires a child as a sexual object. This is a wide-ranging definition, for it encompasses men who seek sex with young girls and those who want sex only with small boys. Some of these longings are of a passive nature; others are sadistic and among the sadistic there is often terrible brutality. There is a strong line of demarcation between young paedophiles who frequently seek only sexual gratification and are prepared to be brutal to achieve it, and older ones who get their satisfaction from a vicarious act like fondling and who are rarely brutal unless they are frightened – although the paedophile killer Albert Fish was certainly the exception to this. There are also paedophiles who are mentally retarded, such as the child killer John Straffen, who died in prison in 2007. Psychiatrists are generally agreed that all paedophiles are both dangerous and cruel, because they attack the morals of children. They are also shrewd and cunning in the methods they use to attract the confidence of young children.

The average paedophile suffers from an acute inferiority complex and is uneasy in adult company. Some of them seek out small children to satisfy their lust because they feel they cannot have satisfactory sexual relations with an adult; they fear impotence. Others are too intellectually undeveloped to function at an adult level. In almost all paedophiles there is a desire to control, a desire which cannot be fulfilled with someone of their own age but which is satisfied with a child. Homosexuals sometimes become paedophiles as a relief from the inner conflict they suffer about their sexuality. Almost all paedophiles are so compelled by their lust as to be able to rationalise the act of perversion, and they grow speedily into a state of euphoria that sees no harm in what they have done to their victims or what they plan to do to the next one.

The problem of monitoring and studying paedophiles is nowhere better exposed than in the statistics about them. In 1996, according to a police report, offences against children had tripled in the previous 10 years. That report estimated that there were 40,000 paedophiles in Britain.

But five years later, at the beginning of 2001, a new police report revealed that there were 250,000 paedophiles in Britain, and that, said Detective Chief Inspector Bob McLachlan, head of Scotland Yard's paedophile unit, was "a conservative estimate." Could it really be that the number of paedophiles in Britain rose more than sixfold in just five years?

The 1996 report was probably inaccurate, for Home Office figures published since then show that 110,000 people in the United Kingdom have convictions for child sex offences. Working on prevalence of victim to victimiser, it is not difficult to suppose that 110,000 convicted would rise to 250,000 known and unknown people who have a sexual interest in children, thereby agreeing the guesstimate of 250,000.

The 2001 report claiming 250,000 paedophiles suggested that more than one in every 200 adults are paedophiles, figures that were bound to give cause for public anxiety. However, that figure must be based on the entire population, which is misleading, since overwhelmingly paedophiles are men. If there are 60 million people in the UK then there are probably 20 million grown men, so the incidence of paedophilia increases to one in 80.

But if that is right, other studies, which have suggested that as few as five per cent of paedophiles are caught and convicted, are open to serious questioning. If 110,000 convictions are only five per cent of the total, then the total is possibly 2,500,000 paedophiles in the UK, or one in every eight men. The problem here is that these various studies reveal these huge differences, ranging from 40,000 to 2,500,000 – figures that demonstrate how inadequate is our knowledge of paedophilia. Even so, even at the lower end, what is revealed is a huge problem of sexual perversion, and one that psychiatrists know will not go away.

The numbers may be unclear, but what is certain is that, worldwide, an underground culture of child abuse is flourishing, and apart from newspapers that report the cases and raise public awareness, too little is done to stamp it out. In Britain a Home Office-funded study carried out at Manchester University in the mid-1990s arrived at some alarming discoveries about official attitudes. Senior police officers, according to the report, "sneer at probing child sex abuse as not being 'real' detective work." Special units set up in the wake of child sex-scandals are regarded with some derision, and one detective commented, "We are seen as a kind of knitting circle."

The attitudes of the courts are also open to criticism for their unsympathetic handling of child victims. Protecting the vulnerable appears to be a low priority – cases are sometimes dismissed because the authorities decide it is too traumatic for child witnesses to have to testify.

It should be said that there is nothing new in this attitude. When Lord Salisbury was Prime Minister at the end of the 19th century his brother, Lord Galloway, 54, was brought before the Dumfries magistrates, charged with molesting a 10-year-old girl – he had put his hand up her skirt. It took the magistrates just four minutes to find his lordship not guilty after he had pleaded that it was all a misunderstanding. It might still have been accepted as such had he not re-appeared in court the following year charged with molesting a 16-year-old girl. This time what really happened was hidden behind that peculiarly Scottish verdict of not proven, and Galloway left the court free to continue his career as a dirty old man. Although as far as anyone knows it did not happen in Galloway's case, some such men left to their own devices gradually re-offend with more serious sexual offences, and can end up being sexual killers.

This same kind of sentencing confusion is still with us

more than a century later. In January, 2007, a judge at Oxford Crown Court ordered a convicted paedophile who had molested a six-year-old girl to pay her £250, and added this advice: "If it buys her a nice new bike, that's the sort of thing that might cheer her up."

Paedophiles are generally men who are failures in love, or who are unable to find love. They look for someone they can dominate and with whom they can feel confident, and when the object of this desire is a child they are effectively regressing to a primitive state. In Victorian England, when the sexes mixed only formally, brothels providing little girls for grown men's delectation were rampant; their customers were the fore-runners of men who nowadays seek child sex in distant countries.

In a report of the Lords Committee in 1881, a police superintendent described his visit to a house in Windmill Street, just off Piccadilly Circus: "I went in with my chief inspector, and in each of the rooms in that house I found an elderly gentleman in bed with two of these children. They knew perfectly well that I could not touch them in the house; and they laughed and joked me, and I could not get any direct answer whatever. I questioned them, in the presence of the brothel keeper, as to what they were paid, and so on. They were to receive six shillings each from the gentleman, two of them; and the gentleman had paid six shillings each for the room. It was four shillings if there was only one girl, but six shillings if there were two girls for the room."

Some paedophiles are highly intelligent. They know how to use international networks, they cover up for each other, and some of them are very wealthy and can afford travel to countries where there is a more tolerant attitude to child abuse. Everything about the paedophile killer can be summed up as cunning. This sets him apart from other sex killers, and makes him the more reprehensible.

Psychiatrists have worked for years to help paedophiles in prison to control and modify their behaviour, exploring their minds to discover motives that lead them to their atrocious crimes. But it is a hopeless task. A lengthy term of imprisonment almost always incubates the sex-offender's desires, so that upon his release he is a time bomb of pent-up lust just waiting to explode.

•

In British prisons, reformers tried an experiment of herding paedophiles together to discuss their own perversions and fantasies. This turned out to be counter-productive because it allowed them to plan future crimes. This was what happened with Timothy Morss and Brett Tyler – and a young boy was to pay for it with his life.

Morss was jailed for seven years in 1985, reduced to five years on appeal, for sodomising nine-year-old twins and an 11-year-old boy. Brett Tyler was jailed for four years in 1986 for attempted sodomy and gross indecency. They met in Wormwood Scrubs Prison where, in a special annexe, sex-offenders attended group therapy sessions. These were conducted not by trained counsellors but by warders. The thinking behind this scheme was that if prisoners could talk about their motivations, they might somehow "cure" themselves.

Prison officer Edward Cook shuddered as he heard Timothy Morss outline his favourite fantasy. Morss wanted to abduct a blond boy, preferably between eight and 13, from the street and take him somewhere quiet to sodomise him. Afterwards, he said with relish, he would strangle the boy and dispose of the body...

Just why paedophiles were allowed to talk openly in these terms to others of the same nature, turning them on with a form of verbal pornography, is difficult to understand. Officer Cook was to remember all that he heard. It was exceptional for a paedophile to be so open and specific about his desires.

Morss and Tyler became lovers, something which is not unusual in prison and which was noted by staff. Morss was previously the lover of another inmate, a 59-year-old man who was serving a sentence for an offence against a minor and who was released in due course, leaving Morss with Tyler.

Timothy Morss, not then 30 but three years older than Tyler, was the dominant partner in the relationship which developed. Of above-average intelligence, he told Tyler about his grim fantasy and got him to share it. They would spend evenings fantasising about cruising the streets looking for a little blond boy.

Like many career paedophiles, Morss was sexually abused as a child. He also dabbled in burglary as a teenager, before briefly joining the army. Then he was jailed for the sexual attack on the twins.

Brett Tyler was also sexually abused as a child. He was abandoned by his mother when a baby, then sent to a children's home where, at the age of four, the sexual assaults began. He returned to his parental home three years later when his father remarried. At 12 he became sexually experienced when he and a male friend had sex on a fishing trip.

Tyler first came to the notice of the police when he was found in possession of a loaded air rifle. He survived through his teens and into his 20s by taking casual work as a waiter or a dishwasher and lying about his qualifications in order to get driving jobs. Then he discovered easier ways of making money by hanging about with rent boys in Soho. He was rather dim, with learning difficulties, someone Morss found easy to manipulate.

During those long days in prison, sharing the same fantasy, it was the dominant Morss who suggested that they team up as a couple when they left prison. Tyler readily agreed, and when they were released they both found jobs working weekends for a minicab firm in south London, a company owned by Morss's former prison lover.

This man, who had served a seven-year sentence for sexually abusing his 10-year-old son, was an exceedingly rare example of a paedophile who had reformed. He sought psychiatric help and never re-offended, but his attempts to persuade Morss to do the same met with scornful rejection. Morss had developed his fantasy painfully over the years and had no intention of abandoning it.

The minicab proprietor also owned a florist's shop in Bristol, where Morss worked during the week. The boss had a house nearby in Bradley Stoke, which he shared with Morss, and they would spend the weekends in London with the cab firm.

The relationship between Morss and his employer slowly foundered because the older man disapproved of Morss's friendship with Tyler, knowing that nothing good could come of it. Tyler lived in London, and he and Morss would meet at weekends at the minicab office. They spent their spare time drinking, smoking joints and cruising working-class areas on a "chicken-hunt," looking for small boys. They chose such districts because they believed that young boys would be less likely to be chaperoned there than in smarter parts of London, and they were right.

They would drive through the streets high on drugs and fuelled sexually by their shared fantasy, seeking a target always within the parameters set by Morss – a blond boy aged between eight and 13, to be abducted from the street. On the afternoon of Sunday, October 7th, 1994, they found him.

They were driving through Beckton, east London, when they spotted a nine-year-old boy with his blond hair swinging in a ponytail as he rode around in circles on his silver BMX bike. Wearing a red boiler suit, Daniel Handley was a familiar figure in the neighbourhood, a cheerful boy always willing to help people load groceries into their cars at the local supermarket.

He was one of five children, two of whom had been taken into care. Daniel had no bed – he slept on a pile of rags on the floor. He lived mostly out on the streets, begging for pennies and wearing hand-me-down clothes that did not fit, and boots that were several sizes too large.

But if the two men cruising in their car thought he would prove to be easily disposable and unlikely to be missed, they were mistaken. Daniel lived with his 34-year-old mother and her new 21-year-old boy friend.

Morss and Tyler, having spotted their prey, dragged him into their car on that Sunday afternoon and drove straight to the flat above the minicab office. There they undressed the boy, tried to make him drink vodka, and took turns sodomising him, filming themselves in the act with a camcorder.

When Daniel did not return home in the early evening his mother assumed he must have gone to one of his friends' houses. But when darkness fell and there was still no sign of him she began to worry. By 10 p.m. she started to fear the worst, and at 11 p.m. she reported him missing.

A massive police hunt began, with 250 officers searching the area and going from door to door with a blown-up photograph of Daniel, asking everyone if they had seen him, and where and when. When daylight came divers searched the nearest docks and a rowing-boat lake and other flooded areas, and by the following weekend police were digging up the garden at Daniel's home. At this stage the nearest relatives were the prime suspects, since the majority of murders are domestic in origin. Mother and boy friend came in for some tough questioning.

The police could not be certain they were dealing with a case of murder – they had no body. But they found a witness, a motorist, who had seen Daniel near the open door of a silver or grey car with two men. One man was standing on the pavement, apparently showing Daniel a map, while the other was in the car's driving seat. This was the last positive sighting of the boy.

Six months passed without any progress in the investigation. Then a fox scavenging for food unearthed the remains of Daniel, buried in a shallow grave near the Woodlands golf club at Bradley Stoke, Bristol. It did not take the police long to identify the body.

When the case was reported on TV it triggered memories for Prison Officer Cook and a consultant psychiatrist who had treated Morss in jail. Detectives had already been trying to establish a link between London and Bristol, looking at known paedophiles who might live in or travel to both places. Cook phoned the police, suggesting that the killer might be Timothy Morss, as the murder closely resembled his favourite sexual fantasy. The psychiatrist was also able to provide significant information.

The result was that the police were able to establish the link they had been seeking for half a year. Morss and his boss – both convicted paedophiles – shared a home in Bradley Stoke, close to where the body was found. Their names shot straight to the top of the suspects' list.

When detectives called on Morss's employer he said that he had been waiting for the knock on his door. He told the investigators that Morss and Tyler were the killers they were seeking. How was he so certain? Because they had told him they committed the murder.

He said he had helped the two men flee to the Philippines, giving them money for the trip, but the pair fell out and Morss returned home alone. Why the Philippines? Because the men had often been there to enjoy themselves with young boys for just a few pence. In a country of grinding poverty their bodies were all that children had to sell – and there were always plenty of eager Westerners willing to pay.

It was apparent that the minicab proprietor was bitterly ashamed of the role he had played and was anxious to make amends. He gave the police an address in Rotherhithe, south-east London, where they would find Morss, and he also supplied the address in the Philippines where Tyler was staying with his Filipino lover and two children.

Morss was taken into custody in London, but he refused to answer any questions and denied any complicity in the murder of Daniel Handley. Meanwhile, the police began a joint operation involving officers from England, Australia and the Philippines, with the aim of effecting the arrest of Brett Tyler.

They learned that Tyler spent several months each year in the Philippines during the 1990s, lured by the easy availability of boys for sex. He was currently sharing a house with a friend and lover, Rolly "Boy" Reyes, in Olongapo City, 50 miles from the capital, Manila. The task was to find him without alerting him. British diplomats asked Superintendent Ken MacTavish, of the Australian Embassy in the Philippines, for help. He organised the arrest with a Filipino agent, after a priest had kept Tyler under discreet surveillance for him.

Then two British police officers flew out to the Philippines to question the suspect. Told that he was believed to have murdered a small boy, Tyler broke down and confessed. "I've been seeing Daniel's face everywhere since," he told the detectives.

His Filipino neighbours were questioned, and they said that Tyler and Morss fought in the house after Tyler warned Morss to stay away from the children. Morss had then returned to London. Now, sitting in a police station office, chain-smoking cigarettes and talking in a low voice, Brett Tyler told his story. The entire interview was videotaped.

He described how he and Morss snatched Daniel from a street corner, showing him a map on the pretext of seeking directions. They drove him to the minicab flat and ordered him to undress. They tried to get him to drink vodka, but he said he didn't want to take part as he had already done it once, didn't like it, and was "blamed" for it.

After taking turns in sodomising the boy, filming themselves in the process, they told him they would take him home. They put him on the floor in the rear of the car, and Tyler stopped at his unsuspecting father's house in east London to pick up a fork and spade to dig a grave. Then they began the long journey to Bristol. The boy slept most of the way, waking occasionally to ask if they were home yet.

During the journey they pulled into a lay-by. There they began knotting a rope. "Are you going to kill me?" the boy asked fearfully. They said they were not, but

Morss made a noose and put it around the boy's neck, gripping one end and telling Tyler to hold the other end and pull. Tyler claimed he kept telling the boy he was sorry as he helped pull the rope tight. They felt the boy's pulse and knew he was dead. It took them nearly four hours to dig a grave in the hard ground.

Following Tyler's arrest, police discovered in his house a letter he had written to his lover, Rolly Reyes, with a PS saying: "Kill the children for me OK."

The Philippine government deported Tyler as an undesirable alien – a device to avoid the problems of extradition – and he was put on a plane with the British detectives. On his return to London in late June, 1995, he was charged with Daniel's murder. His story was that Morss was the killer, and he was an unwilling accomplice. He admitted sexually abusing the boy, but said he never intended to kill him.

The trial of Morss and Tyler began on May 7th, 1996, at the Old Bailey. Morss, 33, pleaded guilty to kidnapping, sexually assaulting and murdering Daniel. Tyler, 30, admitted kidnapping and sexually assaulting the boy, but denied murdering him.

John Bevan, QC, prosecuting, wanted the jury to steel themselves to listen to shocking descriptions of "acts of a callous inhumanity and depravity almost beyond belief." He added bleakly: "What you will hear is about as depressing an example of the dark side of human nature, man's inhumanity to man and downright wickedness as you could imagine." After the two men had fantasised in prison, "the time came when the thrill of imagining it was no longer enough."

Daniel, he said, was "an ordinary, harmless, streetwise London kid." It didn't matter who had actually throttled the little boy. Both were equally guilty in law.

Asked by detectives how long the pair planned to do what they did, Tyler had replied: "The idea we had been discussing for months, but it was not real. It was a fantasy, just something we talked about. It was just talk. I did not think we were really going to do it. I did not think Tim did either. We used to drive around and just talk and fantasise about it. To grab a boy and take him hostage and do everything you ever dreamed about – any sexual perversion you could think about – not to really do it."

Tyler had also claimed that Morss had said he wished he had had more time with Daniel. "He kept saying he wanted to do more but there was not more time." After burying Daniel in a shallow grave the two had returned two weeks later to make it deeper.

The grave was discovered, said Mr. Bevan, only when foxes disturbed the site and Daniel's skull rolled down a hill into a lane where it was found by a passer-by.

When the videotaped confession of Tyler was played to the jury some of them became so distressed that the judge ordered a short break. On the tape Tyler described what happened when Morss pulled into a lay-by as they took their victim to Bristol.

"Tim said, 'You know we have to do this?' and I said 'Yes.' I got into the back with Daniel. He woke up slightly and just asked if we were home yet. I said, 'Not yet.' When Morss got into the back with the rope, Daniel asked, 'Are you going to kill me?' I said, 'No.' He seemed to close his eyes again. Morss had tied a rope around Daniel's neck with a knot at the throat and told me to pull one end. I said I couldn't. He said I'd got to, so I started pulling it. I kept telling him I was sorry until he was dead. He didn't look dead, he just looked asleep."

Telling of how, two weeks later, they returned to the grave to make it deeper, Tyler said, "We took the body out of the grave and just threw it on the floor. I saw a ten pence piece that had fallen out of his pocket, so I took it to get rid of it. We put him back in the hole again and filled it up and went back to London."

When he heard by telephone that Morss had been arrested in England, Tyler continued, he tried to kill himself by taking a drug overdose, slashing his wrists and attempting to hang himself.

In a later interview in England, Tyler told the police that the crime was tearing him up inside, and he burst into tears.

Tyler went into the witness-box to tell the jury that although he was a child-molester he was no murderer. He said he had suggested to Morss that if they grabbed their victim from behind so they could not be identified, there would be no need to kill him. But Morss rejected the idea. "He said he wanted to look into their eyes."

Tyler claimed that he had already fulfilled his own sexual fantasies with boys in the Philippines and had no desire to harm or kill anyone.

The jury took less than an hour to find both men guilty. They were given three life sentences each – for murder, sodomy and false imprisonment. The judge told them: "You are two evil vultures. You are both calculating men and I do not believe that you are truly sorry for what you have done. Because of the nature of the terrible offences and the very, very high risk you pose to little boys, in my book life means life. I promise to recommend that you serve exactly that. You should never be released."

The judge added that the videotape confession and the papers in the case should never be destroyed, and should be shown to anyone who ever thought of releasing Morss and Tyler, "so that they should know of their evil and distorted minds." He also ordered that jury members should receive counselling if they required it. The minicab proprietor was jailed for 30 months for his part in helping the killers flee the country.

The trial of Timothy Morss and Brett Tyler was the trigger that caused the government to set up a register of known paedophiles so that the police could monitor the movements of such men.

What sort of man was Timothy Morss, who will die in prison after spending most of his life there, for sexual deviancy that no normal person can understand? His minicab boss thought that Morss felt "sex was power, revenge and vengeance. He had a warped, twisted view of life." A psychiatrist described him as a brash man with a powerful personality who enjoyed shocking people with his fantasies. He was also quietly aggressive, emotionally cold, and possessed a sadistic sense of humour. The picture is of someone who is prepared to wear his dark, obscene desires on his sleeve, of someone who is prepared to pursue those desires without allowing for any impediment. A very dangerous man indeed.

The more so, perhaps, because of his ordinariness. Now retired, Detective Superintendent Edwin Williams, who led the investigation, thought that both Morss and Tyler would have been difficult to spot as child killers. "They were leading comparatively normal lives. They were friendly, outwardly respectable. There was nothing in their behaviour to lead the public to suspect that they were abusers or murderers."

Edward Cook, who was close to both men as a prison officer, always feared the worst. "I always worried about what was happening on the landing in the evenings, outside the therapy sessions. Even in the therapy sessions you never really got through to the paedophile. He always thinks he's right."

Brett Tyler was much more self-revealing to the police, pointing up some of the motivation of the paedophile. "Immediately after the murder my feelings were a mixture of fear of being caught, and excitement that we might get away with it... if you feel safe it's not exciting. Danger is part of the excitement."

•

The environment in which he does his predatory work is of considerable significance to a paedophile – he will frequently get himself into a position where he is alongside children. The desire to give advice and guidance, to think and play along the same level as children, is no more than a mask for the gratification of his sexual urge. This was the case in an American study of a 34-year-old married man who raped and killed three little girls, a study which reveals much about the state of mind of a paedophile. The man was brought into contact with children by virtue of being an ice cream salesman. He appeared outwardly to be perfectly normal and had never been in any trouble with the police before – in fact he was a regular churchgoer. Psychiatrists found him slightly below normal intelligence, lacking in concentration, and self-effacing.

He told the examiners that he picked up the three young girls because for years he had always wanted sex with someone younger than he had ever had before. Even when he made love to his wife, he said, he imagined her as a young child. He had made up his mind that he was quite ready to kill his victims to satisfy this lust. This desire had been getting worse of late.

His planning was typical of the paedophile, who works out all the details in advance. He visited several likely places deep in the country where he could take the children, and put several scarves in his car with which to strangle them. Then he drove his three victims to the place he had chosen and, on the pretext that if they kept absolutely quiet he would show them, one at a time, a group of young foxes at play, he left two of them behind a tree, took the third about a hundred yards away, brutally raped her and strangled her, and repeated the process with the other two.

As he killed each child he said a prayer beside its body, and when he had killed all three he arranged their shoes neatly in a line, so that whoever found them would think that right to the last the children were unaffected by these events. Throughout the orgy he felt supremely powerful, lording it over the children. He congratulated himself on having done what he always wanted to do, and determined to show his continuing superiority by not getting caught. When the bodies were found, he read newspaper accounts of the crime with considerable excitement, even keeping a scrapbook of the various press stories.

This case is typical of a young paedophile, who is in reality a psychosexual infantile. He has a huge ego which desires to control and exercise power over others, and which has to make do with children, because he is sub-consciously aware that adults will not accept the exercise of such a grandiose ego from such an intellectually inferior person. He is meticulous in his planning, works out everything a long time in advance, and still wants everything to be ordered even when his victims are dead – as in the case of the neatly arranged shoes. The prayers over the bodies of each child indicate awareness that he had done wrong and an acceptance that he should be contrite; the entire episode reveals a man emotionally glacial.

Can the desire for someone younger than he had ever had before be simply a chance to exercise superior powers? The answer to that is not entirely, because this type of youthful paedophile is also excited by virginity. In practice, the younger type of paedophile is always operating at the height of his sexual activity. By contrast, the senile paedophile works on fantasies of past sexual experiences which physically he is no longer able to carry out as well as he once did. This results in a conflict between his brain and his sexual organs – the brain desiring intercourse and the sexual organs unable to fulfil it properly, and this conflict causes the older paedophile to lose control of his faculties. Stripped of the sexual virility of youth, he is effectively regressing to childhood. Among sex offenders, both types of paedophile are the hardest to cure of their condition, if indeed they can ever be cured at all.

•

For generations a disbelieving public has had difficulty coming to terms with the shock and shame involved in the exploitation and cruelty of children. It cannot believe that such offences can exist within its cosy view of modern life. This disbelief went on into the 1960s, with child abuse still unrecognised because of the post-war generation's inability to distinguish between proper discipline and appropriate punishment on the one hand, and physical cruelty on the other. That lack of distinction still lingers on among people who believe they are enlightened liberal reformers, and it is responsible for nurturing crime even today.

Paedophilia; child abuse

The battered child syndrome, "discovered" in the 1960s, initially met with derision. No one could accept that adult men were capable of sexually abusing children who were still learning to walk. But the evidence was pouring in, and with it came dim awareness. More and more children were sent to live in homes as social workers investigated the murkiness lurking within evil families

As in the instance of increasing sexual awareness being linked to sexual crime, so sexual abuse of children within families is linked with the increased incidence of paedophilia. A survey report published by the NSPCC in November 2000 revealed that those responsible for child abuse within families were not, as is commonly thought, fathers, but their siblings. After years in which adult men were cast as the villains, the finger of suspicion had switched to their sons. Here was a nursery for future paedophiles who by definition were much younger and facing a longer sexual career than their fathers or stepfathers.

The survey, of nearly 3,000 young adults who were asked about their experiences as children, found sibling abuse was twice as common as abuse by a father or stepfather. Among those who reported having sex against their will within the family, or with someone who was five or more years older, 43 per cent said the perpetrator was a brother or stepbrother.

The abusers were mainly boys aged 10 to 14 and their victims were mostly five years younger. Most abusers had themselves been victims. Sexual abuse of children within the family occurs in about one in every 30 families. This figure helps to account for the fact that one-third of all sex crimes are committed by under-18-year-olds.

The report's compilers found that age rather than social background is a critical factor. They say that before the age of 10, it is sexual abuse rather than physical abuse that triggers abusive sexual behaviour. After puberty, those abusers who have been physically rather than sexually victimised are more likely to prey on girls. The report's compilers were certain that serious offending behaviour in adulthood could be prevented if abusive behaviour is identified and treated in childhood.

•

Society itself has no cure, no response to the menace of paedophilia, which flourishes like a poison plant in civilisation's neatly planned garden. As a result both perpetrators and victims tend to shroud it in secrecy; it is the crime of deep shame. This is perhaps no better illustrated than by events that occurred in the town of Wollongong in New South Wales in 1997. Within two weeks two prominent townspeople labelled as paedophiles were murdered. In Wollongong, where this sort of thing is supposed not to happen, local newspapers speculated on them having been part of a paedophile ring, and therefore having become the victims of a vigilante.

Yet the killer claimed at his trial for murder that he didn't even know his victims were paedophiles. That they were so was, as far as he was concerned, just a coincidence.

The first victim, David O'Hearn, a 60-year-old antique shop owner, was savagely beaten to death with a cut glass wine decanter in his home. His severed head was placed in the kitchen sink with a cigarette in its mouth. The killer then disembowelled the torso and scrawled satanic symbols in blood on the walls, using the man's chopped-off hand as a pen.

Two weeks later a neighbour found the body of Frank Arkell, who was mayor of Wollongong for 17 years. He had been beaten repeatedly about the head during a running fight that left blood in every room of his home. His Rotary Club badge, awarded for good citizenship and service to the community, was gouged into his eye, and tiepins were stuck in his cheeks. There was no sign of forced entry and nothing of value had been taken.

Arkell had lost his campaign for re-election in 1991

and was striving to get back into the mayoral race when in 1994 allegations that he was a paedophile began to surface. Victims aged between 14 and 18 at the time of the offences were coming forward, obliging the once exuberant mayor to become a virtual recluse in his own home. Then, two weeks before he was murdered, he was charged with 29 child sex offences.

The murderer, 21-year-old Mark Valera, went to the police and confessed. At first he claimed he was the victim of a paedophile ring, and that he had seen media reports saying Frank Arkell was a paedophile. "I felt someone should have killed him because of all the nasty things he did to those kids," he said.

This story was speedily changed. Now Valera maintained that both his victims were total strangers to him. He picked on them at random because he had made up his mind to become a serial killer. But at his trial he told the court that he lost control of himself after each of the two men tried to seduce him into anal sex. The sexual requests from his victims triggered flashbacks, reminding him of the physical – but not sexual – abuse he suffered as a child.

Mark Valera was found guilty of both murders. After being sentenced to two consecutive life terms in prison he was led struggling from the dock screaming, "Paedophiles always get away with it, don't they?"

What was Mark Valera's real intention? Was he a vigilante killer? Or did he really kill two paedophiles by sheer coincidence? Even the purpose of his crimes remains covered up, for cover-ups, it seems are in the nature of anything to do with paedophilia.

•

On a global basis, however, there is nothing to compare with the number of paedophilic assaults that occur in South Africa. More than 67,000 cases of rape and sexual assaults were reported in South Africa in the year 2000, compared with 37,500 in 1998. The number of unreported incidents could have been up to 10 times that number. One disturbing case concerned the rape of a nine-month-old baby girl by six men. Other victims were as young as six months old, a number of whom died from their injuries, while others contracted HIV. Most of these attacks were directly linked with the country's AIDS pandemic.

The increase in poverty, violent crime and unemployment are said to have contributed to the escalation in child abuse, but the most significant factor is the widespread myth that has swept the country that having sex with a child provides a cure for AIDS.

There is a belief across South Africa that a virgin will cure a man of HIV or AIDS. No one knows where the idea came from, but it has been around for a few years and has certainly taken hold. The average 185 child abuse cases that are reported to the police each day represent just a fraction of the true number committed, according to child welfare groups. Of these, only about five per cent result in a successful conviction.

CHAPTER EIGHT

**DOMINATION; PHYSICAL INADEQUACY;
FEAR OF WOMEN**
*Leonard Lake, John Duffy, Christian Jungers,
Manfred Wittmann, Bernardo/Homolka*

We have seen in the previous chapter how some men who are social misfits seek out little children as their sexual object because they are loners, shy and self-effacing, and yet at the same time they feel they need to dominate and control their sexual partner. Domination, sparking male sadism, lies at the root of most male sexual activity, generally in very small doses. In larger doses it can lead to perversion when the need to dominate and control becomes overwhelming. This is what happened to Robert Black, Britain's most prolific child killer, whose case we dealt with in Chapter Four.

Men whose primary motives are to dominate and control frequently resort to torturing their victims, and this was the case with Leonard Lake, an American serial sexual killer. Lake and his mutually supportive partner Charles Ng, a Chinese American, kidnapped their victims – at least 25 of them – in the 1970s and 1980s and took them to an isolated hillside ranch house in Humboldt County, near San Francisco. There they shackled, raped and tortured them before killing them, cutting them up with a chainsaw, and burying them in the three acres of grounds. Sadistic videos found at the ranch house showed the victims strapped naked to a bed in a sex-torture chamber which had hooks fixed to the ceiling and chains and shackles fixed to the walls. Some of the videos were clearly "snuff" movies.

"The perfect woman," Lake wrote in his diary, "is totally controlled" – meaning that he would have total control over her. "She is a woman who does exactly what she is told and nothing else. There is no sexual problem with a submissive woman. There are no frustrations – only pleasure and contentment." For a time he liked to keep his victims imprisoned, using them as sex slaves and sometimes observing them, in the cells he had constructed, through a one-way mirror. Lake's desire to dominate, revealed in his diary entry, also illustrates his profound fear of women – he is not absolutely satisfied until, bound and shackled, they can be no threat whatsoever to his lust. When he grew tired of them he killed them, cut up their bodies, and incinerated them before burying the remains.

Anyone aware of Lake's background would not have much doubted that he would become a sexual killer. His home life was poor and he was surrounded by alcoholics. As a youth he took nude photographs of his sisters and cousins and asked for, and was given, their sexual favours. His brother Donald, an epileptic, was rather less forbearing – he raped the sisters and tortured animals. Donald was eventually murdered by Leonard Lake. When he was a young man Lake persuaded his wife to feature in the pornographic movies he was making. Interestingly, it has been shown that poor living conditions and alcoholic excesses are often in evidence in families where incest takes place. Lake's grandfather, who lived with the family, was a violent alcoholic; both his father and mother came from a family of alcoholics.

Lake was a thief, specialising particularly in stolen credit cards, and with his partner Ng graduated to burglary. Like most sexual killers he was a fantasist and practised confabulation – a symptom affecting psychopaths in which they volubly relate imaginary experiences as true. When San Francisco Police caught him he took a cyanide tablet while being interviewed and died the next day without recovering consciousness.

Ng, from a Hong Kong family, was educated privately in north Yorkshire before he was expelled for theft, despite never being short of money. He went on the run after Lake was captured but he too was caught – arrested while shoplifting in Calgary, Canada. In September, 1991, he was extradited back to California to face murder charges.

Domination; physical inadequacy; fear of women

Some men kill because they are physically inadequate. This was the problem of Britain's serial sexual killer John Duffy, who, in contrast to Leonard Lake, came from a good home. He stood only five feet four inches in his size four shoes, and that worried him. When he married he dreamed of demonstrating his virility by becoming a father, an aspiration that collapsed in ruins when he was told that his low sperm count would prevent him from ever having a child. He quit his job as a British Rail carpenter and his marriage became turbulent.

His wife Margaret left him for a period, then went back to him to try to patch things up. While she went to work Duffy watched horror and kung-fu videos in their two-room council flat in Kilburn, north London. Bruce Lee began to take over his life and he started attending fitness classes and developed an intense interest in martial arts. He studied a book called *The Anarchist's Cookbook*, a manual of urban guerrilla warfare, which taught how to incapacitate, silence, and kill. All these events had a profound effect on Duffy, whose wife was to say, "The nice man I married had become a raving madman with scary, scary eyes."

In June 1985 Margaret Duffy claimed that her husband raped her during their estrangement, when she went back to his flat to collect her mail. "I thought he was going to kill me," she said. Two months later she said he turned up at the home of her new boy friend and attacked them both. They needed hospital treatment for their injuries.

The seeds of violence germinating from his physical inadequacy grew inside John Duffy and he set out to rape and kill ferociously. His serial rapes around the London suburbs caused police to set up a massive manhunt; then, when his traumatised victims were able to describe him, he began to kill them. His first victim was Alison Day, 19, murdered as she left a train at Hackney Wick station, east London, after visiting a friend. Duffy tied her wrists with a piece of her skirt, strangled her with another piece, and stuck a third piece into her mouth as a gag. He almost certainly raped her before strangling her and dumping her body, clad only in her sheepskin coat, which was weighed down with stones, in the River Lea.

His second victim was Maartje Tamboezer, 15, a Dutch girl staying at West Horsley, in Surrey, who he dragged into a wood while she was out cycling in April 1986. When her body was found her wrists were tied together and she had been raped and strangled with a tourniquet. He set fire to her body in an attempt to hide clues.

A month after killing Maartje, Duffy killed Anne Lock. Her body was not found for nine weeks, by which time it had become partly skeletal. There was also evidence that he had tried to burn the body. All three victims were garrotted with a piece of wood inserted into a ligature to make the last strangling turns. Each had their hands tied.

The mind of John Duffy – "the nice man I married" – undoubtedly went through a deep change when, already feeling inadequate because of his small stature, he learned that he could not even do the manly thing of fathering a child. He found some compensation in becoming a kung-fu hero, and then put his martial arts training into horrific practice. All this, it seems, was to prove to himself that he was a man, proof which for the rest of the world revealed that he was also a monster. The evidence for this is so stark that it raises the obvious question: if John Duffy had been born six feet tall and with a normal sperm count, would he have turned out the way he did?

The killer was remarkably well psychologically profiled during the manhunt. He was thought to live in north-west London, to have a turbulent marriage, to be a martial arts fanatic, and a semi-skilled worker in his 20s. All this was true of John Duffy He was also thought to be a loner with few friends, and felt the need to dominate women. He indulged in fantasies and violence with videos and magazines. He was a man who kept some sort of souvenir of his crime, and he might be a carpenter or a plumber. Again, all this was true – Duffy was in fact a carpenter.

Showing no remorse and enjoying all the attention his trial brought him, Duffy was 30 years old when he was sentenced to life on each of seven charges – the three murders and four other rapes. This would mean a minimum of 30 years, said the judge. He will be at least 60 if he is ever released, theoretically in the year 2018.

•

Christian Jungers was also physically inadequate. For him, lovemaking existed only in the mind. At 48 he was still a virgin. When he was nearly 60 he fell ardently in love with a 13-year-old schoolgirl. His first real sexual encounter was with a grandmother to whom he finally surrendered his virginity.

Between puberty and old age Jungers satisfied his sexual drive entirely through his fantasies. He had a special predilection for young girls. The first one he fell in love with was a neighbour, aged 11. He was then 22. He used to spy on the little girl from his bedroom window while she was on her swing in the next garden. One day he snatched a photograph of her while she wasn't looking at him. When the picture was developed he cut out the face, stuck it on the body of a nude woman in a pornographic magazine, and masturbated over it.

He used regularly to arouse himself by pornography and then masturbate over the pictures. For extra perverted kicks he photographed women he knew – neighbours, even strangers in the street. Then he would cut out the face from the photograph, and stick it on the picture of a nude, just as he did with the 11-year-old.

Soon he had amassed a huge "library" of doctored pictures of neighbourhood women stuck upon the naked bodies of other women. He glued them in books and, before he masturbated over them, wrote lengthy obscene and sadistic captions under the pictures, describing what he would like to do to them. These included his desire to stick needles into their breasts, to bite off their breasts with his teeth, and to slit them open with a knife, upwards from the vagina.

All this might suggest that Jungers was seriously disturbed, and that by any means or measure he was a potentially dangerous man. The wonder was that when his activities finally came to the attention of the law-enforcement authorities, no one thought he was dangerous at all.

Christian Jungers was born in 1948 in Arlon, Belgium. His parents separated and he was raised by grandparents for whom he was the centre of their constant attention. At school he was a bright pupil, but very much a loner.

"The other kids used to jeer at me because I didn't know anything about sex," he said. "I didn't know what intercourse was. I thought it was something to do with cuddling, that's all."

An old school friend remembered: "If you talked about anything to do with sex he would blush scarlet and start to stammer. He was very weird. One day he turned up at school dressed like a Scotsman, wearing a kilt."

"That was in homage to English literature," Jungers responded enigmatically.

Leaving school, he joined the post office headquarters at Verviers, near Liège, as a junior executive. He was promoted and well paid, but remained friendless. One day he struck up a conversation with a 15-year-old girl, Brigitte. He took her to an amusement arcade and bought her cakes.

"I'm a keen photographer," he told her. "I'd like to photograph you." Brigitte consented, unaware that her face would be secretly cut out of the photograph and stuck on to a picture of the body of a nude woman. Later he told her: "I'd like to marry you when you're 18." Brigitte laughed. Fifteen years later she was to recall that he never touched her. For her, he was always very generous, rather quaint, and quite harmless.

Domination; physical inadequacy; fear of women

In the mid-1990s, when he was 48, he met Régiane, a grandmother, who thought he was a great catch. She showed him off to all her friends and for the first time in his life initiated him into natural sex. Régiane's daughter, Madame Marie-Clair Pirson, and her two granddaughters, Nadège, 5, and Allyson, 4, all adored Granny's new friend, this middle-aged newcomer to the family, and Jungers responded in the only way he knew – by showering them with expensive gifts.

The mother and her two daughters, who were not well off and lived in a small, cramped flat, simply adored him. Especially Nadège, who became very much his favourite.

Jungers had moved in with Régiane and life seemed so serene now that he had discovered romance that he forgot all about his old apartment on the other side of Verviers. He even forgot to pay the rent. The months of bliss that rolled so quickly by for Jungers were months of chagrin for the owner of his flat, who wanted to know where his tenant was, and the overdue rent as well.

Finally the landlord made up his mind to cut his losses. He used his passkey to get into the flat, intending to throw all his tenant's belongings out on to the street.

But as he unlocked the door he reeled back in horror. Every nook and cranny, every space on the walls, was filled with pornographic pictures. There were videos, magazines, doctored photographs everywhere. This was the time when Belgium was in a collective frenzy over the activities of rapist-killer Marc Dutroux – and horror of horrors, there were photos of two of Dutroux's young victims stuck on the wall, their faces glued to pictures of naked bodies that clearly didn't belong to them. Ashen-faced, the landlord closed the door and called the police.

Jungers, questioned for several hours, was nothing if not bland. "Collecting erotic photographs and changing them to suit my particular disposition is my secret hobby," he explained almost pompously. "It might seem odd to you, but I haven't broken any law. I haven't raped anyone, have I?"

Which of course was true. But the police, still racked by the mayhem that the Dutroux inquiry was causing, reported their man to the prosecutor's office, who told them that they must get a psychiatrist's report before parting company with Jungers.

Accordingly he was taken off to a mental hospital and examined. His life story seemed to astonish the psychiatrist who reported on him. "He tells me he has been behaving like this since puberty," the doctor wrote. And he added: "He is clearly a sadist. But as he satisfies his fantasies with the help of his photos, in my opinion there is no likelihood of him perpetrating anything more serious." So the police decided to let him go, and that should have been that.

Somehow, Jungers had managed to keep from Régiane the raid on his flat, his arrest and his examination at the mental hospital, so, when he returned to her bosom, life went on as pleasantly as before. Only one hiccup marred this serene existence. It came in the spring of 2003, when one of Régiane's granddaughters, Nadège, said she wanted to sleep in the same room as her sister Allyson. Jungers suddenly worked himself up into a fury. He didn't want that to happen. He didn't want Nadège to be influenced by anyone, not even her sister. Nadège – by this time she was 13 years old – was his favourite. She must remain unsullied by anyone.

Later he was to reveal that he was madly in love with her. Just as he did with Brigitte, he asked her to marry him when she was 18. He stroked her long brown hair and, so that she knew his intentions were sincere, gave her a little packet neatly tied up. Inside it was a gem-studded ring.

A ring, of course, is the sort of thing that a girl of 13 can't easily hide, and the ring was a bridge too far for Nadège's mother, Marie-Clair. She told Jungers: "You must stop giving things to my daughters. A ring, indeed! It isn't healthy."

Jungers was distraught. He texted Nadège: "Farewell! I am going," and took an overdose. He was rushed to hospital, where his stomach was pumped out. When Nadège failed to reply to his goodbye message he took another overdose the following week and was rushed to hospital again. Still she didn't reply – so he took a third overdose the week after that.

On July 14th, 2003, Nadège did text him. "I've cut my hair short," she said. That night Jungers couldn't sleep. The thought of her shorn tresses put him into a hundred torments. Next day came another message. "I'm alone at mama's. I need money."

Jungers replied: "I'm coming."

When he got into his car he was carrying a photo of her. On the back he had written: "Nad, your blood and mine are mixed together for eternity." In his coat pocket he carried a kitchen knife.

Nadège was alone, as she had said. The sight of her short hair stunned him. He asked her to get him a drink, giving himself time to take the knife from his pocket and hide it behind his back. As she came back with the glass he sprang at her and drove the knife hard into her chest.

Nadège screamed. "Stop! Stop! I will marry you, I promise!" But Jungers seemed not to hear. Frenzied, he drove the knife into her time and again – 20 times in all. When she crumpled on to the floor, bloody and lifeless, he fell on her, ripped off her clothes, and bit off one of her breasts. Then, with a flourish of his knife, he ripped open her body upwards from her vagina.

He had once written that he would like to do that. And a psychiatrist had once written that because he confined these fantasies to photograph captions, there was no likelihood that he would ever turn the fantasy into reality.

Minutes later, bloodied from head to foot, he staggered into the local police station and announced: "I've just killed Nadège."

Police who arrived on the scene found her lying on her back in a sea of blood. They found her severed breast in the kitchen waste bin. A police doctor said: "He had tried to swallow it, but it was too big, so he spat it out."

Christian Jungers was brought to trial in Liège in January, 2006. In the dock he cut the figure of a comfortable, portly, elderly man with a small greying beard, well groomed, wearing a blue blazer, white shirt and tie. As is the custom in Belgian courts, the magistrates did a re-run through his life, which is how his internalised sex life came to be revealed.

"This child with whom you say you were in love, she was 13 years old," said the president of the court. "She was 43 years younger than you. What have you got to say about that?"

Jungers lowered his eyes. "I would have done anything for her," he said. "I was terribly jealous. Once I saw her talking to a boy. I couldn't stand it. I ran and locked myself in the toilet so that I couldn't see them." And he added: "Each time I looked at her I was in heaven." Weeping, he went on: "But the sight of her shorn hair was too much for me. I was beside myself. This was no longer my princess."

"And the mutilations you performed on her body?" he was asked.

Jungers mumbled: "Mutilations? I don't remember any mutilations."

The last word went to Nadège's mum, Marie-Clair Pirson. Weeping in the witness-box, she told the court that her other daughter, Allyson, had failed to come to terms with her sister's horrific death and was still having counselling. As she turned to leave the box she suddenly addressed the prisoner.

"I want to tell you something, Jungers," she said. "Nadège has gone to live with the angels. But you are going straight to hell. You will never see her again."

Jungers hung his head. It was still hanging when the jury found him guilty. He was sent to prison for life.

•

There is a widespread belief that some rapist-killers attack prostitutes or random strangers because they

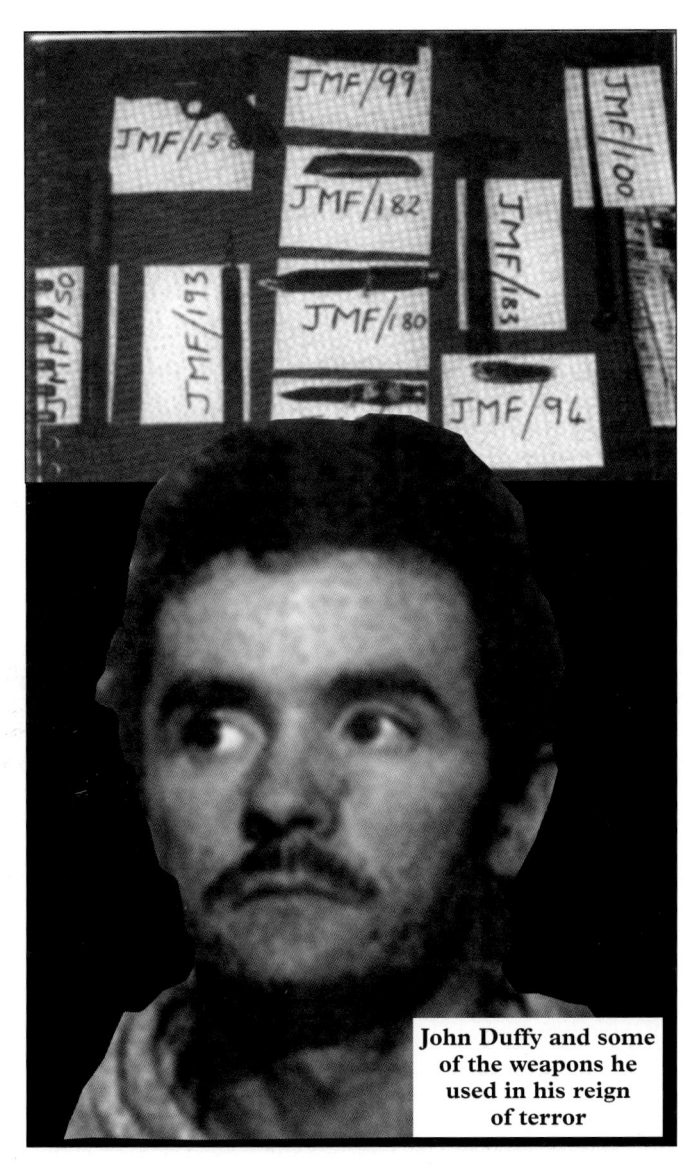

John Duffy and some of the weapons he used in his reign of terror

Domination; physical inadequacy; fear of women (Chapter 8)

Police search a river near Great Yarmouth after Leoni Keating (right) was abducted from a caravan by Gary Hopkins (top)

Voyeurism; Peeping Toms; flashing; mother hatred; Oedipus complex (Chapter 9)

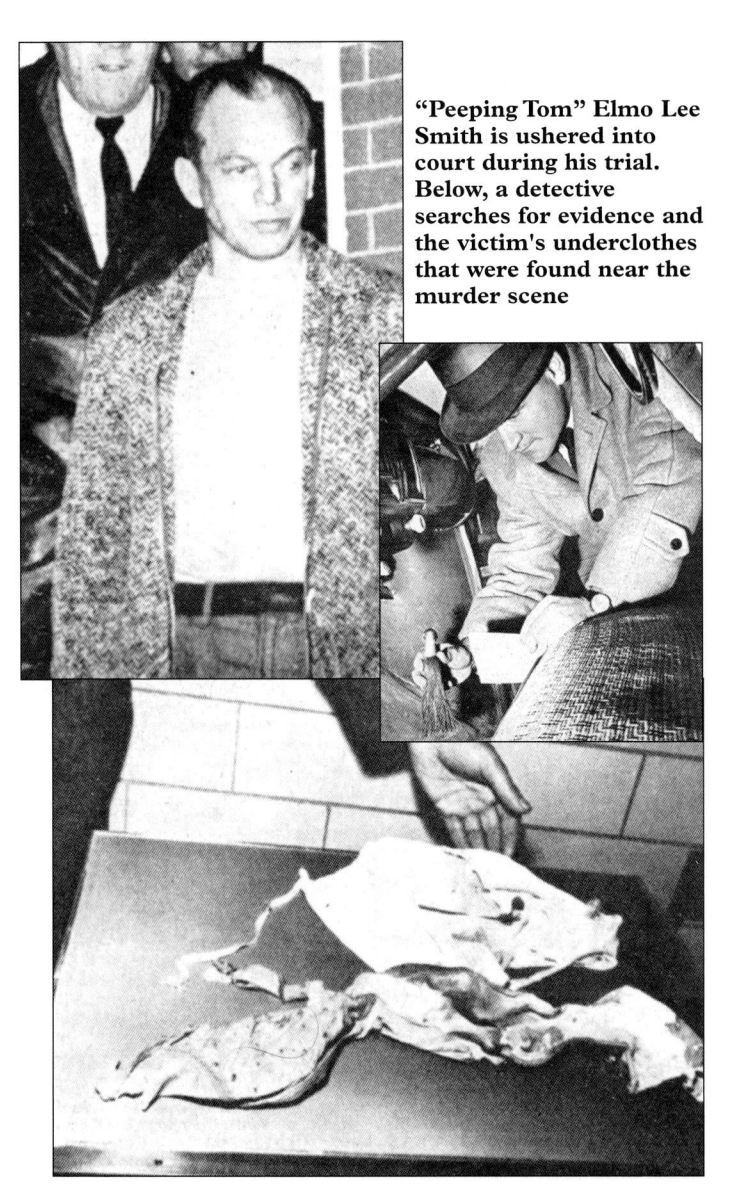

"Peeping Tom" Elmo Lee Smith is ushered into court during his trial. Below, a detective searches for evidence and the victim's underclothes that were found near the murder scene

Voyeurism; Peeping Toms; flashing; mother hatred; Oedipus complex
(Chapter 9)

Werner Boost shows off his shooting skills

Richard Evonitz was the last face seen by three terrified young girls

Voyeurism; Peeping Toms; flashing; mother hatred; Oedipus complex
(Chapter 9)

Richard Chase was convinced he needed to drink fresh blood to survive

Edmund Kemper sliced off the top of a cat's head

Animals; post-mortem voyeurism (Chapter 10)

At his trial, the jury recommended that Steven Parkus receive the death penalty. After medical evidence he was, however, sentenced to life imprisonment

The injury sustained by Phineas Gage over 150 years ago has contributed to the defence that brain injuries can change a person's behaviour. Right, a computer-generated image shows the angle at which the rod went through Phineas Gage's left cheek

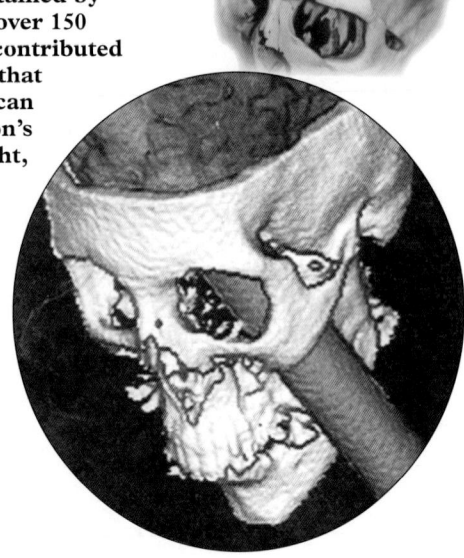

Are sexual killers born or made? VMPC – damage to the prefrontal lobe (Chapter 11)

Donta Page, the 20-stone giant who murdered Peyton Tuthill, below

Jeremy Skocz suffered brain damage after being hit over the head with a baseball bat

Are sexual killers born or made? VMPC – damage to the prefrontal lobe (Chapter 11)

Above and right, Ian Brady, the Moors Murderer

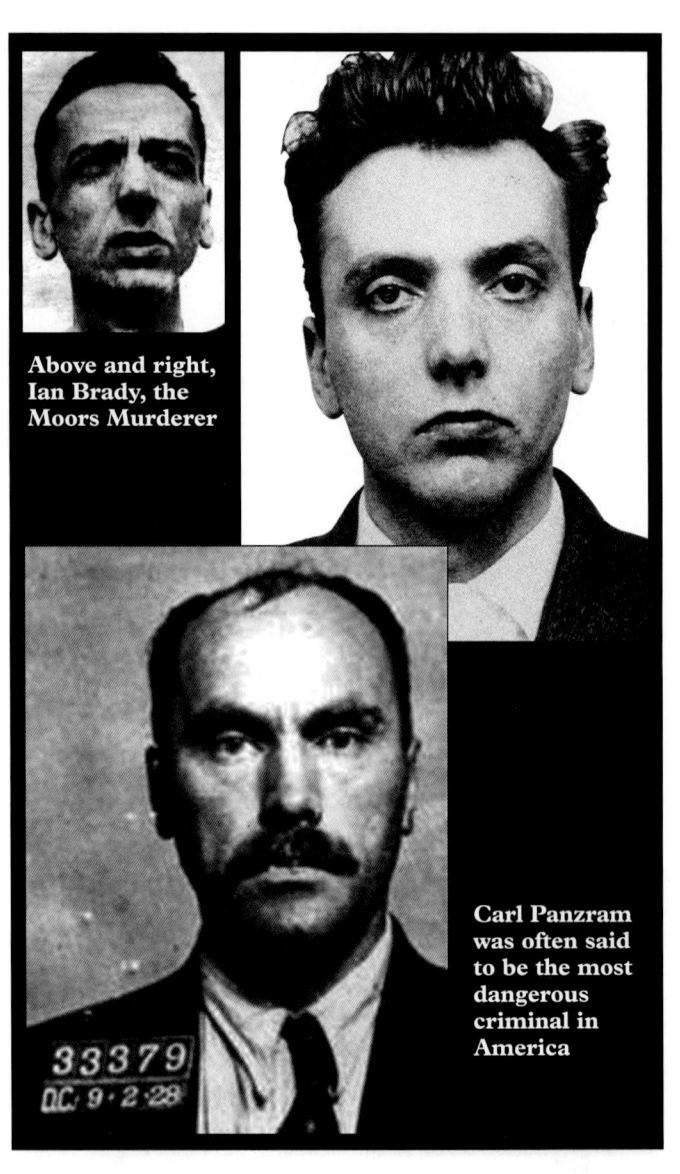

Carl Panzram was often said to be the most dangerous criminal in America

Two sexual killers discuss themselves (Appendix)

hate all women, seeing prostitutes particularly as easy targets for their hatred. Much more likely, however, is that the motive is that they are afraid of women.

In many cases the first sex act is as daunting for a man as it is for a woman. For a man, failure, for whatever reason, can lead to intense psychological problems, which in turn can lead to fear of the act, and of the object of the act. This was the case with Manfred Wittmann, a 26-year-old worker in an asphalt plant at Grossheirath in Germany. He was so terrified of women that his male friends used to joke about it. They did not know the very good reason for his haunting fear.

The spotlight fell on Wittmann in November, 1969, when Sieglinde Hübner, a pretty, vivacious 16-year-old brunette, disappeared from her home in the village of Kaltenbrunn. The police were alarmed, because she was the third teenage girl to have disappeared in two years. The first two were found stripped naked, bound hand and foot with their bras and stockings, and their bodies covered with countless stabs and slash wounds inflicted by their killer, who was to become known as the Beast of Oberfranken. Strangely, however, neither girl had been raped.

The victims could be identified as having been killed by the same man because the knife thrusts in their flesh were so deep that casts could be taken of the wounds. The weapon was a very sharp knife with a 10-inch serrated blade, known as a "Cutting Devil." The casts were so good that analysts were able to say that the Cutting Devil had been sharpened between attacks.

Ten years earlier, on Christmas Day, 1959, the Beast had attacked 19-year-old Irmgard Feder, who miraculously survived to tell the story of her ordeal. She was walking through the snow to her home after visiting the cinema when she was struck violently from behind. As she fell she caught sight of her attacker – he was, she said later, a stocky boy or young man, aged anywhere between 15 and 25. He was holding an umbrella with which he had apparently struck her, and then he produced a long knife.

"Strip!" he said in a sort of strained whisper.

Irmgard realised that he was about to rape her in the middle of the street, within sight of her own home. More angry than frightened, she obediently began to unfasten her clothing.

Still lying on the snow-covered ground, she stripped down to her woollen cap and socks, expecting at any moment to have the rapist fall upon her. But although she could hear him panting with excitement, he made no move. He just stood over her fumbling with the front of his trousers.

When he dropped on her, instead of the anticipated rape, she felt a searing pain in the side of her neck. The man's hand swung upward again, and the streetlight gleamed dully on the blade of his knife. Helpless under his weight, Irmgard realised that she was not going to be raped – she was going to be murdered.

Six times the knife rose and fell, the blade plunging into her throat. And then, as suddenly as the attack began, it was over and the man was gone.

Flopping like a fish on the agonising hook of pain in her throat and with her mouth filled with blood, Irmgard rolled over on to her hands and knees and began crawling to her home. She left a trail of blood the whole way, but she still had the strength to hammer on the door before she lost consciousness. Later she made a full recovery in hospital and a year later, without any repeat attacks, the assault was regarded as an isolated incident.

Then, 10 years after that, Nora Wenzl, aged 14, disappeared. Three months later, in February, 1969, her body turned up in the locks of the River Main at Viereth, 25 miles south of Staffelstein. She was completely naked, her hands and feet still bound with the vestiges of her bra and stockings, her body covered with deep cuts and slashes, and her throat cut from ear to ear. The medical evidence suggested her death was slow and agonising, for she was tortured for a long time before her throat was cut. She died a virgin.

Six months after the discovery of Nora's body, 16-

year-old Helga Luther, a pretty blonde who wore her hair long and her skirts short, set out to hitch-hike from Coburg to her home village of Lichtenfels, 15 miles away. She never arrived. She was found the next afternoon lying in a ditch. She was naked, her hands and feet were bound with her stockings and her bra, she was covered with knife wounds and her throat was cut through to the spine. She had not been raped.

In both these cases the Beast had used the same Cutting Devil for the murder weapon. And now, only three months after the brutal killing of Helga, Sieglinde Hübner had gone missing. She was supposed to have caught a bus in her village of Kaltenbrunn to go to a dance, but inquiries showed that she never got on the bus. The police reasoned therefore that the killer was either a resident of Kaltenbrunn, or there had been a stranger in the village that evening.

The stranger theory was quickly eliminated – the villagers were sharp-eyed and had seen no one around that they didn't already know. That left a group of about 30 potential suspects, all men above the age of 20. While they were being questioned an informer came forward to say that she had seen Sieglinde getting into a grey Audi 60 on the evening of her disappearance.

Only one man owned a car of that description in the village. Manfred Wittmann was single, weighed well over 15 stone and was just five feet six inches tall. He was a popular villager and assistant chief of the volunteer fire department. Questioning one of his friends, the police discovered that the suspect was afraid of women. The friend recalled how he had once gone out for an evening with Wittmann and picked up two girls.

The girls had taken them to their flat in another town and had immediately got down to business, stripping off and making it clear that they were sexually available.

The friend had promptly followed suit, but Wittmann turned brick red and refused to undress. When the girls attempted to strip him, he pushed them away and fled outside into the street.

His secret came out when he was arrested and

routinely medically examined. This revealed that he was no more developed genitally than an average 10-year-old boy. He broke down when the medical evidence was presented to the police.

He confessed first to stabbing Irmgard Feder, the victim who survived. "I didn't want to hurt her," he told detectives. "I just wanted to have sex. But then, when she was lying there all naked, I couldn't. I just couldn't. Do you understand?"

The detectives nodded. They had already been advised by the doctor that Wittmann was incapable of achieving an erection.

Nora Wenzl, he went on, used to cut his hair. On the day he killed her he drove past her on his bicycle, parked his car and came back. "I had to do something. I had to get relief. I didn't want to kill her, but after it was over I felt relieved and better."

He offered a lift to Helga Luther, the hitchhiker, and she got into his car. "She said that since I was going to do something for her, she would do something for me. She pulled up her dress and took down her knickers and wanted me to touch her, and I was like crazy because I couldn't do it."

Finally he agreed to take the detectives to a forest pool where he had dumped the body of Sieglinde Hübner. She was naked, her hands and feet were bound with her bra and stockings, she was covered with deep knife wounds and her throat had been cut. The weapon was the Cutting Devil. The Beast of Oberfranken never varied his killing technique.

Fear of women, and anger at the barrier that nature had put between him and them, drove Manfred Wittmann to his senseless acts of furious revenge. His view of it was that if he was to be tortured all his life, women must be tortured too. Unable to achieve sex, he seems to have gained some satisfaction from stabbing, hence, "after it was all over, I felt relieved and better."

He was sentenced to life imprisonment. The details of his confession were so horrific that few of them were made public. Perhaps the most chilling insight into a

Domination; physical inadequacy; fear of women

mind conditioned by impotency, a mind from which fear of women had been temporarily exorcised, came when he was asked what he had done with the Cutting Devil. "It's back in my drawer at the workshop," he replied. "I use it to cut up my bread and sausage for lunch."

•

Some men become sexual killers with the help of a female partner. Like Ian Brady with Myra Hindley, Canadian sex killer Paul Bernardo used a female assistant and kept her in his power. She was Karla Homolka, an attractive blonde who was 17 when they met. Bernardo raped several girls in Ontario before he met Karla, and raped several more while they were engaged to be married, only now he took Karla along either for company or for procuring virgins for him. Starry-eyed about her good-looking, six-foot-tall beau, she allowed herself to be completely dominated by him to the point where she was adrift without a moral compass.

In such team relationships the male generally identifies some weakness in the psyche of the female and exploits it. Karla Homolka's weakness must have been obvious to Bernardo. She was born brimming with anger. Her father was a refugee from Czechoslovakia, and she was angry that talk at home was always about lack of money. She was angry with Tammy, her younger sister, who enjoyed flirting with Bernardo. She wanted to escape, and marriage was the way out, although she didn't want to be trapped into the sort of impecunious marriage that she felt had trapped her parents. She told her friends she wanted someone who was "going places," someone who was rich. She was in bed with Bernardo within hours of their first meeting. She built him up to such heights that her friends were persuaded she had made the most amazing catch, and whatever happened after that she couldn't allow the illusion she had created to be shattered. That meant she had to go along with everything he suggested.

A few weeks before they married, on June 17th, 1991, Bernardo told Karla he fancied Tammy, who was 15, and a Karla look-alike. When staying at the Homolka house near Scarborough, Ontario, he had been in the habit of masturbating beside Tammy's bed while she slept and while Karla kept a lookout by the door in case her parents should suddenly appear.

When he decided he wanted full sex with Tammy, Karla slipped a drug into her sister's drink, and then held a rag soaked in anaesthetic over her face. He raped Tammy while Karla held her for him, then sodomised her. Karla held a camcorder filming the entire proceedings, except when Bernardo took over the camera, ordering her to suck Tammy's beasts and perform oral sex on her.

During this performance Karla told her fiancée that she was slightly put off by the fact that Tammy was menstruating. He told her to put her fingers into Tammy's vagina and taste her menstrual blood. Karla did as she was told, pulling a face. Bernardo raped and sodomised Tammy again, and only stopped when he realised that they had killed her.

A medical examination revealed that the girl had choked on her own vomit and, since no one was likely to suspect anything else, the verdict was death by natural causes. Amazingly, Karla, who was eventually to be portrayed as an innocent much corrupted by the psychopathic Bernardo, wasn't deterred by this horrific experience. Three weeks later the couple videoed themselves naked and Karla was heard to say: "I loved you when you fucked my little sister." She married Bernardo, then helped him to kidnap and attack two young virgins, taking them to the torture chamber he had created in their basement home and raping and torturing them until they died.

Paul Bernardo was an unusual sex killer because he was a university graduate working at one time with the accountancy firm Price Waterhouse – a CV that helped to protect him from going into the frame as a suspect for the Scarborough, Ontario, rapist being hunted by Canadian Police. His father, also an accountant, was also to get himself a record as a sex offender. Father and son were in fact strikingly similar. Young Bernardo seemed to acquire his contempt for women from his father.

The more Karla worshipped her man, the more he controlled her. He forbade her to go to university, forbade her to take driving lessons. But after their marriage he gradually went to pieces. He failed his accountancy exams, and re-invented himself as a rap artiste. "He'll soon be in the top ten," Karla enthusiastically told friends. In fact, he never recorded anything musical and it is probable that his change of persona was prompted by the knowledge that sooner or later he would be caught and incarcerated for life. He was beating Karla before they were married, and now the beatings intensified. When the last one occurred she needed hospital treatment, and after that her parents removed her from her husband's home.

Criminologists who have studied this case have concentrated more on Karla than on Paul Bernardo, but what is clear is that as much as anything else he enjoyed viciously exploiting his messianic hold over her. When she arrived on the scene she became the partner in crime and the audience he craved, as well as a target for his daily bouts of sadism. Karla, for instance, had an affinity with pets, and one of her favourites was her pet iguana. When it bit her husband he cut off its head, barbecued it, and insisted that she eat part of it. He was a rapist before he met her, but a killer when they were together.

Detectives on the case were at first convinced that she was totally in a grip from which she couldn't escape, and had become a battered wife. This was why they allowed her to enter a plea-bargain, taking 12 years in prison for manslaughter in exchange for testifying against her former husband – she divorced him after the final beating – so that he could be sent down for life. But the plea-bargain was arranged before the videotapes of her participation in the sex crimes were viewed, and they told a very different story about Karla Homolka. She emerged not just as a masochist who had found her sadist, but also as a sadist who had found another sadist.

Very clearly, the videotapes show that everything he suggested was not at all repugnant to her. The tapes showed her instructing girls step by step how to satisfy her husband sexually. They showed her in lesbian activities with the victims and they showed her as being quite unconcerned about the terror she and her husband were causing.

Some analysts have suggested that Karla might just have been one of those women who get turned on by a rapist-murderer, wide-eyed with admiration for a man who was larger than life, which they translate into their man being stronger and more courageous than other men, and therefore a suitable icon to worship. This idea can be carried to such extremes in the woman's head that she becomes thrilled by her partner raping another woman; the rape or other crime becomes a shared excitement that assuages the anger and frustration experienced in her early upbringing.

CHAPTER NINE

VOYEURISM; PEEPING TOMS; FLASHING, MOTHER
HATRED; OEDIPUS COMPLEX
*Patrick Byrne, Gary Hopkins, George Reilley, Niels Falster,
Kevin Fitch, Werner Boost, Richard Evonitz, Elmo Lee
Smith, John Balaban*

A thousand years ago in Coventry a sadistic nobleman named Leofric was taxing his subjects so heavily that his wife, aghast at the condition of the starving poor on her husband's estates, pleaded with him to give the peasants a respite. Leofric agreed, on condition that she should ride naked through the town. His wife, Lady Godiva, accepted these terms and, in gratitude, all the people of Coventry stayed at home, bolting their doors and windows to save her ladyship's blushes. All the people, that is, save one, a certain tailor who peered through a chink, was struck blind, and has ever since been known as Peeping Tom.

Or, as we might describe him today, the first recorded voyeur.

Anyone who has seen a striptease show has indulged in voyeurism in its simplest form. These days the meaning of the word covers a vast canvas – pornography in all its various forms is for voyeurs. Generally speaking, though, voyeurs are people who have an intense desire to watch other people undress and perhaps look on as they have sexual intercourse. The voyeur is driven by curiosity, in itself a childish complex, and the thrill of watching and taking part in this vicarious way gives him his sexual kick.

Voyeurism led 28-year-old Patrick Byrne to a life sentence in 1960. Byrne was a building labourer working at Edgbaston, Birmingham. He had a police record for housebreaking and had been convicted of a drunken assault on a policeman. His reputation was also well established as a Peeping Tom. His friends called him Acky and on the wall of his lodgings someone had written "Acky the Window Peeper." On December

23rd, 1959, he left his lodgings, went to a pub, and then set out for Edgbaston YWCA hostel. According to his subsequent statement he saw a girl enter the hostel and "decided to have a peep through the window."

"I looked through the curtains and saw a girl wearing a red pullover and underskirt," he said. "She was combing her hair."

The sight of the girl, whose name was Stephanie Baird, was too much for Byrne. He crept into the hostel corridor and placed a chair outside the girl's room, so that he could watch her through the glass panel at the top of the door. She heard a noise and opened it, whereupon he pushed his way in and embraced her.

"This got me excited and I kissed her. She tried to shove me away, and I got her round the waist. She screamed, and I put my hands round her neck. She went backwards into the room. Her head hit the floor and I was lying on top of her, kissing her and squeezing her neck at the same time. After a while I knelt up and had a strong urge to have a good look at her. I pulled her red jumper off."

He stripped Stephanie, bolted the door, removed his own clothes except for his shoes and socks, and strangled her. Then he had sex with her corpse. Using a table knife he found in her room, he cut off her head and put it on the bed, and after severely mutilating the rest of her body he wrote a note which he left on a chest of drawers, saying: "This was the thing I thought would never happen."

Something of Byrne's state of mind is revealed by the statement he made after his arrest:

"I got the knife in my right hand then and caught hold of her right breast and carved the knife around it. It was hard to cut round the skin but in the end I got it off. I was very surprised and disappointed it came away flat in my hand. I just looked at it and then flung it towards the bed. I scored her round the chest with the knife.

"I started on the back of the neck, then, catching hold of her hair and pulling her head closer to my bare chest, I kept on cutting away. I remember how the knife broke off close to the handle when I was cutting her stomach, and I carried on afterwards with the blade..."

Byrne then revealed himself as someone who had been taking a studious interest in sex. He said: "It surprised me how easy the head came off. It's been puzzling me since – why I took the head off. It's not connected with sex in all the books I've read. I can understand the breast. I remember when the head came off I had it by the hair and I stood up. I held it up to the mirror and looked at it through the mirror.

"The other times I had been definitely satisfied with peeping, but this time was different somehow."

Again he reveals his state of mind: "I was pretty frantic...I was very excited, breathing heavy and thinking that I ought to terrorise all women. I wanted to get my own back on them for causing my nervous tension through sex. I felt I only wanted to kill beautiful women. I stood by the mirror in the bathroom talking to myself and searching my face for signs of a madman, but I could see none."

In his statements Byrne appears to be analysing what he had done. He cuts off the girl's head but he can't understand why, because decapitation didn't occur in any of the sex books he had been reading. He is disappointed by the appearance of the severed breast, which was flat. Women were the cause of his problems, he says, the cause of his nervous tension. When he looks at himself in the bathroom mirror after the murder and mutilation he expects to see a madman, but he can only see himself. He leaves a note saying that what he had done was the thing he thought would never come – implying that he had given murder, as the ultimate consequence of his Peeping Tom activities, a great deal of thought. He is consummately self-analytical about his sexual sadism and what comes through his analysis is his profound emotional immaturity.

The judge at his trial was evidently intrigued. He asked a medical expert: "Would it be fair to ask that when you get such a marked degree of depravity, that individual cannot be guilty of murder?"

The expert replied, "No, sir."

The judge then asked: "Are you saying there was nothing wrong with his mind except these depraved desires to which he surrenders?"

The expert replied: "Yes."

Another medical expert revealed that Byrne had a long history of gross sexual abnormality, with perversions that had become increasingly bizarre. He was currently suffering from sadistic fantasies, including one in which he cut up a woman with a circular saw.

Another resident at the murder scene hostel, Margaret Brown, was in the ironing room when she saw Byrne's shadow through a glass panel. She opened the door to investigate. Byrne, who was on his way out after the murder, hit her with a heavy stone and, as she staggered against the wall screaming, he fled. Miss Brown called the police and the body of Stephanie Baird was found in her room.

Byrne was caught after seven weeks during which police took 50,000 statements. He had returned to his hometown of Warrington and during a routine interview he suddenly said: "I want to tell you something about the YWCA. I had something to do with that." His statement revealed information that only a man in the room at the time of Stephanie's death could have known.

Medical evidence suggested that Stephanie died from a fracture of the skull after falling backwards on the floor of her room, and that Byrne mutilated her breasts with scissors when she was already dead. The other injuries he caused with the knife were so severe – like Neville Heath, he inserted the instrument into her vagina – that the knife broke under the impact. Byrne was undoubtedly under-sexed, as is often the case with voyeurs, viewing the weapon as a surrogate penis in mimicry of sex.

He was found guilty of murder and sentenced to life, but in July 1960 the Appeal Court changed the conviction to manslaughter without altering the life sentence. Three doctors testified that he was suffering

Voyeurism; Peeping Toms; flashing; mother hatred; Oedipus complex

from an abnormality of the mind that led to violent sexual desires he found difficult or impossible to control – his curiosity, in other words, getting the better of him.

•

Because there is a little bit of curiosity in everyone, the percentage of voyeurs who actually turn into sexual killers is infinitesimal. But case histories suggest that those who do become killers are especially violent, and like Patrick Byrne they frequently have a background of other crimes.

When three young girls were attacked in four separate incidents on East Anglian caravan sites in the 1980s the police mounted a big manhunt. When a fourth, three-year-old Leoni Keating, was abducted from a Great Yarmouth caravan park in the middle of the night, raped, and dumped in a river to drown 70 miles away, the manhunt for this sexual maniac reached epic proportions.

Scanning criminal names on a computer, the police arrived at Gary Hopkins, who had convictions for burglary and indecent exposure. His life story was interesting. He lived in Bedford, had once been a Merchant Navy cook, and had also worked on travelling fairgrounds. He liked to hang around discos and bingo halls at holiday camps.

Hopkins had a juvenile court record in Ipswich, graduating through Borstal to prison. He never knew his father, since his mother did not fill in that relevant detail on his birth certificate. His file revealed that he was a disruptive child at school, with a marked streak of sadism.

In the mid-1970s he lived with an Essex woman and had a son and a daughter by her. But in 1977 the girl became a cot-death suffocation victim. Hopkins was accused obliquely of ill-treating the child. The following day he ran from the house into a nearby park and indecently exposed himself to a young girl. That was recorded on his crime sheet as a "flasher" incident, a crime coupled at the time with assaulting a policeman and driving while disqualified, all of which got him a six-month term in jail.

In 1980 he met another Essex woman, who was a student nurse, like himself, in Hornchurch Hospital. They were married at Havering in June the following year. But it was a stormy affair. Hopkins sometimes dressed up in his wife's clothes – and the couple split up, pending divorce, in 1982.

He surfaced again in Great Yarmouth, working as a bingo-caller, and claiming to be a martial arts expert. Significantly, he spent a lot of time in the area's holiday camps and trailer sites. He frequently stayed at one site with his doting grandmother, spending hours wandering among the rows of trailers, peering into windows and pilfering cash and cigarettes from empty caravans.

He was soon back in jail, this time for a burglary at the Lucky Punter Social Club. When he was released he stayed at an old haunt, the Seashore Caravan Park, this time with a new mistress. Here, in the summer of 1985, he struck twice. He peeped at his first victim at the Seashore Park, a 14-year-old girl, while she was undressing in her caravan. When he attacked her, she fought back furiously and escaped, receiving a knife wound that needed four stitches. His next victim there, a few weeks later, was little Leoni Keating.

So here was a man whose criminal record implied that he was highly dangerous before he actually became a sexual killer. As an ordinary criminal he was a burglar, and he was aggressive with it – he had assaulted a police officer. Then, as a sexual fiend he was a flasher, a transvestite, a child rapist.

At what point was the danger he posed to society actually identified? It can be argued that his name was there and waiting when names had to be fed into the manhunt computer, but it is significant that the detective who decided to scan Hopkins's record initially did so because he remembered him for one crime – the burglary. Hopkins is as good an example as we shall ever have in support of the sex offenders' register, for he almost certainly would have been identified as a sexual predator and isolated before he murdered Leoni Keating. For that crime, and for the three other abductions, he received four concurrent life sentences, with a recommendation that he should spend a minimum 25 years in jail.

•

Voyeurs don't have to be male, and they don't have to be people wanting to hide themselves as they indulge in their fantasies. This can be explained by the thousands of people who visit live sex shows looking for sexual stimulation. There is nothing new in this world: wealthy Romans were known to force slaves to copulate in front of them as an after-dinner entertainment. Infantile regression was undoubtedly as common 2,000 years ago as it is today.

Some secret voyeurs, who plan their peeping and get arousal from watching private moments but who hide themselves while doing so, may be quite harmless. But others may also want to turn their fantasy into reality, and in that case they can become dangerous.

Cases where voyeurs actually rape are comparatively rare. Even more rare is the voyeur who rapes his victim and then stabs her savagely to death or otherwise murders her. That's why police called to the Leamington Clinic in Leamington Spa on the night of August 22nd, 1980, were baffled when they found the body of Suzie Tein-Ahn-Song, an Oriental nurse, raped and stabbed to death, and heard that a Peeping Tom had been seen in the hospital grounds at night. A trap was laid, and the man was caught red-handed and arrested. But doctors who examined him doubted whether he was capable of committing rape at all.

Suzie, the night nurse, had been killed in the staff duty room. She was lying face down on a bed, naked and with her underwear strewn about her. Her buttocks rested on the edge of the bed and her legs were widely spread, the right one drawn up so that her heel rested on the bed frame, with the knee tipped outward. Her breasts and shoulders were studded with deep stab wounds. A doctor testified that prior to being raped she was a virgin.

Police discovered that a carpenter had been doing repair work on cupboards in the staff duty room on the night of the murder. He was George Reilley, 30, but he was not available for interviews because he was getting married that morning to the 21-year-old daughter of a local doctor. Searching his home, police found a cleverly hidden collection of porn magazines, all of them featuring exclusively Oriental girls.

Reilley was brought in from his honeymoon for questioning and he readily confessed. His troubles began in October, 1977, he said, when three Oriental nurses arrived at the hospital. Someone had once told him that Oriental women were the world's greatest experts in eroticism, and he became obsessed with the idea of having sex with one or all three of them. Then Suzie arrived, aggravating his obsession. He fantasised about all four girls, but Suzie was the favourite of his dreams. He used to spy on the girls at night in the hospital grounds.

On the day of Suzie's murder he was working in the staff duty room when he made a sudden decision to leave the window jammed open so that he could return later in the evening. Suzie was alone when he came back, and he attacked her. But for him the rape was a personal disaster. Although he forced the terrified girl to submit to him at knifepoint, it was not the stuff that his erotic dreams were made of. Instead he was trying to enjoy sex with a weeping, passionless girl behaving like any other girl in similar circumstances. With all his fantasises collapsing around him, he lost control of himself and murdered his dream out of sheer disappointment.

On June 12th, 1981, Reilley was sentenced to life imprisonment for murder.

Voyeurism; Peeping Toms; flashing; mother hatred; Oedipus complex

•

Voyeurism is not necessarily confined to peeping through windows. It can and does take place in private homes and involves a couple and a third party, but the raison-d'être – sexual arousal through observing the sex act – remains the same.

In a remarkable case in Denmark in the 1980s the third parties were a group of men who came to watch and indulge their fantasies. The case concerned Chief Inspector Niels Falster who was in charge of Copenhagen's recently formed police section caring for battered women.

Soon after the department was set up, Julie Kiel, 28, was beaten up by her husband Walter. She was treated in hospital, while her husband was arrested and put in a police cell for the night. The man who drove Julie Kiel home after her hospital treatment was Chief Inspector Falster. He followed her into her flat and technically raped her. Technically, because she might have resisted but she felt helpless, for she knew that if her husband was exposed by the police as a wife-beater he would lose his high-powered job.

Chief Inspector Falster also knew that. Which was why he took advantage of her that night.

Falster was evidently a beguiling man, for after that Julie Kiel overcame any aversion she might have felt to being raped and went regularly to his bachelor apartment for sex. And whenever that happened Falster's friends arrived to watch. She didn't mind the sex too much, but she was anxious about all these voyeurs. But she felt powerless, unable to complain to the police and unable to complain to her husband. Several years later, when Falster was finally arrested by his own police department and put on trial, the voyeurs were not identified.

Julie Kiel was not Falster's only mistress. He was having another affair with 40-year-old Mrs. Gertrude Asborg, who had also come to his attention after being beaten up by her husband. Lars Asborg, a reputable Danish lawyer, breathed a sigh of relief when he wasn't charged with wife beating, for a criminal case against him would have cost him his legal reputation.

He soon learned, however, that his wife's rescuer that night was Chief Inspector Niels Falster, who had promptly seduced Gertrude while Asborg was spending his night in a police cell. Gertrude apparently relished the chief inspector's intervention, because she related all the details of the rape, or seduction, to her husband, delighting in the fact that he could do nothing about it.

Lars Asborg was even more furious when he heard that not only had his wife become the police officer's mistress, but so too had his 19-year-old daughter Anna. While the chief inspector was making love to Gertrude, Anna woke up and watched through a crack in the bedroom door. Voyeurism evidently excited Anna, for she returned to her bedroom, changed into a short transparent nightdress and waited for the chief inspector to exit from her mother's bedroom. Falster, clearly a man of some virility, needed no further encouragement, and that night added mother and daughter to his collection of trophies. On subsequent occasions Anna and her mother shared the same bed with the chief inspector. Anna was later to say that for her, the sole attraction was that Falster was good in bed. Like Julie Kiel, Anna and Gertrude were convinced that they were Falster's only mistresses.

Falster's astonishing career as self-appointed "confidant" to the battered wives of Copenhagen lasted 12 years. Towards the end, some of the dozens of wives he raped who were not quite as complacent as Julie Kiel and Gertrude Asborg began making anonymous phone calls to the police department, and soon the police suspected that the callers were referring to a senior police officer.

Investigations began gingerly but urgently, for if one of the cuckolded husbands became sufficiently infuriated the scene could be set for murder. And that is exactly what happened. On November 7th, 1985, a 29-year-old Copenhagen housewife was found battered to death by her husband, who had afterwards hanged himself from a beam in his garage.

Detectives examining the forensic reports on the two corpses concluded that the woman had been badly beaten over a number of years by her husband and had called the police for help. An officer had arrived, neutralised the husband in some way, raped the woman anally and beat her as well. As soon as the husband was free, he killed his wife and hanged himself, for he too was a man whose business life would have been ruined by exposure.

Investigations were getting nowhere, however, until at 4.15 a.m. on Christmas Day, 1985, Mrs. Ingrid Herning, 30, called the police complaining that her husband had beaten her. A bank director, Hans Herning had actually done no such thing. They had been celebrating on Christmas Eve and drunk too much. She slapped him and he slapped her back, but in her drunken state she decided to call the police.

The man who arrived to investigate was Chief Inspector Neils Falster. He arrested Hans Herning, whose protests became somewhat muted when he was confidentially told that publicity would be avoided if he stayed calm. The unfortunate bank director was taken off to a police cell, and when he was safely under lock and key, Falster returned to the house where he had left Ingrid Herning alone.

Ingrid had meanwhile fallen asleep on her bed. When she work up she found herself naked, and alongside her under the sheets was Chief Inspector Falster of Copenhagen Police. She screamed, and when she resisted his advances he blacked her eye and cut her face. Then he dragged her into bathroom, pushed her over the bath and raped her anally, causing such damage that she had to have three stitches. When her husband came home, released early because it was Christmas Day, he found her half-conscious on the bathroom floor.

Deciding that he had nothing to fear from his bank, Hans Herning promptly laid charges. Falster was arrested, and so many women came forward to testify against him that he made a full confession. He was sentenced to four years' imprisonment.

•

The voyeur prefers to go about his business alone, unseen and in the dark, and peeping through lighted, uncovered windows is his special brand of excitement. When one night in April, 1991, Patsy Gray, a single mother living in California, went out to a meeting, she left her 15-year-old daughter Christin alone in their caravan home.

Christin had her schoolwork to catch up on, and when she had finished she took a hot shower and snuggled into bed, from where she called her boy friend on her bedside phone.

Unknown to her, her every action from the moment she undressed and got into the shower was watched by a Peeping Tom. Through the slits of her Venetian blind he had a bird's-eye view of her bathroom and bedroom.

Out there in the darkness he goggled at Christin's nubile virgin body and innocent femininity. She was blonde, pretty, almost voluptuous. A power took hold of the peeper, as if from the boiling brew of a witch's cauldron. A frenzy came over him. He had to have her.

When Mrs. Patsy Gray returned home about 10.30 that night the sight that meet her eyes stunned her. Christin lay in a foetal position on the floor, naked from the waist down, in a pool of blood, her unseeing eyes staring blankly at the wall. She had been raped, repeatedly stabbed, and her throat had been slit with a knife.

A pathologist reported that she had died of 40 stab wounds inflicted on her stomach, chest and back. There were numerous cuts and slashes on her hands, arms and abdomen, which he characterised as an attempt to torture her.

The pathologist had seen murdered girls before,

but not like this one. The first part of her aorta, the trunk artery that carries blood from the heart to the branch arteries throughout the body, was completely severed. She had probably haemorrhaged to death in an agonising way.

"I would say she pumped out blood for several minutes," he said. Christin died probably about half an hour before her mother returned home.

Despite an intensive police search, two years passed and still the knife-wielding sex killer eluded detection. Mrs. Patsy Gray moved out of the caravan park into another community with a security guard patrolling.

The caravan home where Christin was murdered was bought by a mother with a beautiful 17-year-old daughter. The girl undressed and showered in the same room where Christin was sexually attacked and murdered.

On the night of Friday, August 16th, 1996, a Peeping Tom crouched in the darkness beneath her window. He was the killer of Christin Gray, and his silhouette was spotted by a woman neighbour who happened to look out of her kitchen window. The man was peering under the Venetian blinds that did not quite reach to the bottom of the window.

As the neighbour watched she saw the man leave the window when the sprinklers were activated by an automatic system. As soon as the water shut off, he returned to the window, but ducked down when a car's headlights almost caught him. When he came back to the window she called the police.

"I recognised him," she said. "His name is Kevin Fitch. He lives here in the caravan park."

Fitch was 37 years old, unmarried, lived alone and worked as an electronics technician. He had lived in the caravan park for the past six years, and his home was in sight of Patsy Gray's. He had been missed out during the Christin Gray investigation because a detective had knocked on his door, received no answer, and never checked back.

It is a truism that no one knows a voyeur until he

is unmasked, so it's worth examining what other people who knew Kevin Fitch thought of him. He was described as a loner who seldom had company. He rode his bicycle on the asphalt streets of the caravan park. A cat lover, he fed the local cats. A neighbour said he was "a sweet guy, who likes to cook."

Fitch's friends and co-workers also thought he was a nice guy. He was caring and conscientious, they said. Although rather nondescript and unassuming, he was always a delight to have around.

"There is no way that the Kevin Fitch we know and love could have done anything like that," declared one friend. He said Fitch shuddered and called the murder of Christin "grisly" when the two discussed it one day on their way to work.

If Fitch possessed a Jekyll and Hyde personality, none of his acquaintances seemed to be aware of any inappropriateness in his behaviour. They said he didn't have much of a social life. He worked out at a gym four nights a week, and he drank whisky at weekends.

The police decided to put a visible tail on him, in the hope that he would reveal something sinister about himself. He didn't. In fact, even the police who were following him took a shine to him, and reported back that there was no indication that he had any malignant thoughts.

But they still thought that Fitch was their man, so they took out a search warrant and descended on his caravan. They found an extensive collection of pornographic photographs and books about sex with young or teenage girls. Over 100 pornographic magazines, with titles like *Virgin Love, Sweet Young Things,* and *Baby Dolls,* were confiscated. In a chest of drawers they found 20 pornographic videos showing young girls, and beneath the mattress on his bed they found women's underclothes. They also found a magazine article detailing the statutory rape laws in every state in the United States. California was highlighted with a fluorescent marker.

But more important than any of this was the bloody

fingerprint the killer had left on Christin Gray's homework essay. Its genetic structure was shown to be identical to that of Kevin Fitch. It was concluded that only one in every 4.17 million people in California had these same genetic traits. That meant that in a state with a population of 32 million, only eight people could have been in Christin's bedroom that night.

Investigators discovered too that on the day following Christin's murder Fitch reported early to his office medical doctor with cuts on his hands which he said had just occurred in a incident at work. The doctor stitched up the wounds, but doubted Fitch's story because he said the wounds were clearly old ones.

All this was enough to have Fitch charged with rape, burglary, torture and murder. He declined to give evidence on his own behalf, relying on witnesses who came forward to say he was easy-going, non-violent and imbued with exceptional gentlemanly qualities.

The jury didn't think so, and found him guilty, but they were hopelessly deadlocked on whether he should face the death penalty. Rather than start all over again, the prosecutors agreed to accept a life sentence, and Fitch was duly sentenced to spend the rest of his days in the state penitentiary without any possibility of parole.

•

In a celebrated German murder case, the killer, Werner Boost, dubbed "Germany's Son of Sam" by the media, was a voyeur who preyed on courting couples, watching them making love and then shooting the man so that he could have sex with the woman.

Boost made a study of crime and how to perfect it. He was born in 1928, the son of a 17-year-old unmarried mother, and he never knew his father. His mother placed him in a government-run nursing home. When he was older, he was sent to various foster-parents and did farm work from dawn till dark for his keep. He grew up a lonely child, without love or any home life. At school he shocked other children with his cruelty to animals. Though apparently a bright boy, he stayed at school only as long as the law required – until he reached the age of 14.

He was an accomplished thief by then, and had been in trouble with the police several times. During the war, he worked at menial jobs under harsh employers. But he also studied in his spare time to become an electrician. Maturity did not change him, however; he grew up a sullen, embittered youth who hated just about everyone. When he married he took his wife to Düsseldorf, where he got a job as an electrician.

From his wife he apparently received unselfish love for the first time in his life. He reciprocated to an extent, and became strongly attached to their two daughters. For a while he lived a normal family life.

But his early frustrations and the hatred bred in him eventually overwhelmed him. He developed a passion for guns, dabbled in chemistry as a hobby and experimented with poisons that would kill and leave no trace. He tried these out on cats, sometimes putting them in barrels of poison gas to test the effect. He learned how to impregnate bullets with poison to make them even more deadly.

He also began scanning the newspapers for stories about unusual methods of crime. He read a lot about Caryl Chessman, the American serial killer, who became his idol. Here was another man of high intelligence – one from the same miserable background. Chessman had lived by his wits and staged many ingenious crimes that had baffled the police. But Chessman made the fatal error of falling into police hands. Werner Boost was determined he would not be caught.

He spent long hours in the library reading the exploits of notorious criminals, taking notes on their methods, studying how to avoid the fatal slips which led to their downfall. He started prowling the streets of Düsseldorf at night with two aims in mind – robbery and rape. For Boost's ambition to become a super criminal was fuelled by a furious sex drive.

His first major robbery attempt was bizarre. He

placed spike-studded planks across the road at a lonely spot on a dark, rainy night, and, armed with a revolver, hid in a clump of bushes. The first car to be halted by the barrier contained four men, and Boost was afraid to tackle them. The car drove on to the shoulder of the road and passed on. Boost waited for another.

Two more cars arrived and again there were too many people. These cars also skirted the planks. Then a van came along. The driver got down with a gun in his hand, pushed the spiked planks to one side, and drove on. A few minutes later Boost heard a police siren wailing in the distance and hid in a tree while the police searched the nearby bushes. Then he rode home on his motorcycle.

Franz Lorbach, a drug addict who was much under Boost's thumb, said of him: "He practised judo on me until he was perfect at it. He invented a weapon to attack people with – steel pellets in a nylon stocking. He tried that out on me too. He was a first-rate shot with a pistol. He knew an abandoned factory in the country and we'd go there for target practice.

"He made a truth serum. He tried that out on me too, and it worked. I told him things I'd never meant to tell anyone."

Lorbach said that Boost made a powerful odourless gas that he claimed would kill in minutes. "His plan was to fill a balloon with the gas and put it in a cardboard box, with a clockwork device that would puncture the balloon and release the gas at a certain time – say in half an hour. Then he was going to wrap up the box and address it to some fictitious person. He planned to go early in the morning to the post office before there were any customers, and hand it in for mailing. Half an hour later the powerful gas would be released and all the post office workers would die.

"After that, he planned to return and rob the post office. He planned the whole thing meticulously – he even borrowed a book about post office routine from the public library."

According to Lorbach, Boost hated rich businessmen

and planned to kidnap the child of one of them to get some ransom money. He was going to kill the child, he said, because that was the safest way.

"In the ransom note, he planned to instruct the child's father to hide the money at night under the planks of a certain small dock along the Rhine. If the father notified the police and they went there hoping to grab the kidnapper, Boost had a plan. He intended to swim the river under water from the opposite shore, breathing through a snorkel device. He would recover the money under the dock and swim back again. In the morning the police would be amazed to find the money gone."

Boost gave Lorbach instructions to poison his wife, Frau Hanna Boost, with a cyanide phial if he were ever arrested, then to drag her unconscious body to the kitchen and turn on the gas jets to make it seem like suicide.

Boost may have made a practised criminal, or he may have been just a fantasiser, but sex was the driving force in him and his plan was to play Peeping Tom on courting couples, just as Son of Sam was to do decades later when he terrorised young New York couples.

But Boost's first attempt at sex prowling was a disaster. For after tracking a car to a wood he crept up on it, revolver in hand, and shot dead the driver, Dr. Lothar Serve, a prominent local lawyer. The other occupant opened the door and ran off in panic. Only then did Boost realise that this was a man and not a girl.

He was not put off. On the night of October 31st, 1955, Friedholm Behre, young owner of a prosperous Düsseldorf bakery, drove his fiancée, Thea Kurmann, to a lonely lovers' lane. Boost, lurking in the bushes with revolver in hand, crept up on them and watched them through the car window.

Freidholm Behre probably never saw the man who shot him at close range, for he did not struggle. But Thea Kurmann did. She put up a terrific fight as Boost first raped then strangled her. With the dead couple still inside, he pushed the car into a lake where it disappeared under the water and was not found again until some months had passed and the water had receded.

Four months later, a cyclist riding alongside the River Rhine found two corpses, victims of an identical murder. Boost had shot the man, Peter Falkenburg, from only a few inches away, and raped and garrotted his fiancée, Hildegarde Wassing. Afterwards he poured petrol on the bodies and tried to burn them.

"Germany's Son of Sam" was caught literally red-handed. On May 5th, 1956, forest ranger Erich Spath was walking at dusk in woods near Meererbusch, just outside Düsseldorf, when he saw a parked car on its own. It was nearly hidden from the ranger's view by the low-hanging branches of a willow.

The ranger caught a glimpse of a man and a woman in the car and decided to make a detour so as not to disturb them. Suddenly he heard someone moving in the underbrush. He turned and saw the man he later identified as Werner Boost creeping up on the car, a revolver in his hand. As Ranger Spath watched, Boost took several bullets from his pocket and calmly loaded the weapon.

Spath had read all about the killer Peeping Tom, and he didn't hesitate. He swung his rifle into position and crept up silently behind Boost. "Drop the gun and put up your hands," he ordered.

It was all over for Werner Boost. Although the jury at his trial were unable to find him guilty of the murder of the two couples for want of evidence, they found him guilty of killing Dr. Lothar Serve, and sent him to prison for life.

•

Indecent exposure, also known as "flashing" and exhibitionism, is the flip side of voyeurism. The exhibitionist prefers to provide the spectacle rather than be part of the audience, and as such he is a much more sinister figure, for flashing is a sexual offence, and is more likely to be a prelude to more serious sexual offences. A recent survey showed that 243 sex offenders questioned admitted to 40,000 incidents of indecent exposure. A police report suggests that 15 per cent of flashers move up the scale to rape and murder.

The problem for the police is that the other 85 per cent are probably harmless, so how much time can be given to a flasher? In a recent TV documentary on flashing, the narrator, who had herself been the victim of two flashers as a child, attempted to trace the second perpetrator who, she decided, was probably caught and fined. At that time, 1971, flashing wasn't even a recordable offence, and there is little evidence to suggest that it is treated as very much more serious even today.

The first flasher she described was clearly scary. The man came up to her and her mother in a wood and was within touching distance. He wore a mask, shouted in a way that indicated anger, brandished a stick in one hand and masturbated with the other. He ran off only after the girl's mother emitted a piercing scream.

The 85 per cent of flashers who are harmless include husbands, fathers and professional men. They flash on average 70 to 80 times before being caught, and the longer they are at large the more plausible they become at justifying why they do it. In one survey, 75 per cent of British women admitted to having been flashed during their lives.

What was remarkable among the stories presented by other childhood victims of flashing was the lack of adult response at the time. It was as if the grown-ups didn't want to hear, turning their backs on what for a child is at least a disturbing experience. On one occasion after reporting a flasher, the narrator described being interviewed by a policewoman "aggressively." The narrator was also dismayed when, years later and by now an adult, she was walking in the King's Road, Chelsea, and saw a man who had been drinking produce his genitalia to full view. "He urinated against a wall," she said – although it could be alternatively construed that rather than a serious attempt at flashing, this was a silent protest about the appalling lack of public conveniences in central London.

There is no nexus drawing together the differing threads that lie behind the driving force for flashing, but a surprising number of exhibitionists confess to being angry with women after being abused in childhood and feel that by exhibiting themselves they are "getting their own back." Strict fathers and harsh environmental backgrounds are also blamed. In other cases there is a simple desire to be appreciated, or at least to be noticed. The flasher is generally someone with an inferiority complex that he has managed to repress and replace with an attitude of superiority. He is above all an exhibitionist, a complex that exists in many people, although very few of them carry it to the extreme point of physical self-revelation. The exhibitionist is also someone capable of considerable self-delusion, for he frequently thinks that he is doing his victim a favour.

The typical flasher selects a lonely place and exposes himself either in a state of erection or actually masturbating, wherever possible to a woman alone, and slips away before she has time to call the police. In many instances the victims do not even call the police, for the perception has grown up around flashing that it is merely a fringe crime, a bit of a joke that an emancipated woman should be able to laugh off, an experience she should treat dismissively. This is encouraged by the stereotype flasher images of giggling schoolgirls confronted by a pathetic man opening his rubber raincoat to reveal all. The reality may be a long way from this scenario, which fails to take into account that the victim may be profoundly disturbed by the experience, and that the perpetrator is a sinister and possibly dangerous kind of criminal.

In a normal relationship the overture to sexual intercourse is excitement by curiosity. The male is instinctively proud of his accoutrements and is curious about the body of the female; there is subsequent viewing and inspection, which culminates in intercourse. In flashing, the process of exhibitionism serves as a substitute for this preparatory work, and is perverted because it is unfinished.

The selection of the victim, the site for the exhibition, and the clothing selected by the flasher requires a good deal of planning. In one American case a compulsive flasher had the top half of his trousers cut off, and elastic inserted around the top of the trouser legs to keep them in place. In another case the flasher had his entire body tattooed with obscene pictures. In yet another case the flasher deliberately walked around his house in the nude with the windows open so that he was in full view of two women neighbours. When he knew they were looking at him, he said, he became excited. In all cases of such exhibitionism the perpetrator gets his ultimate thrill from the knowledge that his victim has looked at him; if she fails to see him he will do his utmost to confront her again, for without such confrontation he is unable to climax.

•

Richard Evonitz, 38, of Spotsylvania, Virginia, was a flasher with a fetish for young brunettes. He became a violent sexual killer, murdering a 12-year-old girl and two teenage girls. His criminal activities began when, while serving with the US Navy as a sonar technician in 1987, he masturbated in front of a 15-year-old. He parked his car near her school and committed the offence as she passed by. He was caught and ordered to undergo psychosexual treatment after admitting he had a problem.

Evonitz had a short-lived marriage to a teenage brunette before raping and killing the three girls, all of whom were also brunettes. As the hunt for him intensified, the FBI established that he was obsessed with teenage girls, stalking them and masturbating in front of them when the opportunity arose. But they couldn't catch him.

After the three murders he let five years go by before striking again. On a June day in 2002 he saw a 15-year-old girl watering her garden in Richland County, South

Carolina. He forced her into his car, put her in the boot and drove her to his apartment. He tied her to a restraining device set up in his double bed and forced her to watch pornographic films and call him "Daddy" while, for the next 18 hours, he repeatedly raped her. When he finally fell asleep the terrified girl escaped and led police to her abductor's home. Cornered, Evonitz refused to surrender, preferring to put the muzzle of his .25-calibre pistol into his mouth and squeeze the trigger.

Like a true flasher, Evonitz was shy, timid, introverted, and as a result unpopular with work colleagues. His behaviour with the 15-year-old who lived to tell the tale was emblematic of his kind, demonstrating as it does his desire to dominate though only able to do so with the aid of a restraining device, and showing her pornographic forms in the forlorn hope that she might be stimulated and become a willing partner.

•

Elmo Lee Smith, of Pennsylvania, had a long history of violence, robbery and sexual offences that began with flashing, followed by voyeurism and culminating in rape and murder. Describing the first time he indecently exposed himself, he told the police that after driving past a woman pedestrian he stopped, got out of his car and took off his trousers.

"I had the lower part of my body exposed. She stopped and stared and then started running. I threw my trousers at her. I didn't say anything, just threw my trousers."

In one of a string of Peeping Tom incidents he had looked through a window, seen a girl sleeping on a couch, broken in and fractured her jaw with a frying pan.

After he was caught and jailed following another Peeping Tom and breaking and entering offence, he wrote in a letter to his wife: "Honestly, darling, I'll never really know just what causes me to do these things." He thought his too-warm nature had got the better of him. "When I saw a woman getting undressed, or nude at a window, I tried to get her to satisfy my desire."

A prison psychiatrist who examined him reported in rather unscientific language: "The prisoner shows sexual psychopathic trends, with sudden impulses which lead to caveman tactics."

In December, 1959, only two months after his most recent release from prison, where he had spent many years of his life for a catalogue of offences, Smith murdered Maryann Mitchell. He picked her up at a bus stop, dragged her into the rear seat of his car and raped her.

"She begged me to take her home," he said. "I said to hell with her. I told her she could walk home."

Instead, he drove with her still in the back seat for another five miles, stopped the car and tried to rape her again. But she put up such a fight that he grabbed the iron arm of a jack and beat her over the head. 'She was unconscious after that," Smith said. "I drove for another mile and a half, pulled her from the car and rolled her down a gully."

Maryann's body was found next day with "101" – Smith's motel room number – written in lipstick on her abdomen – and Smith was identified through the testimony of another women he had attacked in the street. When he was sentenced to death he replied: "May God have mercy on all of youse." Eighteen months after the sentence, on April 2nd, 1962, he went to Pennsylvania's electric chair.

•

We tend to think of sexual killers as lonely, deprived, disadvantaged social misfits who are less well off than most people. While this is often true, the universality of sexual interest and experiment that has surfaced during the last few decades embraces people from every stratum of society. Many men who work hard find recreation in hard sex, and sometimes it doesn't always end in pleasure.

Daniel O'Brien, a practised voyeur, paid with his life for his involvement in a sexual liaison that became punctuated with jealousy. He was a divorced, wealthy businessman and a workaholic, usually leaving home at 5 a.m. and not returning until 11 p.m. All his weekends were devoted to sex. He paid £50 a year to have his name placed on an internet site's sex files list which entitled him to have phone sex at £1.50 a minute. He expressed an interest in escorts, including transvestites, males and couples, aged 25 to 34, and was sent a list of 18 women in the Wakefield area where he lived, and four transvestites and 10 men nationwide.

One of the women who responded was Janet Charlton, 35, a former escort girl, who moved into O'Brien's home with her daughter in 2000.

Very soon the couple were into what is known as "dogging and piking," which is having sex with strangers in public places and watching each other doing it. Doggers and pikers were much in evidence at Bretton Country Park, a local beauty spot. Once O'Brien invited a stranger in the park to have sex with Janet Charlton. She got out of his Mercedes wearing a short skirt, took off her top and the stranger had sex with her on the car bonnet. "She was all for it, she was enjoying it," the stranger said. "She was moaning, 'Give me more, give me it.'" He then watched O'Brien have intercourse with Janet Charlton.

What lies behind this bizarre behaviour is a combination of voyeurism and exhibitionism linked to the thrill of getting sexual satisfaction by risk-taking that drives back the frontiers of conventional behaviour.

Before O'Brien met Janet Charlton he had had a four-year relationship with a 42-year-old hotel manageress who described sex with him as "very exciting – he had the most wonderful eyes." They had sex with strangers in car parks, hotels and at his home, where he hosted parties for "swingers" who he recruited by advertising in contact magazines. They would phone him on his business line, which he called his "naughty phone." Her photograph appeared with their advertisement, which read: "Professional attractive couple, both late thirties, seek new sexy friends. Both mildly bisexual. We would like to hear from singles, couples, whether bi or straight, and TVs and TSs. We are both extremely broad-minded. Both can be submissive, therefore Masters are always welcome. If compatible, ultimate always sought on first meeting. We would love party invites especially if male-orientated to service slut wife. She is tarty and is extraordinarily orgasmic."

O'Brien and his girl friend had a code word which she would use any time she wanted what was happening to stop. She had only to say "toast" and he would immediately end the sex session.

She wore a Zorro mask with no eyeholes while having sex with 12 men in one day, including three men at once while O'Brien watched. "We rang a lot of people that day and these 12 men turned up." Another visitor, known as "The Master," brought a leather whip and nipple clamps. "I didn't like the nipple clamps – they were too painful," she remembered.

At other times they wore rubber gloves while playing "doctors and nurses" role games, and they were always together when they had sex with other people. Ninety-nine per cent of these were men, although she once experimented with another woman but didn't like it. O'Brien liked to watch her having sex with other men, and he liked to be in control during the group sex romps. He also twice proposed that she should have intercourse with a teenage boy and his father, but she said no.

She did, however, once have sex in a hotel with a stranger who paid her £80. "It was a fantasy I wanted to fulfil."

Her relationship with Daniel O'Brien ended in July, 2000, after she developed a blood disorder that made sex painful for her. "I walked out as I did not want the relationship to dwindle away and spoil our many wonderful memories. But I remained besotted with him."

Then Janet Charlton came into O'Brien's life. At least at first she acquiesced in his overwhelming unconventional sexuality. A man to whom she had given oral sex at Bretton Country Park at O'Brien's request described her as "quite willing; there were no problems, no hesitation at all." Afterwards, he added, O'Brien lifted her long black skirt and "started messing around with her. They were both happy."

O'Brien seemed as besotted with Janet Charlton as he had been with his former girl friend. He told his cleaner that he had met the woman he had always wanted – "Janet is the only one for me." But that proved not to be the case. They began to argue. One day, according to Janet Charlton, O'Brien became "frisky' and suggested having sex. They went upstairs, where he stripped naked while she removed her turquoise bikini and put on fishnet stockings and a leopardskin-effect suspender belt.

She said O'Brien wanted to use his sex toys, which included latex gloves, a whip, handcuffs and "poppers" – capsules that intensified sexual arousal. O'Brien told her, "Get the gag out, get the handcuffs." They had oral sex, "and I stroked his – with the whip, but I didn't hit him with it." They were interrupted by the arrival of her daughter.

That was Janet Charlton's story. But there was another version – told by the prosecutor at Leeds Crown Court on April 11th, 2002, when she stood trial for O'Brien's murder. The couple had talked about separation, said the prosecutor, he having made plans to go back to his former girl friend. But Janet Charlton wanted a lot more than the payoff of £67,000 and a sports car that O'Brien offered her in compensation for the impending loss of her home and the sex-crazed man with whom she had developed an intense relationship.

"It was Janet Charlton who seduced Danny O'Brien, no doubt a very willing partner, to go to the bedroom that afternoon," the court was told. "Earlier, she had taken an axe from the garage to the dressing-room of the master bedroom. Ten of the 20 blows she delivered with it struck the victim's head. One blow that missed sliced through the carpet, another sheared chips from the doorframe, and pathologists believed she changed positions during the attack. The room was spattered with O'Brien's blood and brain tissue."

When O'Brien was dead Janet Charlton removed her fishnet stockings and threw them on top of his body. She left the axe embedded in his head, her leopardskin-effect suspender belt draped over its handle. She attempted to clean up the room, and then, "as if nothing had happened, she took her daughter to the park."

The jury spent four days considering the evidence, and at the end of it they found Janet Charlton not guilty of murder but guilty of manslaughter, accepting her plea of provocation. They decided that it must have been O'Brien who had taken the axe into the bedroom, and that he threatened her with it before allowing himself to be placed in a vulnerable position. "This was not self-defence. You lost your self-control and lashed out in a frenzy," said the judge, jailing her for five years.

•

Ten-year-old John Balaban, a Romanian, became a Peeping Tom involuntarily. One night his father came home more drunk than usual. He woke his wife and tried to make love. When she fought him off, Balaban *père* dropped to his knees at the foot of the bed and, sobbing, tried to wheedle her into embracing him. She sat up in bed, her face twisted with hatred, lashing the unhappy man with obscene taunts into greater self-humiliation.

Through a crack in the door young John Balaban watched all this, fascinated. He was both convulsed with shame for his father and with rage against his mother. The experience incised itself on his memory.

Hatred of one's mother (or father) is not infrequently cited in the psychological condition of some sex-murderers. It springs from an interference to the proper adjustment of the Oedipus complex and may arise from neglect or brutality caused by one of the parents. In psychoanalysis, the Oedipus complex is a group of emotions, usually unconscious, involving the desire of a child, especially a male child, to possess sexually the parent of the opposite sex, while at the same time excluding the parent of the same sex. An inadequate personality may extend his dislike of women – misogyny – by way of an antagonistic attitude to females in general; this almost always springs from a sense of inferiority coupled with fear of rejection as a result of the earlier experiences with the mother.

A year after young John Balaban had watched the bedroom incident involving his parents, his father came home late again and drunk, and his mother gave him her characteristic bellicose welcome. On that occasion she emptied a bowl of dishwater over his head and chased him out of the apartment. That same night he fumbled up to the attic and hanged himself. When the tragedy was discovered John was forced to help his mother cut down the body.

The Second World War came to Romania, and when it was over Balaban went to Paris. He was a gauche, tongue-tied young man, haunted by his loathing for his mother and his sub-conscious desire to transfer her sins to all women and punish them for them. As we have seen, in such cases the perpetrator often vents his impotent rage on prostitutes, because they are the most vulnerable. One evening he picked up a girl in the city centre and, notwithstanding that she was not a prostitute, she invited him back to her flat.

Balaban said later: "She just fell into my arms. She was shameless and reminded me of the prostitutes on the boulevards. She was like a dirty animal that should be destroyed...I leaned over her naked body that offered itself to my eyes with its stillness of a foul cadaver. I put my hands around her neck and squeezed. Her face was ugly in death. I had to punish her some more. I got my knife and dug into her."

The killer decided to flee to the other side of the world – to Adelaide. There in July, 1952, he met Joyce Cadd, a 29-year-old divorcee who had a six-year-old son and who owned the Sunshine Café. Two months later they married, and almost immediately Balaban was feeling uneasy about their physical relationship. Joyce tried to show him more affection, but her husband's reaction was a growing distaste for her.

One night he exploded: "You're a filthy slut! You make me hate all women." He packed his bags and went. The marriage had lasted three months. Later he wrote: "Joyce was insatiable. She would exhibit herself with the shamelessness of a prostitute. I was greatly relieved to have left."

Balaban met another girl, Zora Kusic, who asked for money for sex. "That disgusted me for good," he wrote. "I got out my knife and threw her on the bed. It gratified me to slash her abdomen, to cut off her breasts and slice her throat from ear to ear. To punish her foul body gave me immense satisfaction." After he killed her he had sex with her body.

The Romanian had now killed twice and he was explicit in his self-justification – on both occasions he had used the word "punish." In fact, he was no different from the lust murderer who kills for love – such killers want to possess something they love or hate, and in Balaban's case the operative word was hate. He was never to forget his mother's treatment of his father, and the "punishment" he was meting out was punishment that, in his sub-conscious, he was inflicting on his mother. He saw his mother as a low woman, and so was Zora. "I did not feel sorry to have cut Zora Kusic's throat. I think I was quite justified in doing so. She was a low woman and deserved to die."

Balaban was arrested for the murder, but there was insufficient evidence against him to justify a guilty verdict, and he was acquitted. In January, 1953, his wife Joyce, who had stood by him during the trial, took him back, although he slept in his own room and they never resumed normal marital relations.

Two months later he went for a walk along a riverbank, where the courting couples "made my blood boil." He found an iron bar and, "I went on the hunt for the filthy-minded couples that befoul the lawns along the river. I hate to see public kissing and necking." He "slugged" two courting couples, who miraculously survived their terrible injuries, then went to a café, where he spoke to a young girl. When she told him she was 14 he replied that he would teach her a lesson, and beat her into unconsciousness. That same day he left his wife for the second time and booked into a hotel.

The next night Balaban crept quietly back into the marital home. Armed with a claw hammer, he beat to death his wife, her son, and his mother-in-law. He was arrested by an armed policeman while walking on the roof of the house next door.

During his trial he wrote his autobiography. "Joyce was like a prostitute," he said. "She made me feel I was nothing but a stud to her. Any red-blooded man would have done what I did. I didn't mean to kill my mother-in-law, but she kept interfering."

Psychiatrists decided that John Balaban was neither mentally disordered nor deficient. His trouble, they said, was abnormality of character, combined with an unwillingness to conform to the ordinary standards of society. He knew he was wrong, but liked to see himself in the role of a judge of morals. They had heard about how he had grown to hate his mother, and about the searing images of his childhood, but in their view that wasn't enough to save him from the hangman three days after Christmas, 1953.

CHAPTER TEN

ANIMALS; POST-MORTEM VOYEURISM
Ed Kemper, Alan Victor Wills, Richard Chase, John Norman Collins

An American psychiatrist has reported on cases in which men with sadistic tendencies have avoided execution by diverting their murderous compulsions to animals. In one such case the man always took a chicken with him when he was visiting a brothel. In front of the recumbent prostitute he would wring the chicken's neck – an act which, he felt, was necessary to prepare him for sexual intercourse. Without the chicken he was impotent.

What held his attention was not the woman but the sadistic cruelty he was practising on the chicken – the role of the woman in such cases is only to gratify the desire once the man has been aroused by his perverted cruelty. Of course, the man with the chicken needed to find prostitutes willing to acquiesce in his bizarre behaviour, and fortunately he did find them. Had he not done so he might have had to acquire a woman by force; then, abandoning the chicken surrogate, killed her instead. For in such cases, the assault on the chicken is a substitute for an assault on the woman – the animal is killed for sexual gratification instead of the prostitute.

The chicken, obviously, resists being killed, and its resistance also helps to arouse the pervert. Without the chicken he might seek out a woman who doesn't want sex with him, and resists him, and the more she resists the more excited he becomes.

The killing of animals linked to sexual killing of women is not confined to America. After buying 28 ferrets, a duck, a polecat and 40 chickens at an auction, John Taylor, a serial killer living in Bramley, Leeds, killed them all. It was said that Taylor, who sold pet food from a market stall and from his terraced home, enjoyed torturing and destroying animals.

He turned to humans by waylaying Leanne Tiernan,

16, seizing her by the shoulders and "stifling her after she had emitted one scream." He blindfolded her with his scarf, threw his hooded coat over her, and then frogmarched her on the 20-minute walk to his home. There he forced her into his bedroom and bound her, before strangling her with his scarf and tie.

When Leanne's body was found there was no evidence of sexual assault, the prosecutor told the court at Leeds Crown Court in July, 2002, but "the motive for killing her was for the purpose of sexual gratification."

John Taylor, who was divorced and lived alone, owned four dogs and killed all of them because, investigators believed, newspaper reports of the murder mentioned a dog-walker seen using the footpath where Leanne was seized. The police subsequently unearthed the dogs' skeletons, one with a smashed skull, in Taylor's back garden.

When police appealed for information from anyone who knew the area and the killer, some women came forward to testify about Taylor's appetite for bondage. This would not surprise a psychiatrist, because sexual murders often involve a complication of motives. The most obvious motive, perhaps the one the killer confesses to, may have behavioural significance only because of some deeper and less recognised motive. It was not determined in Taylor's case which was the most clearly recognised motivational determinant – the killing of animals or the tying-up of victims – and which was the least recognised. One woman said Taylor had tied her with twine to the four corners of the bed and self-locking plastic cable ties, fixed round her wrists and ankles. Tight cables were tied around each of her breasts. Another said Taylor told her he wanted to bind her so that she couldn't move, and he could do whatever he wanted with her. He also told her he would like to tie up her 15-year-old daughter and have sex with her. These remarks were made only four months before he murdered Leanne.

Taylor had still another, possibly still lesser, motivation of necrophilic voyeurism, in that he kept Leanne's body at his house for anything between three weeks and nine months. He had three deep freezers in which he kept the pet food he sold, and medical examination of Leanne's cardiac tissue suggested that her body had been refrigerated.

Taylor was given two life sentences, one for Leanne's kidnapping and one for her murder, with a corollary that he should never be released. But the problem of determining what goes on inside the mind of a sexual murderer is best illustrated by comments made by his customers, who confessed to being stunned when he was charged with murder. "He was just an ordinary bloke. It's just unbelievable," said one. And another said: "He was as normal as anyone else around here."

•

Sexual stimulation from animal suffering is not as rare as it might seem. Porn queen Tracey Seward, of Sale, Manchester, also killed animals – mice and frogs – although this was for the sexual satisfaction of her clients. She performed her killings on videos, and there was apparently a regular demand for them. Ms. Seward, 38, the daughter of a high-ranking police officer, called herself Stiletto, and dressed in leather gear and high heels. She tortured and killed the defenceless creatures while the probing lens of her common-law husband, Philip Brierley, recorded everything. They posted the films on the internet and spent hours in chat-rooms talking to fans. She built up a cult following of fans who would do anything for her.

One of the fans, Giona Previtali, 26, a Swiss, became her lover. When Philip Brierley objected, Ms. Seward persuaded another of her fans, Christopher Cassidy, 37, to murder Brierley by shooting him. Giona Previtali then cut up the body into seven parts, set them in quick-drying cement, and dumped them under an M60 motorway bridge. Finally overcome by remorse, Cassidy went to the police and confessed, and in July, 2002, Tracey Seward and her two accomplices were each given a life sentence.

It goes without saying that the instigators, the cult and the "fans" of this kind of sexual perversion are all exceedingly dangerous, because obtaining vicarious thrills by participating in the death of an animal can easily be transformed into obtaining thrills by participating in the death of a human being.

•

When Ed Kemper was a teenager he was six-foot-four and had a "superior" IQ. Despite that, his very strict mother thought he might become a homosexual and needed toughening up, so she locked him in the dark basement every night, dragging the kitchen table over the trap-door to make double-sure he stayed there until morning. She was able to do this because Kemper's self-esteem was at the bottom of the scale – he despised himself.

His mother had other doubts about her son, with good reason. Young Ed had buried one of the family's cats alive, subsequently digging it up and slicing off its head, which he kept in his bedroom, praying to it. He had also killed his sister's pet cat, burying part of it and hiding the remainder in a cupboard.

Ed Kemper went to live with his grandparents in the foothills of California's Sierra Nevada Mountains in August, 1964. Finding his grandmother an even worse harridan than his mother, he took a gun and shot her through the head, then stabbed her repeatedly. Shortly after that, his grandfather returned home and Kemper shot him dead too.

For the next five years Kemper, a paranoid schizophrenic, was incarcerated in a state hospital that housed both sex offenders and the criminally insane. There he enjoyed listening to the recollections and the boasts of the rapist inmates. They all seemed to have been caught through their victims identifying them, which suggested to him that the way to become an accomplished rapist was to leave none of the women alive.

In 1969 this ticking time bomb was released – into the care of his mother, despite the fact that the authorities believed she was responsible for his problems. He was now six-foot-nine and a muscular 20 stone.

His killing spree began by picking up female university student hitchhikers as he cruised the access roads of the freeways in San Francisco. After killing the first two students in his car, he took the bodies home to his bedroom, stripped them, decapitated them, and dissected them in the bath, recording his progress with a Polaroid camera. Later he buried the body parts in the mountains, keeping the heads as trophies.

He raped his next victim, a 15-year-old schoolgirl, after he had rendered her unconscious, then strangled her. While her body was in his car boot he went to talk to his mother, to determine for himself whether he could keep cool in the knowledge of what he had done. His mother noticed nothing unusual in his manner, and he returned to his car, well pleased with himself. Decapitating the girl's corpse, he left the head in his car boot and took the body to his room for dissecting.

It is worth remembering that this young giant had a "superior" IQ, because he was using it to convince himself that he could cover up his horrific crimes. With the head of the girl still in his car boot, he drove to an appointment with two psychiatrists appointed by the state hospital to monitor him as part of his condition for release. They told him they were so pleased with his progress they would recommend the sealing of his juvenile record. This would virtually erase his past, and it would allow him to buy a gun.

The psychiatrists reported: "We are dealing with two different people when we talk of the 15-year-old boy who committed the murders [of his grandparents] and the 23-year-old man before us now."

Kemper bought his gun in January, 1973, and pushed it into the ribs of an 18-year-old student who had thumbed a lift, before shooting her dead. He took the corpse home, hid it in a cupboard, and after his mother had gone to work next morning he committed necrophilia on it, before dissecting it and tossing the body parts over a hilltop road. This time he buried the head in his back garden, beneath his bedroom window. "I talked to it," he later told police. "I said affectionate things, like you would say to a girl friend or a wife."

Two more girl hitchhikers were shot and decapitated. He took one of the headless bodies to his room and had sex with it, then threw both bodies into Eden Canyon, near San Francisco.

Kemper said to himself, "What's good for my victims is good for my mother." So he slit his mother's throat and cut off her head. Later that evening, Sally Hallett, a friend of his mother's, phoned. Kemper told Mrs. Hallett that he had been trying to contact her to invite her over for dinner with his mother and himself that night. The rendezvous was fixed for 7.30 p.m. and when Mrs. Hallett arrived he put her in a stranglehold that crushed her larynx. After undressing her and having sex with her body on his bed, he went for a drink. On his return he cut off Mrs. Hallett's head and then went to sleep on his mother's bed.

When he woke up he did the only thing that was left for him to do – he fled. Police broke into his mother's home, found the two corpses, and tracked him down. Today he is serving life imprisonment with no chance of parole. A model prisoner, he spends much of his time recording books for the blind. He was chosen for this role because of his pleasant voice.

•

Kemper's intelligence helped him to become overtly and articulately self-revealing. His younger sister recalled him cutting off the head and hands of one of her dolls. His elder sister told how he confessed to having a crush on his schoolteacher. "Then why don't you kiss her?" his sister had asked. "I can't," he told her. "I'd have to kill her first."

Talking about his victims he said, "Alive, they were

distant, not sharing with me. I was trying to establish a relationship...I had to evict them from their human bodies...if I killed them they couldn't reject me as a man. It was more or less making a doll out of a human being, carrying out my fantasies with a doll, a living human doll." Fear of rejection was finally obscured in an encrustation of fantasy.

He had kept and eaten parts of some of his victims, he said. Decapitating also turned him on. "There was almost a climax to it. It was kind of an exalted, triumphant-type thing, like taking the head of a deer or an elk or something, would be to a hunter."

When he picked up a hitchhiker he became elated. "When someone put their hand on that doorknob, that's it. They're giving me their life."

One student hitchhiker had kept cool before he killed her, and that profoundly impressed him. He regarded her with reverence, revisiting her grave to be near her. "I loved her and wanted her." Significantly, she was the only victim who had talked to him when she began to realise his intention. But like the true schizophrenic he was, buried in his conscious mind was a solid wall that blocked out his murderous role. For Kemper gave lifts to many students without incident. As he drove along many of them talked about the "Co-ed Killer," as the press were dubbing the murderer, speculating on what he was like. He was never able to bring himself to kill a passenger who introduced this topic of conversation because he knew that such an act would confront him with his own guilt.

It emerged that after the first killing he became engaged to a 17-year-old girl, who was still his fiancée when he was arrested. He was "a perfect gentleman," she said, and their relationship was purely platonic. Ed Kemper, after all, preferred sex with corpses.

The case of Ed Kemper shows that sexual killing – lust murder – and necrophilia are closely akin to each other. This was certainly known to De Sade, who wrote about men who tortured women, killed them during intercourse, then found their greatest sexual gratification in having sex on their corpses. The necrophiliac is able to relax completely knowing that his sexual partner is dead for, as with Kemper, he holds himself in low self-esteem and fears rejection. It does not matter that the female partner cannot respond, for he calls upon his imagination to feed his brain with all the visual images necessary to satisfy his lust.

•

Trying to reach conclusions about the state of mind of sexual killers is never helped by the conflict of medical evidence in court. It almost always happens that the prosecution will call expert medical evidence that will be rebutted by expert medical evidence called by the defence. Both medical witnesses are obviously telling the truth as they understand it, so it is left to a somewhat bewildered jury of non-experts to decide who is right. One such typical case – one of thousands – was the trial of Alan Victor Wills, a 33-year-old kitchen porter at the Palace Hotel in Birkdale, near Southport, for the rape and strangulation of a six-year-old girl in his room in the hotel's staff quarters.

Wills forced intercourse on the girl, holding her throat with one hand to stifle any cries for help, but claimed that he could not remember anything about the crime.

Called by the defence at Liverpool Crown Court in November, 1961, Dr. William Sharpe, medical superintendent of a local hospital specialising in the treatment of the mentally subnormal, said Wills had a mental age of 11. In ordinary conversation he was cheerful, co-operative and apparently normal. But he had a histrionic attitude, as though he were acting a part, and this was incongruous in view of his situation. He was on the borderline between definite sub-normality and "the low average." He had an abnormal mind, and he had less mental responsibility than a normal person.

If there was amnesia suggested, it was "emotional," said the doctor, and he agreed it was an easy refuge for anyone to take when something dreadful has happened, to say they didn't remember anything about it. He thought that Wills had the ability to form a rational judgment as to whether an act was right or wrong, although his capacity for self-control was limited because of his mental sub-normality.

When Dr. Sharpe stood down the prosecution called their expert, Dr. W. J. Gray, senior medical officer at Walton Prison. He thought Wills was mentally alert, with a good appreciation of the situation.

"Only yesterday I observed him in the exercise yard, and he was walking briskly and chatting with others. But when he was called from the yard and I interviewed him, it was as though a curtain was drawn over our conversation and I was seeing someone quite different."

Wills, he went on, was not suffering from any mental abnormality sufficient to substantially impair his responsibility for his actions.

"I formed the opinion that he knew more than he cared to admit or was willing to discuss about the events on the night of the murder."

Dr. G. P. Egan, a psychiatrist, told the court that Wills could judge between what was right and wrong, but he was less able than an ordinary man to resist temptation and control his impulses. He was emotionally immature, writing letters to his estranged wife that he never posted, and this was an abnormal "fantasy relationship."

Did Wills have an abnormal mind, or didn't he? Should the full force of the law be brought to bear on a man with a mental age of 11, on the borderline of being subnormal? Or was he covering up, as the prosecution's witness – in marked contrast to the defence evidence – suggested? And to what degree can a man guilty of rape and murder claim that he is less able than ordinary men to resist temptation and control his impulses? It may be said that even less is known about the minds of jurors than about the minds of sexual killers, so none of this apparently gave much of a problem to the jury in the case of Alan Wills. They took only 40 minutes to convict him, and he was jailed for life.

In the eyes of the law, Dennis Nilsen, Jerry Brudos and Peter Kurten were not insane. So it is important for the psychiatrist to understand what the law regards as sanity, so that he can separate criminals who appear to act in the same way as such men, but whom the law would classify as insane.

At trials in crimes of sexual sadism where there is irrefutable prosecution medical evidence that the defendant is sane within the legal meaning of that word, the defence customarily resorts to the argument that he was insane "at the time." The point made is that you can bounce in and out of insanity, which is convenient if you are going about committing crimes.

But what if the defendant is mad anyway, before, during and after he has committed the crime? In that event it is the prosecution, of course, which has to prove its case.

One case – it is almost certainly the only one – in the criminal history of human vampirism where the vampire was probably not a sadist killer but was simply deranged, was the case of the "Sacramento Vampire" Richard Chase, who murdered six times.

Before he turned murderer, Chase habitually killed rabbits and birds and drank their blood. He would also take buckets of blood from cattle and drink that too. When he became a killer he would shoot his victim, then slit open the abdomen and drink its blood.

There was neither sadism nor sexual gratification in any of these acts – Chase was acting under the delusion that his body was continually running out of blood and the only way he could keep himself alive was to kill and take it from other people.

His condition was caused by massive and chronic depression, for which he was treated while under arrest with drugs handed out daily. Although clearly insane, he was sentenced to die by lethal gas in San Quentin. At some point, though, he had begun to hoard his drug supply, and on December 26th, 1979, he swallowed the whole of his secret cache, laid down on his cell bunk and died.

It is difficult to analyse the mind of a sexual sadist who is already crazy, because one needs to go deeper and find out what made him mad in the first place. Take, for instance, the child-killer John Straffen. He argued that he killed little girls to show the police that he wasn't mad. It is easy to label such a man as wilfully evil, but it is much more likely that his reasoning faculties simply don't exist, and he is therefore completely insane.

So sadistic child-killer John Straffen was mad, and sadistic child-killer Robert Black, whose case we covered in Chapter Four, wasn't. Yet there are similarities in the backgrounds of the two that may make us scratch our heads over the meaning of insanity.

The key to Black's psyche lies in his depressing upbringing, punctuated by the schoolmaster sexually abusing him. A man who is sexually abused as a boy and then sexually abuses little girls is taking on the role of the abuser, and the girl becomes representative of his weak victim self. Black grew up to detest his weaker self, and therefore detested the little girls he killed. In the nature versus nurture dialogue, there is a strong argument here for nurture, for surely it is in such cases as that of Robert Black that our society creates its own criminals,

•

We may not yet be able to identify sex killers through their genes, but there are visible similarities in the backgrounds of young men who kill for sex. John Norman Collins was a student at Ypsilanti University in Ann Arbor, eastern Michigan, before he became the principal suspect in the rape and killing of six students in 1969. Like Ted Bundy, Collins was good-looking, superficially good-natured and highly intelligent, and as with Bundy the seeds of his violent behaviour were probably sown in his childhood. His mother divorced, married a new husband whom she divorced after only a year, then married for a third time a man who turned out to be an alcoholic and a wife-beater. By the age of nine John Collins had had three fathers and was entitled to be somewhat confused about his identity.

His sister Gail was 18 when she became pregnant and had to get married. The marriage didn't last and a few years later Collins met her in the company of another man. He beat the man unconscious and hit Gail until she bled. At that time Collins was just 18. When his behaviour was analysed at his later trial for murder he was said to have fantasised about beating and torturing women.

At university Collins was suspected of stealing $40 from the entertainment fund and dropped out. Other petty thefts were revealed and Collins seemed to be the culprit. Then he became a burglar. The pattern of childhood problems followed by petty crime was thus set – the next step was sexual killing.

Collins became a compulsive post-mortem voyeur during his violent killing spree. When the body of his first victim was at the undertakers he called in and, introducing himself as a friend of the dead girl's family, asked if he could take a photograph of her as a keepsake. He was refused, of course, the horrified receptionist noting as he left that he was not carrying a camera.

After brutally beating, raping and then strangling his victims, Collins would hide their bodies in remote places, like disused buildings, and return to them several times, when he probably committed necrophilia on the corpses. Yet there were two personae named Collins. We have seen the psychopath; the other one was religious. Brought up by his Roman Catholic mother who had been excommunicated because of her divorces, he claimed to hold to the tenets of the Catholic church and once severely reprimanded a girl with whom he was dancing for holding herself too close to him. This religious streak is very common in Collins's psychopathic type.

The killer in 1947 of Elizabeth Short, otherwise known as The Black Dahlia, arguably the most talked-about murder in Hollywood, has never been found. In a recent book, *Black Dahlia Avenger*, published by Arcade Publishing, New York, author Steve Hodel, a former Los Angeles Police Department homicide detective, claims that the man who committed the crime was his father, Dr. George Hodel, who was a celebrated physician in Los Angeles in the 1940s.

Steve Hodel also claims that his father, teaming up with an artist friend, murdered most of the other 11 lone women killed in LA between 1943 and 1949.

If Steve Hodel is right – and his case is compelling – Dr. Hodel was an unusual serial sexual killer because he had an IQ of 186 – that is one more than Einstein.

At the time of the murder, in which the victim was tortured and mutilated, the consulting psychiatrist of the LAPD was Dr. Paul de River who, two days after the murder, profiled the killer as a man who "hates womankind" and was "a sadistic fiend." He was not typical because "in his act the murderer was manifesting a sadistic component of a sado-masochist complex." He was evidently following the law of analytical retaliation, "what has been done to me, I will do to you."

Dr. de River commented: "These types of killers are usually highly perverted, and resort to various forms of perversion and means of torture to satisfy their lusts. Above all, they seek the physical and moral pain and the disgraceful humiliation and maltreatment of their victims. They have a superabundance of curiosity and are liable to spend much time with their victims after the spark of life has flickered and died." Such a killer may be a studious type delighting in feeling in himself the humiliation of his victim. He is "the experimenter and analyst in the most brutal forms of torture."

If Dr. Hodel was the killer, it was likely that he was overwhelmed by two things: his sexual appetite, and the enormous inner superiority he felt over the rest of humankind as a result of his genius-level IQ, a superiority that brooked no refusal to his expressed will. The Black Dahlia refused to marry him, therefore he had to have his revenge upon her. In such a person nothing must stand in his way – retribution will if necessary include sadistic and violent murder to expunge the hurt he feels. Just as frighteningly, Dr. Hodel was to all outward appearances perfectly normal, a pillar of society, much respected by his patients. Few would have guessed that inwardly he was in turmoil.

CHAPTER ELEVEN

Are sexual killers born or made?
VMPC – damage to the prefrontal lobe
*Phineas Gage, Donta Page, Jeremy Skocz,
Steven Parkus*

To find out how men become sexual killers, we might do well to study how children learn about right and wrong, good and evil, in the first place. McGill University psychologist John Macnamara believes that they learn it in much the same way that they learn about geometry and mathematics. Moral development isn't merely cultural learning, coming about through innate principles that have evolved through natural selection – it involves the construction of a formal system that makes contact with the external world in a special way.

Commenting on this proposal, Paul Bloom, Professor of Psychology at Yale, says: "This cannot be entirely right. We know that gut feelings, such as reactions of empathy or disgust, have a major influence on how children and adults reason about morality." Nor, he adds, can the role of natural selection in shaping our moral institutions be ignored. But Macnamara's proposal helps us to "reject the nihilist position...that our moral institutions are nothing more than accidents of biology or culture." And so he too believes that the development of moral reasoning is "the same sort of process as the development of mathematical reasoning."

In an attempt to answer the question of whether or not we are responsible for our actions, scientists are continually searching for clues to the mental flaws that might produce a serial killer. To this end they have started to preserve the brains of criminals. One such is Harold Shipman, the Hyde, Cheshire, doctor who hanged himself in Wakefield Prison in 2002, after being jailed for life for killing 15 of his patients. An official inquiry concluded he had murdered between 215 and 265 patients, making him Britain's worst serial killer.

Tissue from Shipman's brain has been genetically tested and analysed with imaging cameras, using the latest techniques of brain mapping, to find out whether there are traits that could cause behavioural abnormalities. It has also been examined for signs of degenerative disease or structural abnormality, but reports suggest that nothing unusual has been found.

The subject is a controversial and sensitive one, and officialdom doesn't like talking about it. After earlier denials, the Home Office admitted in 2004 that the brains of mass murderers Fred West and Michael Ryan have been kept for similar analysis. The brain of the gangster Ronnie Kray was also secretly removed. Those in the scientific team who are responsible for the tests on these brains include scientists from Broadmoor.

To date there is no evidence of characteristics that could identify potential murderers in advance. But there is considerable interest in the field. The brains of notorious killers are being preserved until research moves forward sufficiently for brain tissue to yield information about major "mis-wiring."

The view of scientists in this field is that our biology affects the way we think, how our emotions are expressed, and everything about us. If they can discover why a particular set of genes interact with particular life experiences to create violence, they may be able to develop ways of preventing it.

Harold Shipman had bequeathed his body to scientific research, but it was thought that medical students would not be too happy about dissecting his body after recognising its owner. So his brain was removed for investigation and the rest of the body is being kept in long-term frozen storage at Sheffield University's Medico Legal Centre.

The analysis of criminals' brains is not new. Studies were made on the brain of Thomas Hamilton, who murdered 16 children and their teacher in Dunblane, Stirlingshire, in 1996. They revealed a thyroid disorder associated with violent behaviour.

That this is a science with a promising future is no

better illustrated than by the fact that researchers at the Institute of Psychology in Camberwell, southeast London, have identified an association between MAOA, a gene controlling signals in the brain, and anti-social behaviour. Another related project has used the latest generation of imaging techniques to examine the structures of the brains of dozens of patients at Broadmoor and other hospitals treating violent mentally disordered offenders. Scientists working on this project have already found patterns associated with particular traits.

In America scientists have been searching for years for physiological indications of criminal tendencies, concentrating on genes rather than brain structure. But there is plenty of opposition to their work. There was for instance much public disgust at a plan to conduct research on the brain of Jeffrey Dahmer, the cannibal homosexual killer who murdered 17 men before being bludgeoned to death in prison. The idea was abandoned.

The objections to this type of research are legion, raising as it does all sorts of issues. Suppose, for instance, scientists find genes that turn people into monsters. What are they then going to do with them? Suppose, too, that a rogue scientist then planted these characteristics into normal people. These are the ethical considerations that plague so much scientific research.

One eminent forensic psychiatrist who believes that serial killers are born and not made is Dr. Helen Morrison, of Illinois. She has made a special study of John Wayne Gacy, executed in 1994 for torturing, raping and killing 33 men and boys. She keeps Gacy's brain in the basement of her home for research purposes, with the permission of Gacy's family.

Dr. Morrison doesn't believe that serial killers commit their crimes because they were abused physically or sexually by their parents when they were young. She believes that their addiction to killing stems from a genetic anomaly – a fault in the hypothalamus, which is the part of the brain that regulates emotions and moods. Other indicators are chemicals in the body, such as oxytocin and vasopressin, that trigger emotions. She seeks to discover whether a killer has an imbalance of these substances or a lack of receptor attachment in the brain, or whether he experiences a neurochemical change that kicks in with puberty.

Dr. Morrison, who has interviewed more than 80 serial murderers, describes in her book *My Life Among Serial Killers*, co-written with Harold Goldberg and published by John Wiley, the moment when she interviewed Michael Lee Lockhart, who specialised in eviscerating his victims. He is thought to have killed up to 20 women before his arrest in Texas in 1987. He told her how he got up late one morning and while he was in the shower: "It hit me. I had to go out and get me one."

For Dr. Morrison, this was a key sentence. "In my psychiatric practice I treat drug addicts. They have to get their drug and nothing else exists. The drugs for people like Lockhart are the people they murder. They are addicted to killing."

•

So can people really be born bad? Is it inevitable they will turn out to be morally blind, raping and killing? A scientific study published by the University of Virginia in 2007 proposed that the answer might be yes. The study suggests that character defects such as criminal behaviour are interwoven in our DNA. More surprising, it suggests that such inherent defects have little or nothing to do with influences to which we are subjected in infancy. In other words, a criminal is predestined to be a criminal.

It is a study that won't be taken seriously by many scientists because there remains deep division in scientific circles about whether we are born bad (nature) or become bad (nurture). Where the "born bad" notion falls down is that if criminal tendencies are linked to DNA, why is it that someone like Jeffrey

Dahmer becomes a cannibal serial killer and his brother is perfectly normal? It is much more probable that we have a choice as we mature – to behave badly or to behave well. The first option is an easy one; the second needs to be learned. The Roman philosopher Seneca summed it up: "Nature does not give a man virtue. The process of becoming a good man is an art."

•

American investigators have discovered that serial sexual killers have very high levels of testosterone – the chemical that causes men to act on their impulses. These high levels are at their peak in men aged between 16 and 30 – when men are most likely to commit sexual crimes and murder.

In America, this condition is treated by drug injection – prisoners call it chemical castration. After treatment, obsessive thoughts and fantasies begin to diminish. "The monster is still present but the medication has rendered him impotent," is the way that serial killer Michael Ross, who raped and murdered eight women and became the first man sentenced to death in Connecticut for 25 years, put it.

Ross kidnapped his victims along the same road he drove while on his way to work, and took them into nearby woods to satisfy his lust. He told investigators that an irresistible urge would come over him to satisfy his craving for a woman; when he was arrested after someone reported a young woman getting into his car, he took police to each of the graves in which he had buried his victims, but said he couldn't believe what he had done. Dr. Fred Berlin, a psychiatrist who studied the Ross case, says that with such men "it makes sense to lower their testosterone levels."

In Germany castration isn't chemical but physical. Any prisoner found guilty of sexual violence who feels he has an abnormal sex drive can volunteer to have his testicles surgically removed. Each case is put before the "Castration Committee." When a prisoner has been castrated his release date is speeded up because, say researchers, a sexual criminal is 20 times less likely to re-offend after he has been castrated. Not everyone is agreed about that, however, as we have already seen in Chapter Five.

It does not follow that a man with high levels of testosterone will become a sexual killer. Testosterone levels rise in a man when he succeeds in any contest – for example; when he is watching his football team winning – or in any exhilarating situation when, in the classic contemporary cliché, he is "on a high." Increased testosterone levels don't bring murder into his mind, but high levels of it can cause some men to want to kill.

Medical researchers have also demonstrated that the bodies of violent men contain low levels of the chemical serotonin, and these low levels promote anti-social behaviour. They believe that a mother's touching and comforting of her baby can have a permanent effect on serotonin levels in the brain. So if the baby is a victim of disruptive care, his serotonin levels are permanently lowered – the mother, in effect, is determining the sort of man her child will become, for the way she cares for the infant will have a direct consequence on his behaviour in adulthood.

If this is right, we are one step away from a sexual killer pleading that he can't possibly be held responsible for his actions any more than he can be held responsible for the chemical imbalance in his body. It should be said that not everyone is convinced. A detective involved in the case of serial killer Michael Ross laughed off suggestions that Ross's problem was a chemical one. "He cold-bloodedly raped those defenceless women to satisfy his lust," the detective said. "When he was arrested he told us that he killed them just to stop them identifying him. He knew exactly what he was doing all along the line."

Courts are familiar with the defence of diminished responsibility, the defence lawyer arguing along the lines of, "This man has done something which no man in the full possession of his senses would do." They are familiar too with the defendant who is said to have had a bang on the head when he was young, a bang which completely changed his personality and which must be held accountable for his current criminal activities. Let us see how much truth can be extracted from this hypothesis.

We know that since the Second World War the average IQ of children has been steadily rising, while their social and emotional skills – tools that should be vital in the community and in community living – have been declining. There are a number of reasons for this, including the proliferation of visual media, the rise of the single-parent family, and the over-organisation of young lives resulting in the loss of "quality" togetherness time.

While today's children cope with these situations, the last part of their brain to become anatomically mature is still in formation. This is a small region behind the forehead that contains the ventromedial prefrontal cortex (VMPC) – the neural circuitry crucial to the acquisition of social and emotional abilities. The VMPC will not be properly formed for life until after the age of 21, perhaps not until the mid-20s. What this means is that the images, the experiences, much of the information a child needs for its social skills development, will not be there to be processed.

The results of this are there for all to see in steadily changing behavioural patterns such as increased aggression, immodesty, and lack of care and thought for others. Now, if the prefrontal-limbic part of the brain becomes damaged before its owner has reached full development in the mid-20s, these patterns may remain in a state of immaturity, or the individual's personality may be permanently changed.

One of the first such cases on record happened more than 150 years ago when an American construction worker named Phineas Gage received a bang on the head which his friends said completely changed his behaviour. On September 13th, 1848, Gage was using a yard-long iron rod to tamp blasting powder into a hole when the powder exploded and propelled the rod through his head. It entered his left cheek and exited through the top of his skull, passing through the front of his brain on the way.

Miraculously he survived. Not only survived but, according to one witness, walked away "talking with composure and equanimity of the hole in his head."

Friends said that before the accident he was an easy-going, well-mannered, sociable young man. After it, they said, he was completely different. He became a foul-mouthed, irascible drifter, an impenitent liar who behaved obnoxiously to everyone around him. He was unable to plan anything or hold down a job. In the words of his doctor, Gage's brain injury destroyed the balance "between his intellectual faculty and his animal propensities."

His accident revealed the function of the prefrontal lobe of the brain in controlling emotions, judgment and general behaviour. Subsequent research confirmed that injuries or diseases that damage this part of the brain can erode inhibition and judgment, promoting behaviour that is at best anti-social, at worst downright criminal. It can turn a model citizen into a dangerous psychopath, and a severe bang on the head causing concussion can be sufficient to damage that critical frontal brain-lobe.

VMPC abuse can also be caused by shaking a child, damaging its delicate brain tissue. The damage may not be investigated until the child grows up and turns to criminal activities, although researchers have noticed that people suffering from prefrontal lobe abuse generally have a short fuse.

Phineas Gage's injury set off the bang-on-the-head defence beloved of advocates when there is very little else to offer in mitigation. At 18, the serial sexual killer Fred West fell off a fire escape, struck his head on a concrete floor, and was unconscious for 24 hours. Before that accident, his family said, he was never aggressive. After it, he began to have violent rages and mood swings to such an extent that his doctor thought he might have suffered brain damage. Whether that was so or not we shall never know because West avoided justice by hanging himself in his cell before he could be tried.

But had he gone to trial his medical history and condition would surely have been investigated, and offered as a plea of diminished responsibility. The inference would have been that West could not be held totally accountable for what he was doing, an argument which, had it been upheld, might have reduced his murder charges to manslaughter.

In a recent Harvard University study neuroscientists traced abnormal moral choices – notably cold-blooded "utilitarian" judgments where one person's life is sacrificed for the greater good – to damaged emotional circuits, revealing how, in such cases, moral judgment fails without feelings. This is a discovery that will inform the philosophical debate about the degree to which moral judgments are based on norms or emotions.

One of the co-senior authors of the study, Professor Marc Hauser, said: "Our work provides the first casual account of the role of emotions in moral judgments." He emphasised that not all moral reasoning depended strongly on emotion. "A wide class of moral judgments are completely normal even without emotional input, showing that we have a cold moral calculus that operates without emotional inspiration," he said. But for a certain class of moral judgments the VMPC is important.

Researchers studied six people with damage to the VMPC who behaved in a matter-of-fact way when considering difficult dilemmas, such as, would you kill someone in the knowledge that they are about to kill six other people, so that one life is sacrificed instead of six? Most people would probably choose not to, even if they agree that in theory they should. But the study found the subjects with damage to the VMPC came to the logical conclusion that one life should be sacrificed in order to save several. These subjects stood out in their willingness to harm an individual. "Because of their brain damage, they have abnormal social emotions in real life. They lack empathy and compassion," said one of the researchers. Another said: "Most people without this specific brain damage will be torn. But these particular subjects seem to lack that conflict."

•

Now let us consider three American murder cases that have a common link.

Case No. 1: Donta Page. He was living in a rehabilitation centre in Denver, Colorado, in 1998. His stay at this halfway house was not proving much of a success and a decision was made to send him back to prison for the rest of his sentence. On the day that he found this out, six-foot-two Page, who weighed in at 20 stone, broke into a house two doors away from the rehabilitation centre. He hadn't been there for more than a few minutes when pretty 24-year-old Peyton Tuthill returned home to change her clothes. She had been to a job interview and was getting ready to return to work.

Peyton walked in on Page as he was rummaging through her kitchen searching for valuables. She ran screaming up the stairs, desperately trying to escape. But he caught her. He yanked an electric flex from its socket and bound her hands and feet. Then he left the way he'd come.

But as soon as he reached the street he changed his mind. He went back into the house, took a knife from the kitchen drawer and, threatening Peyton with it, raped her twice. She pleaded for her life, begging him to spare her. Instead, Page slit her throat and stabbed her repeatedly.

Case No. 2: Jeremy Skocz. At the age of only 18 in 1995 he left his adoptive parents, went to live with his father on a trailer park in Florida, and became one of America's most infamous child-murderers.

In one of the adjacent trailers lived four-year-old Shelby Cox. This angelic little girl with blonde hair and blue eyes was a favourite in the trailer park. Her parents were on good terms with Jeremy and his father. Shelby's father said the 18-year-old was "just like any other kid of that age." So much so, it seems, that one afternoon Mr. and Mrs. Cox asked Jeremy to baby-sit. When they left little Shelby was playing happily on their porch. When they came home again she had vanished.

Five days later Jeremy Skocz led police to where he had hidden her body. He admitted raping the child before binding her arms with electrical tape and murdering her.

Case No. 3: Steven Parkus. As a teenager he was sent to reform school, where he promptly assaulted a teacher, and while awaiting trial escaped and assaulted a local woman.

At his trial Parkus pleaded guilty to three felony charges and was sentenced to 17 years in the Missouri State Penitentiary. In November, 1985, he went into the cell of another inmate and bound him hand and foot to the bunk. While having sex with his victim he choked him to death.

Page, Skocz and Parkus are typical of the murderers who are executed in the United States every year, and in all three cases the prosecution demanded the death penalty. But all three were examined by the same psychiatrist, Dr. Dorothy Otnow Lewis, professor of psychiatry at the University of New York. As a result of her efforts, all three were saved from execution.

For 20 years Dr. Lewis has been studying the workings of the criminal mind., interviewing America's most infamous murderers and delving into their childhood histories. She trained as a psychoanalyst at Yale medical school – a perfect start for anyone hoping to become wealthy by listening to the problems of America's affluent professionals. But she was immediately intrigued by the conundrum of why some people are able to control their violent impulses while others commit heinous acts of murder.

This is of course a conundrum addressed by every criminologist and every politician responsible for law and order. But Dr. Lewis set out to seek the answer from the murderers themselves.

She and her research partner, Yale neurologist Professor Jonathan Pincus, reported their findings in a book, *Guilty by Reason of Insanity: A Psychologist Explores the Minds of Killers*. Its conclusions are currently having a considerable impact on the foundations of American justice.

Dr. Lewis concludes that all the killers she studied suffered childhood abuse and neglect, resulting in brain injuries and psychotic symptoms, especially paranoia.

"Long before these men wound up on Death Row," she writes, "their parents had battered them. They used them sexually. They sold their child's body to buddies in exchange for drugs or food or money. They neglected them. Sometimes they even tried to kill them. These brutish parents had set the stage on which our condemned subjects now found themselves playing out the final act. They had lived to perpetrate on others the violence that had been visited upon them."

The killer cocktail – abuse, brain damage and mental illness – produces someone programmed to murder. Dr. Lewis devotes most of her book to backing up her theory with detailed accounts of the backgrounds of the killers she has studied. Donta Page, Jeremy Skocz and Steven Parkus receive a great deal of her attention. There is no doubt that their experiences fit the thesis she expounds.

Case No. 1, Donta Page, was born to a 16-year-old single mother who was suffering from gonorrhoea. He never met his father and grew up without any parental care. His medical records chronicle a history of mental illness that showed itself in criminal behaviour, and a long history of drug and alcohol abuse.

Page was battered from birth. By the time he was nine months old he was a regular visitor to the local emergency hospital. At six months he fell from a top bunk on to his head. Three months later he fell out of a moving car, landing on his head again.

Later abuse took the form of violent shaking, punches

to the face and head, and beatings with electrical cables. When he was 13 he was taken to a casualty unit after his mother hit him on the head with an electric iron. Doctors found his body was covered with cigarette burns.

Apart from physical abuse, he suffered dreadful neglect. His mother would only feed and clothe him if he was able to pay. As a result, he spent a great deal of time living on the streets and sleeping in derelict buildings. At 10 he was taken to casualty, suffering from rectal bleeding resulting from a neighbour's savage sexual assault. His mother had made no effort to prevent this predatory neighbour from repeatedly abusing her son.

Convicted of a series of robberies and burglaries, Donta Page was sentenced to 20 years' imprisonment. He was then 18 years old.

Dr. Lewis claims that it is obvious to anyone who has spent some time with Page that he is mentally ill. A brain scan confirms this. It shows that the blows to his head have damaged the frontal lobe of his brain – the area that controls violent impulses.

Case No. 2, Jeremy Skocz, was born to parents who were heroin addicts. He spent the first seven years of his life in an atmosphere of violence, abuse and neglect. Then his fortunes changed. He was taken into care and eventually adopted by Mary Skocz. In the security of a loving home, he developed into a happy, normal adolescent.

But at the age of 15 Skocz became the victim of random violence. His assailants beat him over the head with baseball bats. X-rays of his skull did not show any serious damage, but the change in his personality was sudden and profound. He became violent, volatile and prone to fits of anger. Sometimes he behaved as if he were invincible. There were frequent arguments with his adoptive mother and he spent more and more time on the streets, eventually leaving home and setting out for Florida to look for his father. When he found him he also found hard drugs, causing an even steeper deterioration in his behaviour.

It was while he was living with his father in Florida that Mr. and Mrs. Cox asked him to look after Shelby.

Unusually for a convicted murderer in Florida, Skocz was spared execution and sentenced to life imprisonment. One of the principal reasons for this was that Dr. Lewis was able to produce brain scans showing that early abuse and the attack with the baseball bat had damaged the frontal lobes of Skocz's brain.

Case No. 3, Steven Parkus, is the saddest of all. He was born in 1960 to Linda and J. W. Parkus. Linda, a schizophrenic, spent most of her days drinking and taking drugs, even when she was pregnant. J. W. Parkus was a heavy drinker with a record of car theft. The family lived in a bug-infested apartment in the St. Louis area until Linda took the children and left J. W.

She continued to drink heavily and would not feed, clean or care for little Steve and his brother Chester. She was prone to terrible mood swings, and often her indifference turned to outright abuse. On one occasion she locked Steve and Chester in the bathroom. Steve climbed out of the window and wandered around until a police officer found him and brought him home. After the police left, his mother took a knife, held it over the stove and burned his buttocks with the hot blade.

In November, 1997, Steve and Chester began living with their great-aunt and uncle, Mr. and Mrs. Taylor Hampton. Any hopes Steve may have had that his life was about to improve were quickly dashed. Taylor Hampton was an alcoholic paedophile who regularly beat and savagely raped his nephew. He flogged Steve with a belt on a number of occasions, battered him with his fists and hit him on the head with a monkey wrench. Once he repeatedly slammed a door against the boy's head.

Taylor Hampton regularly tied Steve to a bed, beat him and forced him to perform oral sex, and to submit to anal sex.

On one occasion Chester lost his uncle's cigarettes. Hampton blamed Steve, and told him to put his hand on a kitchen worktop. Not knowing what was going to happen, he did as he was told. His uncle then hit Steve's hand with a meat cleaver, nearly severing the right index finger at the base.

Not surprisingly, Steve was a very disturbed child. He would run away from home at any opportunity and frequently became lost on his way home from school. At the age of eight years doctors diagnosed him as mentally retarded, with serious psychiatric disturbances. Tests revealed that "his consciousness seemed flooded with threatening, hostile thoughts." An examiner concluded that Steve "was very unstable at this time and may be psychotic."

During the next two years he alternated between in-patient treatment at St. Louis State Psychiatric Hospital and survival at the Hamptons. But his problems deepened. Juvenile delinquency landed him in the Booneville Training School, and when he was jailed for assaulting a teacher he escaped and assaulted a local woman, but did not injure her. Then came his 17-year prison sentence at the age of 17.

He was a small youth, and his size and age made him an easy target for other inmates' physical and sexual abuse. Early in his prison life he was gang-raped by 16 inmates. Prison documents indicate that one of them sold him for $60 for use as a sex slave. At one point he was stripped naked and paraded up and down a cellblock by prison guards who asked other inmates if they wanted him in their cell for sex.

On November 24th, 1985, Steve went into the cell of Mark Steffenhagen, with whom he was having a consensual homosexual relationship. Like Steve, Steffenhagen was small and he too was being victimised by predatory inmates. He and Steve had discussed suicide as a way to end their suffering. After choking Steffenhagen to death while having sex with him, Steve maintained that he had killed him to save him from further sexual abuse.

At Steve Parkus's trial the jury recommended the death penalty, but, after Dr. Lewis and other medical experts had testified, he was instead sentenced to life imprisonment. The defence testimony included the findings of Dr. Adrian Raine, an English psychologist who began his career in Britain's top-security prisons and is now an American university professor. For 23 year he has studied two questions: how are those who commit violent crimes different from the rest of us, and how do they get that way?

His brain-imaging studies of 41 convicted killers showed they all had malfunctioning of the prefrontal cortex of the brain. This, he noted, was liable to promote impulsiveness, immaturity, loss of self-control and an inability to modify behaviour. Dr. Raine suspects that the defects can be present at birth, and that if combined with childhood abuse and neglect they can induce violence.

Dr. Lewis's findings are also echoed by the results of research conducted by two American-based Portuguese neurologists, Antonio and Anna Damasio, who in 1990 found that people who had suffered damage to the front of the brain, and who previously had normal personalities, had since developed abnormal behaviour with a tendency to be aggressive, and with their ability to plan and make decisions diminished. Similar observations have been made by Swedish researchers who studied 21 violent criminals and found brain abnormalities in all but five of them.

Tests carried out on psychopaths – egocentrics without conscience – have also found them to be less fearful than normal people. They were not fazed by sudden loud noises that would startle most of us, and this indicated that they need greater stimulus than normal people in order to get their thrills. We have already seen this lack of normal feeling in the case of serial killer Ted Bundy. He knew what he was doing when he went killing, but he is believed not to have felt the emotions that such brutality would have evoked in ordinary people.

Taking their researches a step or two farther, some experts believe it should be possible to identify dangerous psychopaths through brain-scanning. Other experts believe it can't be as simple as that: the brain is highly complex, the frontal lobe being connected with other areas of which little or nothing is known, and it is impossible to make positive judgments from only part of the picture.

"There are a lot of factors involved in crime," says Dr. Raine. "Brain function is just one of them, but by understanding it we will be in a much better position to understand the complete causes of violent behaviour."

The time when dangerous psychopaths may be authoritatively identified by brain scans, taken out of circulation and treated with drugs developed for their condition, is remote and may never come. And as the law stands it is not an offence to be such a psychopath – we have to wait for him to commit his crime and be caught before he can be put away. He cannot be detained under the Mental Health Act because he is not mentally ill, and his condition is untreatable. Only the treatable can become mental patients.

The much larger issue is that if such killers commit their crimes involuntarily, programmed to behave as they do by their brain abnormalities, should they be held accountable and punished for acts they cannot help committing? This question is raised by those who believe that the psychopath's problem – to which he is indifferent – is biological, and the proper place for him is not prison but hospital. The same sort of reasoning eventually triumphed after much heart-searching during the First World War, when shellshock was not officially recognised. Many military men thought that men suffering from so-called shellshock should be shot for cowardice; the more enlightened, who won the day, knew that they should be treated in hospital.

If the argument about psychopaths is extended to its logical conclusion, however, there would be a lot of secure hospitals and a great number of redundant prisons. Prisoners like Roy Whiting, little Sarah Payne's callous Sussex murderer, and Michael Stone, the Kent killer of a mother and a daughter, could become patients, not prisoners, in a world in which no one is responsible for their actions.

Both Whiting and Stone displayed all the hallmarks of the psychopath, but they had the right to remain at liberty until they offended because being a psychopath is not classed as a mental illness. For this reason the judiciary tends to be sceptical of the psychopaths' lawyers' claims of diminished responsibility. The plea is often regarded as an excuse for the inexcusable, and there is equal suspicion of stories of personality disorders caused by bangs on the head. Such sceptics will be heartened to learn that the brain damage evidence given by Dr. Dorothy Lewis as a defence witness is not always successful.

In 1991 her testimony failed to save the Arkansas killer Ricky Ray Rector from the death penalty, but, as she said afterwards, you didn't have to be a psychiatrist to know there was something terribly wrong with him. When he ordered his last meal before his execution he requested the pecan pie to be set aside so he could have it later.

Psychologists have debated for decades whether human character is formed by nature – that we are born the way we are – or by nurture – that we become the way we are as a result of our environment. Sir Francis Galton, the inventor of fingerprinting, held that criminality was inherited; while in the same era Socialist reformers of the 20th century blamed it all on poor social conditions. Two Harvard researchers, James Wilson and Richard Hernstein, have demonstrated that criminals are generally less intelligent and have a lower level of self-control, apparently due to their slowness in responding to the their nervous systems. That icon of sex worshippers, the Marquis de Sade, was not unintelligent, but he accepted that he suffered a slow response system. He told his wife that he needed to be flogged and to inflict pain on others because of the dullness of his senses, which needed violent stimuli to arouse them.

Research into brain damage in childhood should not lead us to rule out the probability that some people deliberately choose violence. Experts cannot agree about how free will operates inside the criminal mind; in looking for reasons why people kill we should not jump to seemingly obvious conclusions. For instance, Al Capone killed a man after he got tertiary syphilis and people said, "Ah, he killed because he had syphilis." The problem that was conveniently ignored was that he had already killed a few other people before he got syphilis.

In his short story *Erostrate*, the French author and philosopher Jean-Paul Sartre wrote about a man named Paul Hilbert who decided of his own free will to become a murderer. First Hilbert wrote to a number of celebrated authors explaining his decision: "As soon as you meet a fellow human being you have empathy for him; a human being has human ways about him which you eulogise in your works." As a result, ordinary people devour the authors' works and praise them.

"I suppose you might be curious to know about someone who doesn't like human beings," Hilbert went on. "Such a man is me. I dislike them so much that soon I am going to kill half a dozen of them. Perhaps you will ask, why half a dozen. That's because my revolver has only six bullets. But I have to tell you that I am completely unable to like humankind. What attracts you disgusts me. But it is quite wrong that you should be admired and that I should not be. I am free to like lobster thermidor, but if I don't like people I am branded a misery."

Hilbert uses his torment to bring attention to himself – hence the title of the story, *Erostrate*. Told by a friend that Erostrate was a Greek who wanted to become famous, and that he thought the best way to go about it was to burn down the temple at Ephesus, one of the seven wonders of the world, Hilbert asks, "What was the name of the architect of that temple?"

His friend replies: "I don't remember. In fact, I don't believe anyone knows his name."

Hilbert laughs. "Really? Yet you remember the name of Erostrate. It seems he got it right!"

So perhaps Hilbert, like Erostrate, was seeking

self-aggrandisement and, being a nobody, chose the only method he was capable of to achieve fame – killing a fellow-human being. The phenomenon is not unknown.

•

This book has travelled only a short journey, but one that, if nothing else, makes it clear that the search for the dark secrets inside the minds of sexual killers must go on. To that end there follows an appendix in which two high-profile sexual killers talk about themselves, their motivations and the nature of what we call crime.

They are of interest, to be sure – but are they truthful? Many will say the confusing ego trips of Carl Panzram and his admirer Ian Brady are not helpful, and we should perhaps consign them to the margins where they belong. You be the judge.

APPENDIX

Two sexual killers discuss themselves
Carl Panzram, Ian Brady

In Chapter 11 we described the work of Dr. Dorothy Otnow Lewis, who talks to sexual killers about their motivation. Some sexual killers do not need too much coaxing to talk about themselves – they are only too willing to say why they killed. In recent times two high-profile sexual killers have been extremely articulate, recording their evilness for all of us to analyse and sigh over.

Carl Panzram died being exactly what he always wanted to be – a horrific serial killer. His boast – it could have been his epitaph – was chillingly simplistic:

"In my lifetime I have murdered 21 human beings," he declared. "I have committed thousands of burglaries, robberies, larcenies, arsons and last but not least I have committed sodomy on more than 1,000 male human beings.

"For all of these things I am not the least bit sorry. I have no conscience. I don't believe in man, God, nor Devil. I hate me. I hate the whole damn human race including myself. I preyed upon the weak, the harmless and the unsuspecting."

Half a century later Panzram was to excite the attention of a man whose appraisal of him he would have enjoyed immensely. That man was Ian Brady, the Moors Murderer, who with Myra Hindley raped, tortured and killed five youngsters. He described Panzram as "a killer fierce enough to send shivers of apprehension down even the spines of hardened criminals."

Panzram, Brady wrote in his book *The Gates of Janus*, was "a killing machine as lethal and remorseless as a shark."

In the early years of the 20th century, when serial killers were still something of a novelty, Panzram stood apart from the few others because he was also something of a philosopher. He wrote down his theories on serious crime and hardened criminals, and for social reformers this was something new – a literate serial killer.

Here there is a marked parallel with Ian Brady. For Brady too is a literate serial killer. His book was described by a psychiatrist who read it as "a remarkable document."

Panzram was also different from most serial killers because he was a rampant homosexual who enjoyed "committing sodomy," as he liked to put it, on his victims before killing them. He had quickly accepted from a very early age that he wasn't very bright, but he resented the constant beatings he got for his poor disciplinary reports. Early in the 20th century the undisciplined were seen as offending the Lord, and anti-social behaviour was therefore a sin that needed to be beaten out of the miscreant.

When he was sent to reform school he was put to work in the warders' kitchen, where he avenged himself on his tormentors. "I used to urinate in their soup, coffee or tea and masturbate into their ice cream or dessert and then stand right beside them and watch them eat it."

Panzram was the worst kind of killer because he was untroubled by any feelings of conscience; he was lacking in any remorse. But he attracted the attention of criminologists because in prison, where he spent a total of 22 of his 39 years, he read books on philosophy. Or at least he tried to. He generously admitted that he couldn't fathom out Kant and gave up his writings as a bad job.

It didn't matter to a new generation of reformers that what Panzram wrote was mostly conceited mumbo-jumbo about his criminal life, all that mattered was that here was a killer who could think, read and write – qualifications which would surely open the way to his own reformation.

Although, as we all now know, that simply isn't true, the liberal bleeding hearts still thought they were on to something exciting. They didn't even believe Panzram when he told them it wasn't true. "I know all about reforming people," he wrote. "I reform them regularly. How do I do it? I just kill them."

Even that didn't seem to overwhelm one prominent psychiatrist who examined him, and who wrote afterwards, "I carried away a vivid image of this earnest, very intense, very profane, very ugly, but obviously thoughtful individual faced with the problem of evil in himself and in the rest of us.

"He was a remarkable man in his fierceness, in his restless mental activity and his great embitteredness. I have always carried him in my mind as the logical product of our prison system."

How Panzram would have chuckled at that, for there was nothing he enjoyed more than someone else taking the blame for his misdemeanours – in this case the prison system. He knew the learned doctor was talking gobbledegook. "I have been a human animal ever since I was born," he said.

And when he was hauled before a court for being drunk and incapable he could hardly have held the prison system to blame, for at the time of that first offence he was eight years old.

His parents were German immigrants, and he assured the world that they always treated him like an animal from the day he was born in June, 1891. His father walked out of his Minnesota farm, leaving his mother with six children to bring up. As soon as he got home from school he was put to work on the farm until sundown. He was kicked and beaten regularly until he was about 11 years old, when, he says, he had a sort of Road to Damascus vision.

"At about that time I began to suspect that there was something wrong about the treatment I was getting from the rest of the human race. I began to see and hear that there were other places in the world besides my little corner of it. I began to realise that there were other people who lived nice, easy lives, and who weren't kicked around and worked to death."

The visionary decided to run away from home, but not before burglarising a neighbour's house. He was soon caught, yanked before a court, and sentenced to pass a few years in a reform school. There he was regularly whipped for failing to learn his Sunday School lessons.

Panzram claimed that he was beaten sometimes five times a week. He was sometimes stripped naked and tied, face downwards, to a large wooden block. An officer would soak a towel in salt water and spread it on his back.

"The man who did the whipping had a strap with a lot of little round holes punched through it. Every time the whip came down on the body the skin would come up through these little holes in the strap and after about 25 or 30 times of this, little blisters would form and then burst, and right there and then hell began. The salt water did the rest. About a week or two later a boy might be able to sit down on anything harder than a feather pillow."

Panzram nurtured his burgeoning hate and vowed that if he couldn't injure those who injured him, then he would injure someone else. Anyone, in fact. Meantime, he took his revenge by burning down the punishment room.

Reform school failed to make a Christian out of Carl Panzram. In fact it had exactly the reverse effect. "I was taught by Christians how to be a hypocrite and I learned more about stealing, lying, hating, burning and killing. I learned that a boy's penis could be used for something besides urination and a rectum could be used for other purposes than crepitating. All this made me decide that I would live my life robbing, burning, destroying and killing everywhere I went. I figured that if I was strong enough and clever enough to impose my will on others I would be all right." Something of the hopelessness of trying to break him must have got through to the authorities, because when he was 13 they discharged him from the school.

Panzram became a railcar hobo – riding the freight trains across America, a dangerous but nonetheless popular means of free travel among early-20th-century vagrants. Twice he was gang-raped by other hoboes. He made no particular complaint; the reverse, in fact. "I had discovered there were a lot of nice things in the world, among them whiskey and sodomy."

A petty theft landed him back in another reform school, where he regularly fell foul of an officer named Bushart, "who made it his special duty to make life miserable for me. He kept on nagging at me until finally I decided to murder him."

Panzram was then 14, and this was probably the only time he failed in a murder attempt. He hit Officer Bushart with a plank – "it didn't kill him but it made him pretty sick." He was beaten mercilessly for this, but he was too young to be sent to prison. Instead, he claimed, they took him to hospital and clipped off his foreskin to stop him from his habit of masturbation.

One night Panzram and another boy escaped from the school and lived on the road by robbing churches and setting them alight. When the cold weather set in he decided on a whim to enlist in the US Army. He was only 16 but he was already over six feet tall, and the recruiting sergeant had no difficulty in believing he was 18. But his military career was to last only a matter of weeks before he was court-martialled for stealing army property. His legs shackled, he was sent in a chain gang of other prisoners to Fort Leavenworth Military Prison, an institution that was to loom large in his later criminal career.

By day Panzram swung a hammer in the rock quarries while he was shackled to a 50-pound iron ball. He quieted his simmering rage and resentment by burning down the prison shops. He was 20 when his sentence, and his army life, was over, and thirsting to get his own back on society.

He returned to the railroad boxcar trail where he raped and murdered an Indian before crossing the Mexican border. "I burned down old barns, sheds, fences, chicken coops, anything I could, and when I couldn't burn anything else I set fire to the grass on the prairies, or the woods, anything and everything."

Back in the southern states and riding the Southern Pacific railroad, he raped hoboes and if he got caught, which happened a couple of times, he would pull a Bible out of his pocket and "tell 'em how much I loved Jesus and what a hard-working, honest fellow I was."

Boxcar riding has long been painted as a romantic time for travellers in the early years of the 20th century, but Panzram put a different slant on the romance of it. When a railroad brakeman tried to put him and two travelling companions out of a freight car Panzram pulled his gun.

"I told him I was the fellow who went around the world doing people good. He gave me all he had, and then he gave me his watch and chain as well. Then he was so kind as to pull his pants down while I rode him around the floor of the freight car. When I was through riding him I told the other two bums to mount him but they declined. But by using a little moral persuasion and much waving around of my pistol, they also rode Mr. Brakeman around."

Panzram was arrested twice more. He escaped from custody while on remand the first time, and served eight months in jail the second time before escaping again. But at least at this stage of his life he seemed to enjoy himself in prison, for, "I knew more about sodomy than old boy Oscar Wilde ever thought of knowing. I would start the morning with sodomy, work as hard at it as I could all day and sometimes half of the night."

He does not appear to have been a born homosexual, for in his youth he had an encounter with a prostitute, from whom he caught gonorrhoea. In the early years of the 20th century sexually transmitted diseases were difficult to cure and the experience seems to have chastened Panzram. After that he avoided women like the plague, and vowed never to sleep with another one. It is difficult to believe they avoided him, though, for he was a huge, powerful man, good-looking in a hard, mean way.

The year 1914 found Panzram in San Francisco trying to sell items stolen from a bank president's home.

He was arrested and got seven years in the Oregon State Prison where he was regularly stripped, flogged, and thrown into the Hole, a tiny dungeon where prisoners could not sit or lie down, and where they were kept sometimes for days on end.

He proved to be a violent prisoner and was regularly tortured for it. Once, chained hand and foot, he was put into a steel bath filled with water and rubbed down with a sponge connected to an electric battery. After two or three minutes of this intense agony, he said, he was "ready for the grave, or the madhouse."

Other torture refinements he had to endure included being put into a strait jacket until his blood stopped circulating and being beaten with a baseball bat while strapped down on a bed. Swearing he would never serve seven years, he set fire to the prison. "They kicked the hell out of me and put me in the cooler for 61 days on bread and water and then carried me out to the bullpen, where you had to walk constantly around a circular path without stopping until it got dark."

He again set fire to the prison, and again he was put in the Hole. Released, he went berserk with an axe until he was felled by guards and returned to the bullpen. Later he was chained to a door and targeted by a high-pressure fire hose, until he was "black and blue and half blind."

The hosing incident was leaked to the press and the Oregon state newspaper decided that while it did not approve of "hosing" prisoners, neither did it approve of the state having to "feed and fatten an unregenerate animal in his sodden and ugly bestiality."

For Carl Panzram, the newspaper declared after conducting its own investigation, was "lawless, unruly, revengeful and treacherous," and no amount of solitary confinement seemed to have any effect on him.

It had, in fact, the opposite effect. After the hosing punishment Panzram was unconscious. When he came to he was nearly blind, and "all swelled up from head to foot...my privates were as big as those of a jackass. The full effects of this didn't ever wear off completely. Since then, every time I catch an Oregonian and get him in a corner, I give him hell."

Reformists pleaded with the state government that the prison regime was far too harsh and in response the state put in a new prison governor who reduced the severity of discipline and created a relaxed atmosphere. Panzram's response was to escape.

After robbing a house he was cornered and fought a gun battle with a deputy sheriff. Even when he was caught he grabbed the deputy's gun and tried to shoot him. Returned to jail, he discovered that the reformist regime was over – at least for him. He was handcuffed and chained to a cell door for eight hours a day for three days.

The state's retribution was even more severe. Charged in May, 1918, with burglary and attempted murder he was given 10 years to add to the four he already had to serve. Within days he escaped again. Changing his name, he got a job with an oil company and, when he was fired for fighting, burned the oil well rig. Then he became a merchant seaman.

"I robbed the ship and everyone on her, for which I got a short bit in Barlinnie Prison, Glasgow. After that I sailed to Bridgeport, Connecticut, where I robbed a jewellery store of about $7,000-worth of stuff. I robbed another house and got about $40,000-worth of bonds, with which I bought a yacht. I figured it would be a good plan to hire a few sailors to work for me, get them drunk on my yacht, commit sodomy on them and then kill them. This I done."

He killed 10 sailors in this way, he said, dropping them overboard after shooting them through the head.

In Angola, West Africa, Panzram renounced his vow to eschew women and paid $11 for a Negro girl on the promise that she was a virgin. Next day he demanded his money back. claiming breach of contract, and was given another girl instead.

"This girl was about eight years old. I took her to my shack but she didn't look like a virgin to me. I took her back and quit looking for virgins. I looked for a boy. A little Negro boy, about 11 or 12 years old, came bumming around. I took him out to a gravel pit, committed sodomy on him and then killed him. His brains were coming out of his ears when I left him, and he will never be any deader.

"At Lobito Bay I hired a canoe and six Negroes and went out hunting for crocodiles. I shot all six Negroes, firing a single shot into each one's back, and dumped them in the water. The crocks did the rest."

Panzram wrote that he would have gone into the murder business "on a wholesale scale" if only he had had a more efficient gun. "Instead, I killed only 21 human beings. My intentions were good because I am the man that goes round the world doing people good."

At Salem, Massachusetts, he sodomised an 11-year-old boy then killed him by beating his head in with a rock. He stole another yacht and tried to sell it to a man who held him up at gunpoint. "But I was ready for him and I shot him twice. I tied a big hunk of lead around him and threw him overboard."

At New Haven he killed another boy. "I committed a little sodomy on him and then tied his belt around his neck and strangled him. I threw his body behind some bushes." But in White Plains, New York, he was caught red-handed trying to rob a post office. Throughout his trial no one seemed aware that this was the same prison escaper, notorious killer and arsonist who was wanted for a 14-year sentence in Oregon.

He had been free, except for a few months in jail, for five years – for most of the next five years he would now be incarcerated in one of America's harshest prisons, at Dannemora, in New York State.

At Dannemora prisoners were not allowed to speak to each other. They ate, worked, and exercised in total silence. The regime was sufficient to drive many of them insane, whereupon they were removed to the prison's own lunartic asylum.

Panzram made a bomb and tried to burn down the workshops. Next he tried to murder a fellow-prisoner.

When he was released from solitary confinement he made a failed escape bid, falling 30 feet from the wall and breaking both legs, fracturing his spine and rupturing himself.

"My broken bones were not set. The doctor never came near me. I was left like that for eight months. At the end of that time my bones had knitted together and I could stagger around on crutches. At the end of 14 months of constant agony I was operated on for my rupture and one of my testicles was cut out. Five days later I tried to see if my sexual organs were still in good order. I got caught trying to commit sodomy on another prisoner. I was thrown into a cell where I suffered more agony for many months, crawling around like a snake with a broken back. This went on for five years and the more they misused me the more I was filled with the spirit of hatred and revenge. I hated everybody I saw."

Still nursing that hatred, Panzram was finally discharged at the end of his sentence. Eighteen days later he had committed nine or 10 burglaries and another murder. He was caught on the last burglary and taken to the police station where he insisted that the charge was a joke.

"Why is it so funny?" asked the interrogating officer.

"I've killed far too many people to worry about this kind of charge," Panzram replied. "Don't you know people are better off dead?" The police officer became interested.

Carl Panzram was now 37 and had only two more years to live. Like his latter-day admirer Ian Brady he was to insist on his right to die – and in his case the way it turned out was just the way he wanted it to be. He was sent to Washington DC Prison, where a new warder named Henry Lesser took an interest in him. Lesser was a young Jew who had singularly failed to come up to his rich family's expectations and, after a variety of insignificant jobs, had ended up as a prison warder. He was never to forget Panzram; there was, he said, "an air of quiet stillness about him."

Lesser was to become the only friend Carl Panzram

ever made. He was to be the intermediary in Panzram's writings about the motivations for his life of crime. Apart from Lesser, almost everyone else Panzram met he tried to kill – but not until he had "practised a little sodomy on them" as he delicately used to put it. But while the young prison officer was putting himself on nodding terms with the old lag, he failed to notice the prisoner's hands working steadily on the bars of his cell. Gradually, millimetre-by-millimetre, the massive, 17-stone Panzram was loosening the bars in the concrete that held them.

This was to be yet another escape bid. He had been in so many of them he had lost count.

What Lesser failed to detect was discovered a few days later by a prison search. Panzram was yanked out of his cell, taken to the prison basement and handcuffed to a post. A rope was slipped through the handcuffs and he was pulled off the floor until only his toes touched the ground. And there, Lesser was afterwards to say, he hung virtually crucified for 12 hours, cursing his mother for bringing him into the world and yelling that he would kill her and everything human.

From the isolation cell which routinely followed such punishment he called a passing warder a son of a bitch. For that, four guards knocked him unconscious and then dragged him back to the post, where he was again hung up for a whole night.

His only method of retaliation now was to boast about all the murders he had committed. Jeering, scoffing, shouting, yelling, he told anyone who would listen how he had killed a little boy here and a youth there, filling in all the details of times and places.

Warders took notes, and passed them to lawyers, and lawyers passed them on to the police, and the burglary charge for which he was being held began to pale into insignificance as the confessions were painstakingly linked to unsolved crimes.

Panzram jeered: "Where would you be without people like me? You all make a nice soft living out of crime. You all revel in it. You don't produce a damn thing. You just shoot off your mouths and push a fountain pen."

The same idea, that people involved in law enforcement – crime writers, newspapermen…anyone involved in any innocent job which touches on the business of crime – is doing well out it – is echoed in Ian Brady's book. How this should be regarded as a justification for serial killing is never made clear.

Another Panzram idea, that society made him what he was, is also developed by Brady. Panzram said: "From the age of 11 I have lived among moral and mental misfits…in an atmosphere of deceit, treachery, brutality, degeneracy, hypocrisy, everything that is bad and nothing that is good. I have absorbed these things and become what I am today, a treacherous, degenerate, brutal human savage, devoid of all decent feeling, absolutely without conscience, morals, pity, sympathy, principle, or any single good trait. Is that unnatural in the circumstances? I did not make myself what I am. Others had the making of me."

This idea that if we commit a crime it must be someone else's fault and not ours was of course to become well developed in the 20th century.

Panzram never seemed to stop talking, writing, passing notes to his friend Henry Lesser, and the result of all his singing was inevitable – he now faced murder charges constructed out of his own evidence.

While he waited for his trial he was transferred to the dreaded Fort Leavenworth, once a military prison from which many years earlier he had escaped, and which now ranks in the annals of criminology alongside Alcatraz. The governor at Leavenworth interviewed the notorious prisoner and assigned him to the laundry. Panzram told him icily: "I'll kill the first man that bothers me."

The first man to bother him was bespectacled Robert Warnke, who was the laundry foreman. When Warnke discovered that Panzram was running a moneymaking racket in the laundry, he sent the prisoner to a punishment cell and reduced his grade status to a level that meant every hour of his life would be like purgatory.

It was time, Panzram decided, to finish with this world. On June 20th, 1929, he strode into the laundry room from where he had been banned, carrying a 10-pound iron bar. He walked straight up to Robert Warnke and brought the instrument crashing down on the warder's head with all the brute force he could muster behind his 18-stone frame. Warnke sank to the floor already dead.

"This is my lucky day!" whooped the serial killer, swinging the bar over his head as other prisoners scrambled away in fear of their lives.

He was swiftly overpowered and taken to an isolation cell. Expecting to be beaten to death, he was amazed to find bed sheets and slippers, magazines, books and writing paper laid out for him. From now on the prison killer was to have the good life – something he had never experienced before. The only problem was that it was to be all too brief.

Now he kept up a regular correspondence with Henry Lesser, who was still a warder at Washington DC jail. He wrote to no one else and refused all interviews. Even Leavenworth's most famous prisoner, canary student Robert Stroud, later to be celebrated as The Birdman of Alcatraz, failed to make contact with him.

From those letters, and from the things he said while awaiting trial for Warnke's murder, there was no doubt that Panzram had made up his mind to die. He was asked by the prosecutor who visited him: "Did you intend to kill the warder when you hit him with that iron bar?"

Panzram stared back at the lawyer in astonishment. "What the hell do you think I hit him with it for?" he replied.

To Lesser he wrote: "You asked me if I get a kick out of killing people. Of course I do. If you don't think so, imagine five or six big huskies walking in on you, hammering you unconscious, then dragging you to a cellar, chaining you to a post and working you over some more. Imagine forgiving and forgetting after something like that, then write and tell me about it. I had 22 years of that kind of stuff.

"Besides, you put them out of all their misery when you knock them off."

From the prison cell where he was well aware that there was only one exit, Panzram kept up a stream of letters to Lesser about his early life.

"I learned so much about the Christian religion that I finally came to detest, despise and hate everybody connected with it," he said. "I still do. You asked me about my mother. I first liked her...my feelings gradually turned to distrust, dislike, disgust, and from there it was very simple for my feelings to turn into positive hatred towards her."

But he liked his new prison lifestyle. "No one abuses me in any way – this is the way it's been for the past three or four months. I figure that if I had been treated the way I am now, there wouldn't have been quite so many people robbed, raped and killed."

This was somewhat at odds with his continued protestation that if he were allowed out he would go right on killing people, "because I still think that that is the best way to reform them."

Panzram's trial was finally fixed for April, 1930. Judge Richard Hopkins, who was appointed to preside, refused to accept the prisoner's request to act as his own defence lawyer and appointed a court lawyer. Panzram was furious and wrote to Hopkins:

"You have acted without my consent. I refuse to accept the services of any counsel the court may appoint. If I am found guilty of murder and then sentenced to death, it is my wish that that sentence is carried out."

While the man who had ended the lives of 21 people was making it clear that he had himself lost the urge to live, he was aware that it might not be as easy as all that, for there had been no state execution in Kansas for nearly 40 years, and lots of people did not want that situation changed, even for Carl Panzram.

First, he was arraigned before a commission to inquire into his state of mind. Panzram told the commissioners that if his parents were living he would kill them for bringing him into the world. He would like to hire chemists to prepare poison gas and germs with which, "I would be able to exterminate a great mass of human beings...Society should build me a great monument because I have never propagated my kind."

He later wrote to Lesser: "I intend to leave this world as I have lived in it. I expect to be a rebel right up to my last moment on earth. With my last breath I intend to curse the world and all mankind. I intend to spit in the warden's eye or whoever places the rope around my neck when I am standing on the scaffold."

He made a change of plan, however, for three months before the execution date he tried to commit suicide by taking poison and cutting an artery. But the noise of his suffering was quickly relayed to warders, who pumped out his stomach and bound up the wound. They too were determined that Panzram should die – but in their way.

Panzram's trial in Topeka, Kansas, on April 15th and 16th, 1930, was short and swift. He called no witnesses and said he was delighted with the verdict of guilty and the sentence of death – he was to be hanged on September 5th, 1930, at Fort Leavenworth Prison. He wrote angrily to the Society for the Abolishment of Capital Punishment, which tried to intervene:

"I prefer to die that way, and if I have a soul that burns in Hell for a million years I still prefer that to a lingering, agonising death in some prison dungeon or a padded cell in a mad house. The only thanks you or your kind will ever get from me for your efforts on my behalf is that I wish you all had one neck and that I had my hands on it.

"I have no desire to reform myself. My only desire is to reform people who try to reform me, and I believe that the only way to reform people is to kill them. My motto is, rob them all, rape them all, and kill them all!"

The death sentence, he added, was "absolutely just" and in welcoming it he claimed to be in full possession of his faculties. Just in case anyone else intervened, he even wrote to President Hoover requesting that the sentence should be carried out.

No one else did intervene. At 6 a.m. on the appointed day Panzram, still describing himself as "the most criminal man in the world," went hustling to his execution. He was true to his braggart image to the last. When he was told that two priests were there to offer him comfort, he roared: "Run 'em out, or any man I get my hands on is going to hospital."

As the two priests were quickly escorted away he was asked by the executioner if he had any final words.

"Yes, hurry it up, you bastard!" he snapped. "I could hang a dozen men while you're fooling around!" The hangman duly obliged.

•

Ian Brady was exhilarated by Panzram's grand exit. He wrote: "I laugh with delight even now at Panzram's magnificent final performance on earth, full of such tremendous innocence and spirit. Those were Panzram's final words, his contemptuous goodbye to a world he loathed having to breathe in.

"The lever was pulled, the trap-door opened. With that fall, the world became a duller place. A great spirit had flown. A star had been extinguished. The air seemed subdued."

Brady's literary message from Ashworth Hospital, where he is a long-standing resident, is that serial killers think that conformists (a group of people roughly comprising you and I) are sanctimonious, timid bores who preach traditional morality, all the time remaining unaware that the serial killer has his own quite different morality.

The majority of serial killers, he tells us, create their own god, or rather they believe so devoutly in a form of personal philosophy, predominantly nihilistic, that it has the psychological power of a religion. They become gods in their own kingdom, sampling everything that was once forbidden, "eventually taking the lives" of those who have entered their private domain and witnessed their darkest desires.

"The killing also affirmatively defines their new powers. That is why, in this primarily metaphysical context, some [killers] can often regard destruction as an act of creation – an 'act of God.'"

The serial killer is a rebel who daily observes people throwing their lives away on repetitive jobs, territorial obsessions, promotion to a particular desk, key to the executive toilet, etc. He thinks that such objectives are insane. He craves excitement, but it never seems to come. He goes out searching for it and he will not draw the line at any border "which others have had the arrogance to draw for him."

Traditional morality to such a killer reduces life more than it enhances. And then comes a typical Brady climax, an onrush of verbosity sufficient to deafen:

"It could be impartially argued that he inhabits an almost poetic fourth dimension, where dreams and reality naturally meld, a world of esoteric certitude and applied will. A psychic state in which common reality is seen merely as a lace curtain, visually recognised and noted but too insignificant to interfere with the more fascinating visions he sees beyond.

"He intuits that those around him can only see the lace curtain, and he keenly appreciates his advantage. While they blankly daydream behind the lace, he acts... the natural prize due psychic penetration and a superior altered state."

The book opens with the publisher himself telling us that it is a remarkable work (well, he would say that, wouldn't he?), and then proceeds to a thoughtful Introduction by Colin Wilson, the celebrated criminologist, who discusses crimes of intellectual rebellion that may not be classified as sex crimes. Then, somewhat curiously, as Brady gets under way with his part of it he becomes highly critical of, guess who? – Colin Wilson.

Brady writes in a style that is halfway between a psychiatric journal and a tabloid newspaper. Hence every half-dozen paragraphs or so he begins with "As previously stated," or "As already indicated," or "As already posited," like some learned fellow, and then he fills in the gaps with sentences without verbs, that come at you like machine-gun fire straight out of the *Sun* newspaper.

Every so often in this oddly structured book there is a quotation which appears to have nothing to do with what the author is saying at that point. Henry James, Oscar Wilde, the Bible, Sun Tzu, Pindar – Brady has picked them all out from his dictionary of famous quotations. The writer who is probably most quoted is Dostoevsky, who is clearly much admired.

The first part of the book wanders aimlessly all over the place. It is mostly concerned with the Ian Brady philosophy, peppered with aphorisms like the sayings of Chairman Mao, and it picks holes in society's infrastructure as a basis for self-justification – "law-abiding souls have their victims too," he sneers, meaning that the best of us have our nasty side, though omitting to say that we don't go about killing and sexually abusing children.

A typical Brady aphorism is, "The vibrancy of evil requires the threat of external force for its containment, and the drive to be good requires narcissistic self-interest or delusions of grandeur." And another: "There are no saints in this world, only liars, lunartics and journalists."

The second half is a regurgitation of the evil deeds of a collection of serial killers, including the Yorkshire Ripper, Carl Panzram, Ted Bundy and the poisoner Graham Young. Why this should be so is unclear, because Brady adds absolutely nothing to what is already known about all these individuals.

A psychiatrist, Dr. Alan Keightley, who wrote the Foreword, tells us, "The author speaks with great authority and originality." It seems that Dr. Keightley wrote that when he didn't know who the author actually was. Sadly, what is really missing from the author is any sign of remorse, any mention of the suffering of victims, any attempt at humanising.

When Brady tells you that most people would be tempted to kill anyone who got in their way in exchange for a complete guarantee that no suspicion would fall on them, you are left in no doubt that he is a man with a very sick mind.

truecrimelibrary

at your bookshop now, or use the coupon below

✓ *Please send me the book(s) I have indicated:*

☐ FORENSIC CASEBOOK OF CRIME	£5.99
☐ A DATE WITH THE HANGMAN	£4.99
☐ TONY MARTIN AND THE BLEAK HOUSE TRAGEDY	£5.99
☐ STRANGE TALES FROM STRANGEWAYS	£4.99
☐ WOMEN ON DEATH ROW	£4.99
☐ MURDER WITH VENOM	£4.99
☐ CELEBRITY SLAYINGS THAT SHOCKED THE WORLD	£5.99
☐ BRITAIN'S GODFATHER	£4.99
☐ FROM WALL STREET TO NEWGATE	£5.99
☐ CAMINADA THE CRIME BUSTER	£5.99
☐ FROM THE X FILES OF MURDER	£5.99
☐ FAR FROM THE LAND	£5.99
☐ THE BOOTLEGGERS	£5.99
☐ MURDER MYTH AND MAKE-BELIEVE	£5.99
☐ INSIDE THE MIND OF THE SEX KILLER	£6.99
☐ BRITAIN'S LAST HANGMAN	£6.99
☐ WOMEN ON DEATH ROW 2	£6.99

Total £ ....

Name ....

Address ....

....

.... Post Code ....

Send to: True Crime Library, PO Box 735,
London SE26 5NQ.
Enquiries and credit card orders ring:
020 8778 0514.
Or order from our website:
www.truecrimelibrary.com

Get more of the world's best true crime stories – every month!

True Crime Library is about more than books – we also publish the world's first and best magazines of non-fiction crime. They're packed with authoritative reports, astonishing photos and must-read stories of crime, detection and punishment – all 100% true!

Find our magazines at all good newsagents in Britain and Ireland.
Alternatively, call us on **020 8778 0514**
– or visit our website:

www.truecrimelibrary.com

- True Detective • Monthly
- Master Detective • Monthly
- True Crime • Monthly
- Murder Most Foul • Quarterly